LAND OF ENCHANTMENT, LAND OF CONFLICT

NUMBER ELEVEN
Tarleton State University
Southwestern Studies in the Humanities

LAND OF ENCHANTMENT, LAND OF CONFLICT
NEW MEXICO IN ENGLISH-LANGUAGE FICTION

DAVID L. CAFFEY

Texas A&M University Press
College Station

Library of Congress Cataloging-in-Publication Data

Caffey, David L., 1947–
    Land of enchantment, land of conflict : New
Mexico in English-language fiction / David L. Caffey.
— 1st ed.
        p.   cm. — (Tarleton State University south-
western studies in the humanities : no. 11)
    Includes bibliographical references (p.   ) and
index.
    ISBN 0-89096-891-8 (alk. paper)
    1. American fiction—New Mexico—History and
criticism.   2. New Mexico—In literature.   I. Title.
II. Series.
PS283.N6C34   1999
810.9'32789—dc21   98-55985
                                        CIP

FOR MARY

CONTENTS

ILLUSTRATIONS

PREFACE

The late Alice Bullock, Santa Fe traveler and writer, liked to say that she was born in New Mexico at the age of eight. The year of her birth as a New Mexican was 1912, when New Mexico attained statehood and her family moved to the Colfax County coal-mining town of Gardiner.

I too was born in New Mexico and in Colfax County, but at the more advanced age of fifteen, when, in August, 1963, I camped for two weeks at the Santa Fe Trail settlement of Rayado, on the Philmont Scout Ranch. I had never before seen the Rocky Mountains up close, and they made a big impression. It was an adventure to hike up into bear country, to hear the creek splashing down through Rayado Canyon, to breathe the cold mountain air after a hailstorm. Even when viewed through the rain that persisted during most of that brief stay, those mountains — the Sangre de Cristo — were wild and beautiful. I had to see more of them, and I did, through twelve summers on the Philmont staff.

I saw what was left of the gold-mining era on Baldy Mountain and of the logging camps and abandoned railroad grade in Ponil Canyon. The scars on Baldy were plain to see, as were the effects of clear-cutting in the Ponil country, but my response to these visible ruins was mostly romantic rather than critical. In the tailing piles and other debris, I saw not nature despoiled, but history strewn across a mountainside, much of its residue overgrown with weeds, grass, and aspen trees. I learned some things about the culture of the Jicarilla Apaches who once lived in the area, but I didn't think to ask what had happened to the people. I heard —

and told — campfire tales of Juan de Oñate, Popé, and Diego de Vargas; of Lucien Maxwell, Kit Carson, Clay Allison, and Thomas E. "Black Jack" Ketchum.

With an audience of several thousand campers and leaders each summer, we did our share, I'm sure, in making and perpetuating western myth — despite the best efforts of Larry Murphy, who monitored our programs and tried with mixed success to keep them true to known facts and free of improvisation. Murphy, then in the process of becoming a first-rate western historian, pointed us toward solid keys to New Mexico — *Sky Determines,* by Ross Calvin; and *The Maxwell Land Grant,* by Jim Berry Pearson, for example. Somewhere along the line, someone gave me a copy of Frank Waters's *The Man Who Killed the Deer.*

As with many who came to Philmont from distant places, there came a time when I just didn't go home at summer's end. I stayed, found work, spent a year in Santa Fe, and another in Cimarron. But I backslid into Texas for more school and, finally, a real job.

Midland College was well funded, a comfortable and congenial place to work. I was not mistreated or made to feel unwelcome, but I did think I might die of boredom if I didn't do something soon. After four years in Midland, I decided to look for a way to live in New Mexico. I watched the want ads and filled out applications for state and federal employment. I applied to be director of the Harwood Foundation of the University of New Mexico, a library and art museum in Taos. Situated in a sprawling adobe compound of nineteenth-century origin and appointed with Spanish Colonial furniture reproductions from the WPA era, the Harwood was a widely revered community institution, though fiscally challenged. To my amazement, I was offered the position.

I went to Taos very much aware of the ethnic composition of Taos County — more than 75 percent of residents were Hispanic or Native American — and of the high rates of unemployment in the area. The first thing I did, U-Haul still in tow, was stop at the Motor Vehicle Division office and apply for New Mexico license plates. My cautious approach was validated by a four-column headline in the *Taos News:* "Harwood Defends Director Selection"; but the discomfort was short-lived, and I went about the business of trying to make myself useful in the land of Cíbola.

Taos in the 1980s was an ideal place to investigate the history and cultural riches of New Mexico. It also was, as John Nichols had discovered, a setting in which to learn about ancient conflicts and discomfiting social and historical realities.

The Taos Valley, in addition, was an ideal place to explore works of fiction and their relationships with the people, times, and places they portrayed. Working writers were visible and accessible. Ron Querry and Stan Crawford, residents of downriver communities between Taos and Española, were heavy users of the Harwood Library. Nichols was a routine presence, his frantic motions before the copy machine usually signifying a deadline. Though enfeebled, Frank Waters still enjoyed summers at his home near Arroyo Seco and occasionally relayed requests for library materials. Tony Hillerman came to town from time to time, as did Elizabeth Tallent, Max Evans, and other New Mexico writers.

A short drive to Santa Fe or Albuquerque could put me in the presence of other resident and visiting writers — Edward Abbey, Richard Bradford, Fray Angelico Chavez, and N. Scott Momaday, for instance.

Our crumbling files of El Crepúsculo and the Taos News contained a handful of strident opinion pieces and funky editorial cartoons — testament to Abbey's brief editorial career. Mabel Luhan and D. H. Lawrence had departed long ago, but their shadows remained. The personae of Padre Antonio José Martínez and Kit Carson, too, were much in evidence, despite the fact that both had been dead for more than a century.

Clovis is distant from the literary centers of New Mexico, but the past few years have brought Rudolfo Anaya, Denise Chávez, Natalie Goldberg, Kate Horsley, and Kevin McIlvoy as guest lecturers at Clovis Community College. Portales, just down the road, is the longtime home of science fiction pioneer Jack Williamson and the site of an annual science fiction lectureship. So the elements germane to this study — the New Mexico landscape, the state's literature and history, and contemporary writers interested in the area — have been remarkably and delightfully accessible.

This project began in Taos, was slowed by changes in employment and location, and was sidetracked temporarily for a complete overhaul of format and approach. That the selection of works discussed is, to some extent, a reflection of personal interests and preferences, may go without saying. While I have tried to provide a reasonable balance and breadth of authors and works within the scope of the study, it has not been possible to examine all pertinent materials or to transcend entirely the limitations of my own background and experience. Had this volume been written by someone with a different set of experiences, I'm sure it would have been a different and quite possibly a better book. To the extent that it helps advance anyone's understanding of the myths and realities of the land and people of New Mexico, I'm glad.

I acknowledge with gratitude the help of staff members at numerous libraries and cultural institutions: Harwood Foundation Library and Museum, Taos; San Juan College Library, Farmington; Center for Southwest Research, University of New Mexico, Albuquerque; Huntington Library, San Marino, California; Bancroft Library, University of California, Berkeley; Harry Ransom Humanities Research Center, University of Texas at Austin; Rupert and Pauline Richardson Library of Hardin-Simmons University, Abilene, Texas; Golden Library of Eastern New Mexico University, Portales; Special Collections Department, University of Iowa Libraries, Iowa City; Clovis-Carver Public Library, Clovis, New Mexico; Rio Grande Historical Collections of New Mexico State University, Las Cruces; General Library, Texas Tech University, Lubbock; Lincoln Library, Springfield, Illinois; Southwest Museum, Los Angeles; and History Library and Photographic Archives, Museum of New Mexico, Santa Fe. I am grateful, too, to colleagues at Clovis Community College, my employer for the past seven years, for assistance with photographs and for library and computer support essential to the completion of this work.

Thanks also are due, posthumously in some cases, to Rudolfo Anaya, Emily Otis Barnes, Octavia Fellin, John Pendaries La Farge, Edith O'Rourke, Harvena Richter, Patricia Skarda, C. L. Sonnichsen, and Frank Waters, for information, print and photographic materials, and encouragement.

I am also grateful to the New Mexico Endowment for the Humanities for opportunities I have had to develop and refine some of the material included in this work through my participation as a presenter in public programs of the Endowment.

This project probably could not have been accomplished but for the work of Saul Cohen, who compiled an initial checklist of New Mexico fiction; and Tom Lewis, whose more comprehensive bibliography of New Mexico novels was an essential reference.

I am deeply appreciative of helpful comments provided by Tom Pilkington and Robert Gish, both of whom long since have achieved distinction as students of western literature. Richard W. Etulain and Robert R. White also offered helpful words of encouragement.

Finally, I wish to thank the members of my family for their continued tolerance of my biblioholic tendencies and of other distractions occasioned by this work.

LAND OF ENCHANTMENT, LAND OF CONFLICT

1 SOME WRITERS AND A PLACE

Exploring New Mexico in Fiction

For some time, historians of literature and popular culture have known that, if they want to learn about the attitudes, values, and concerns of a particular society or period, they can find much of what they want to know by digging into the fiction literature of the time and place in question. The body of popular fiction is apt to contain some cogent observations and descriptions, as well as a record of ideas and attitudes. If such material suffers from obvious deficiencies relative to other sources of information, it also offers some distinct advantages.

It is sometimes the intention of the fiction writer to provide a faithful portrayal of the subject matter — to reveal truths about a time and place, about human events, in a realistic manner. Writers are applauded for doing this successfully. Max Evans is recognized for showing a side of ranch life that rarely appears in popular Westerns. His northeastern New Mexico cowboys don't carry six-guns or run down outlaws. They actually work cattle and horses. They get dusty, dirty, weary, and buttsore, discouraged and lonely. They work for low wages and endure perpetual servitude for the privilege of working outdoors and enjoying a measure of freedom from bureaucratic regulation and social norms.

In *The Delight Makers* (1890), Adolf F. Bandelier hoped to show life as it may have been in prehistoric Tyuonyi, when the ancestors of today's Pueblo Indians lived and worked there. Bandelier applied years of research in archeology and ethnology to produce a work he hoped would reveal the "truth about the Pueblo Indians" to a popular audience. Fiction allowed the author to appeal to nonacademic readers. By interesting readers in the experiences of characters with whom they could identify, he could enliven otherwise musty accounts of prehistoric life and culture and make them relevant.

Like Bandelier, Eugene Manlove Rhodes, chronicler of the last days of the open range in southern New Mexico, meant to inform and influence as well as entertain his readers. Rhodes drew characters from life and insisted that his portrayals were faithful to the people, places, and times of which he wrote. Discouraged at the careless handling of his books by publishers who failed to appreciate his purpose, and at a disappointing lack of critical acclaim, Rhodes consoled himself with the conviction that his works would preserve significant ideas and images for posterity. "They may or may not be 'art,'" he conceded, "but they are Archeology, or will be when the few survivors of that bright, brief day are buried" (Hutchinson, 344).

But novels and stories need not be literary works of art or offer accurate portrayals of time and place in order to provide useful information to the reader. In a groundbreaking study, *Virgin Land: The American West as Symbol and Myth* (1950), Henry Nash Smith demonstrated that popular fiction of little or no intrinsic merit could provide insight into widely held perceptions about the West. Smith proved that popular novels and stories could be useful in identifying compelling ideas that emerged from the frontier experience to shape an enduring mythology of the West — ideas that influenced political ideology, policy, and action.

C. L. Sonnichsen says much the same thing about fiction in general, and western fiction in particular. He takes as an example Edward Abbey's *The Monkey Wrench Gang* (1975), a book that crystallized the inarticulate thoughts of many readers who were troubled by events in the contemporary West:

Fiction has always reflected, as well as shaped, popular tastes, prejudices, and admirations. Propaganda novels like Abbey's do it openly and obviously, but stories with no apparent axe to grind do it also. A writer who seems not to be taking a stand on anything, aiming only to amuse, reflects more than he realizes of the basic attitudes of his time. Thus the assembled fictional output of any specific period contributes to social and intellectual history because it offers a guide to what people think and believe, thereby providing a key to what they do, or would like to do. (1978, p. 4)

If one accepts these modest premises, then the slagheap of popular fiction becomes an interesting and inviting body of ore.

Journalism, history, and the social sciences are accepted and useful sources of information and insight concerning human affairs, but none of these is infallible, and all of them operate under severe handicaps. The journalist is expected to find and corroborate sources, verify quotations, and produce a product which will stand against conflicting accounts. His work must be proof against charges of libel or slander. The scholar is under duress to substantiate his assertions — to provide credible evidence, to document the analysis upon which his conclusions are based, and to refrain from invoking suspicions or prejudices which cannot be so supported. No such obligation exists to encumber the fiction writer.

Writers may go back and forth among fiction and nonfiction modes, depending on the materials at hand and the purposes to be accomplished; several have done so with remarkable success. Paul Horgan worked in a variety of literary forms over a career spanning some six decades. Much of his creative life was devoted to works of fiction, but he also produced an epic history of the Rio Grande, *Great River: The Rio Grande in North American History* (1954), and a highly acclaimed biography, *Lamy of Santa Fe: His Life and Times* (1975). Regardless of the form, his intent was to convey factual or literary truth in an elegant and engaging manner. Horgan's devotion to style and story perhaps was better suited to fiction, but it was evident in his nonfiction works as well; while he twice won the Pulitzer Prize for history, he incurred the disapproval of academic historians who felt that he had allowed scholarship to slide in favor of aesthetics.

A journalist by training and experience, Tony Hillerman relished the freedom he found as a mystery writer. "Working with facts, as a journalist must," he observed, "is like working with marble. Truth has its beauty but it doesn't bend" (1986b, p. 131). In fiction, Hillerman could follow where his imagination led, inventing characters to suit his purpose and simply conjuring up many of the facts that, as a journalist, he labored over.

When Bandelier, the anthropologist, turned to fiction as the medium of choice for his exposition of prehistoric Pueblo life and culture, he shed a great many bothersome restraints. The tyranny of accountability bars the scholar from indulging in whim or fantasy, leading to what Rhodes called "a brutal prejudice against guessing." Like the sadly maligned good man in Rhodes's *The Trusty Knaves* (1933), the responsible academician proceeds with caution, "always fussing about the rules, stopping for Sunday and advice of counsel" (Rhodes, 1933, p. 111). The fiction writer labors under no such constraint. Such inhibitions may be necessary for the scholar, whose credibility derives from the discipline of systematic inquiry, but they are abhorrent to the artist, whose authority depends upon fidelity to beliefs, feelings, and hunches.

In fiction, the writer has virtually unlimited license to say whatever he or she pleases, without regard for public taste, political correctness, or the approval of patron or sponsor. The writer is under no obligation to prove anything to anybody, nor is there any compulsion to adhere to the facts, even when dealing with familiar events and personalities.

Like the mischievous *koshare* of the Rio Grande pueblos, at liberty to act in outlandish ways so long as his identity is submerged in that of the costumed clown, the fiction writer enjoys certain exemptions from responsibility. The writer is free to exaggerate, to rearrange, to indulge in flights of fancy, to invent, to guess, and if necessary, to offend and outrage readers; to put forth bold assertions that he will never have to prove. The writer is free to err, but free as well to tell truths that may elude the responsible journalist and the sober practitioner of academic inquiry.

Such freedom allows the fiction writer to comment in ways that those bound by the facts cannot. The creative writer is free to stray from the relative safety of observable phenomena — facts and behavior — to explore the inner world of feelings, values, motivation, and personal meaning. The writer can let the air out of exalted personages in society, as fiction writers once delighted in lampooning Taos salon matron Mabel Dodge Luhan. The fictionalist can broach sensitive or controversial subjects with relative ease; if unpopular sentiments need to be expressed, they can be attributed to a character who lives beyond the grasp of enraged readers. The fiction writer can also take a remote social issue and make it real and personal, as John Nichols did in *The Milagro Beanfield War* (1974). And, like Abbey in *The Monkey Wrench Gang*, he can invent acts of outraged heroism that he would like to commit if not for the practical consequences.

The fiction writer is a recorder, a commentator, an artist, an unconscious reflector of norms and attitudes; a maker, a keeper, and sometimes a destroyer of hackneyed stereotypes and cherished myths. Whether functioning as one or more of these, the writer cannot help but reflect something of the larger society. If the creative writer pays attention to the world from which his fictive world is drawn, he is likely to tell much about the values, attitudes, preferences, and prejudices of people in a particular time and place. Like Abbey, the writer may be relating such observations in pursuit of a specific agenda, but it's just as well if they are no more than unpremeditated reflections of assumptions and attitudes absorbed along the way.

To be sure, the reader whose interest is in learning about times, places, people, and events must approach fiction materials with a good deal of caution and discernment. He or she is well advised to consult reliable historical sources where factual matters are concerned, to consider carefully the writer's purpose, and to develop a healthy curiosity concerning the writer's background and the circumstances and attitudes prevailing in the period when a given work was produced. The reader who is willing to do all this, however, stands to learn quite a lot.

What is proposed here is an exercise in literary archeology, involving the excavation and sifting of a major portion of the English-language fiction set in New Mexico from 1826 to the present, approximately 1998. Of interest are clues to New Mexico — the land and people, social patterns, values, and attitudes, as related by the fiction writer. Structure, style, and other traditional objects of literary criticism are of marginal interest.

The idea is to examine novels and stories with New Mexico settings in order to discover patterns of commentary on the land and its people. What are the recurring themes in these works? What judgments are rendered? What incisive observations emerge? Do the prevailing views expressed in works of fiction tend more to reveal truth or to betray it? These are questions that must concern anyone who wants to learn more about his own home country or someone else's through works of fiction.

There are limitations, certainly. Some novels and stories, though nominally set in known places, reveal little or nothing of those places. This is especially true of many western adventure novels, which require only the basic elements of a western setting and which do not necessarily concern themselves with the intricacies of place. It is also true of some very fine literary works in which setting is incidental and the author's concern is, for example, with human dilemmas and relationships.

Where the writer does attend to the sense of place, the reader must decide whether he or she is a reliable observer and take into account the possibility of prejudice based on the author's background and experience. It is noteworthy that a disproportionate share of the fiction literature of New Mexico has been produced by Anglo men from other places. While some of these authors have produced excellent, sensitive, insightful works, the search for truth requires a greater diversity of experiences and perspectives. Until recently, published novels and stories by Hispanic and Native American writers have been few in number, a circumstance which, thankfully, is changing for the better. The proportion of works produced by women has increased dramatically; this, too, works in the direction of an inclusive body of literature that readers actually might be able to learn something from.

It is also true that the traditional novels and stories of English-language fiction comprise a restricted and, some might say, inherently biased body of literature. For the universe of New Mexico literature is much larger and would include, for example, poetry, drama, and essay, as well as works in varied languages. It would encompass the many novels and stories written expressly for younger readers. It could include the stories and legends of several Native American cultures, as well as the *cuentos* and narrative songs of Spanish tradition. All of these would bear looking into.

As it is, most of the works cited here are novels created in, or translated into, the English language and containing significant portions set in New Mexico and adjacent, culturally related areas. Many would be classified as "general fiction." Some attention has been given to short stories and to works representing familiar genres — mystery, romance, science fiction and fantasy, Western — but no attempt has been made to examine any of these specialized bodies of material exhaustively. Works from all eras have been included, and some care has been taken to consult the perspectives of native and nonnative writers, and of writers representing varied cultural experiences.

The book's essential emphasis on place-related content of works of fiction, and its lack of emphasis on critical analysis, may give rise to the impression that all novels and stories are created equal, which they are not. In fact, the works cited vary considerably in quality, from dime novels derided as products of a subliterary genre, to Pulitzer Prize–winning novels and other works long enshrined as classics of American, western, or southwestern literature.

As both a "Land of Enchantment" and a "Land of Conflict," New Mexico invites — indeed, fairly compels — response. Writers, artists, musicians, and poets, whether celebrated or laboring in obscurity, whether native, immigrant, or visitor, all seem to have something to say about their infinitely varied surroundings. D. H. Lawrence, though worldly-wise when he arrived in New Mexico, felt himself changed forever by a land of immense beauty, spiritual resonance, and mystery. "It had a splendid, silent terror," he wrote, "and a vast far-and-wide magnificence which made it way beyond mere aesthetic appreciation" (1931, p. 154).

New Mexico is also characterized by a time perspective that spans prehistoric civilizations and the Atomic Age, and much evidence of the whole span remains observable. "This finally has come to be its chief distinction," wrote Harvey Fergusson in *Rio Grande* (1933), "that here alone change has not wholly obliterated all that went before, that the past is present in patterns of life and types of men, that the face of the earth is not much altered" (286).

An illustrious and accessible past invites consideration. Had Willa Cather not beheld the graceful mission churches and the old pueblo of Acoma, could she have grasped the early missionaries' faith and determination, which inspired *Death Comes for the Archbishop* (1927)? Had she never marveled at the ruins of Colorado's Mesa Verde, could she have conceived the story of Tom Outland and Blue Mesa in *The Professor's House* (1925)? Perhaps not.

New Mexico is enchanting, all right; but fiction needs conflict, contradiction, irony perhaps, and suspense. Despite exaggerated and widely disseminated reports of three cultures dwelling in harmony, New Mexico is a land of many conflicts. These include conflicts among cultural groups, conflicts over land use, conflicts over scarce water, conflicts between stability and change. These clashes stem from conflicting legal and religious traditions, conflicting views of the individual's place in society, and opposing values concerning civilization and progress.

The nature of such conflicts varies and may depend to a considerable extent on one's point of view. One person's war of liberation may be another's war of aggression and conquest. Likewise, the conflict between native cultures and outside developers in northern New Mexico may be viewed by some as a clash of interests played out within the accepted rules of a market economy; to others, it's an example of class struggle, pitting privileged capitalists against an exploited rural, ethnic-minority underclass. One writer's frontier hero may be seen by others as the unwelcome agent of a dominant colonial power. A literary work concerned with such conflicts, then, may have one set of meanings for the writer and other, perhaps conflicting meanings for various readers, since each person brings her or his own values, perspectives, and experiences to the work.

Of New Mexico and its many contradictions, Oliver La Farge wrote:

It is a vast, harsh, poverty-stricken, varied, and beautiful land, a breeder of artists and warriors. It is the home, by birth or by passionate adoption, of a wildly assorted population which has shown itself capable of achieving homogeneity without sacrificing its diversity. It is primitive, underdeveloped, overused, new, raw, rich with tradition, old and mellow. It is a land full of the essence of peace, although its history is one of invasions and conflicts. It is itself, an entity, at times infuriating, at times utterly delightful to its lovers, a land that draws and holds men and women with ties that cannot be explained or submitted to reason. (1952, p. 46)

Remarked the sagacious Tony Hillerman of the land's fabled spell and its effect on him, "As for me, I can only say that New Mexico seems to make me want to write" (1976, p. 4).

Apparently New Mexico has made a lot of others want to write, too. By 1991, bibliographer Tom Lewis had identified more than twelve hundred novels set wholly or partly within the state's modern boundaries. Stories must run into the thousands, although their production surely has been slowed by the demise of many of the magazines that once made a substantial market for short fiction. Faced with such a wealth of material, one can hardly hope to examine everything. C. L. Sonnichsen once advised would-be historians of fiction to "take soundings and samplings and make generalizations with caution" (1978, p. 8), an approach that will have to suffice here.

As on the white sands of the Tularosa Basin and the talus slopes of the Truchas Peaks, there is no sure footing on this uncertain terrain. It is hoped, however, that this study may serve as a primitive map to parts of New Mexico's literary landscape, highlighting some keys to the understanding of people and place, and inspiring readers to undertake further explorations of their own.

2 FIRST REPORTS

In an 1851 novel by Mayne Reid, *The Scalp Hunters,* Dr. Henry Haller, an Englishman, goes west from St. Louis in search of adventure. He finds plenty. Separated from his companions on the vast western prairie, he finds himself in the path of a buffalo stampede.

"God of heaven!" he exclaims, "I am in their track. I will be trampled to death." When Haller's rifle shot fails to turn the herd, his demise seems assured. With more than three hundred pages to go in a tale barely begun, it is clear that something must be done for Dr. Haller, and fast: "A huge bull, ahead of the rest, furious and snorting, plunged through the stream, and up the slope. I was lifted and tossed high into the air. I was thrown rearwards, and fell upon a moving mass. I did not feel hurt or stunned. I felt myself carried onward upon the backs of several animals, that, in that dense drove, ran close together" (23–24). Unharmed, the startled traveler manages to drop his legs over the sides of one of the beasts and ride him down to a smooth landing. Thus he is able to continue his journey to northern Mexico.

So it goes, page after page, in this story by Captain Mayne Reid, and in dozens of other nineteenth-century novels of incredible exploits on the great American frontier. Apparently this was the way readers in distant places liked their West. They didn't mind being kidded; they just didn't want to be bored.

Until the last years of the century, English-language fiction portrayals of New Mexico and the West were few and generally undistinguished. In the main, they catered to an insatiable demand for tales of romance and adventure — the more fantastic, shocking, and improbable, the better. Any resemblance to literature was mostly coincidental. A few books, like George Frederick Ruxton's *Life in the Far West* (1849), offered reliable reportage on the western country, but they were in the minority.

As literature, most nineteenth-century novels of the West have little to recommend them. They have elicited somewhat greater interest as evidence of the values and aspirations of their readers, and of prevailing perceptions of the frontier. Henry Nash Smith, in *Virgin Land: The American West as Symbol and Myth* (1950), found popular fiction a powerful influence in the creation of a durable and compelling mythology of the West. This mythology, he said, looks to freedom and self-reliance as its cardinal virtues and adopts as its ends the extension of Anglo-American political and cultural dominance and the exploitation of western lands for material gain. Ray Allen Billington (1981) has noted the importance of early novels for their influence on European perceptions of the frontier, where western stories enjoyed enormous popularity.

The number of nineteenth-century works of fiction with significant New Mexico settings is small, but these works are typical of significant patterns and movements in early fiction of the American West.

PRE-CIVIL WAR NOVELS

New Mexico appears as a significant setting in scarcely half a dozen novels published before the Civil War. Like many western novels of this period, most of these can be traced to James Fenimore Cooper and the popular *Leatherstocking Tales*. Other novels of the period demonstrated greater originality and helped popularize themes and approaches that would recur time and again in western fiction.

The pre–Civil War novels of New Mexico and the West manifest the influence of the Romantic movement of the eighteenth and nineteenth centuries — a movement that profoundly affected literature and the arts in England and the United States. As a term used to describe and classify literary works, "romanticism" carries multiple meanings and connotations, but some generalizations can be made with reference to the romantic qualities commonly found in early western fiction. The romantic novel typically emphasizes action over character, exalts the constancy and durability of true love, and idealizes nature as an ennobling influence. A strong melodramatic quality often is evident in story and prose style. A good deal of imaginative license is assumed; the early novel billed as a "romance" was not intended to be taken literally, nor was a literal reading likely.

The past frequently is idealized in romantic novels; but, as Edwin W. Gaston, Jr., observes, American writers of the mid–nineteenth century found little to idealize in the brief history of European settlement in the New World. For indigenous materials, they turned instead to contemporary features in which they perceived edifying qualities: "the Indian, the frontiersman, and the wilderness setting" (13). The white man's ambivalence toward native peoples was apparent immediately in fiction and nonfiction works about the West, but the "noble savage" had his day in the tales of a handful of die-hard American and European romanticists.

The earliest appearance of New Mexico in an English-language novel occurs in *Francis Berrian; Or, The Mexican Patriot*, published by the Boston firm of Cummings, Hilliard and Company in 1826. Its author, Timothy Flint (1780–1840), was a native of Massachusetts and a graduate of Harvard College. Following a sixteen-year career as a pastor and missionary, he sought fame and fortune as a man of letters, exploiting a growing interest in the American frontier. Between the end of his pastorate at Lunenburg, Massachusetts, and his death in 1840, Flint traveled extensively and relocated numerous times, enjoying his greatest productivity during a six-year residency in Cincinnati, Ohio, in 1827–33 (see Folsom). He produced works of fiction, history, and biography, including his *Biographical Memoir of Daniel Boone* (1833), based in part on Flint's personal acquaintance with Boone and members of his family. Flint apparently never ventured west of the Mississippi Valley and the states of Missouri, Arkansas, and Louisiana, but he developed an interest in the borderlands of Mexico and the present-day American Southwest. This interest found expression in his first novel, *Francis Berrian*. True to the literary conventions of his time, Flint insists in prefatory remarks that his improbable tale is "any thing, rather than fiction" (iii).

In *Francis Berrian*, Flint helped to blaze a trail that would become a well-worn rut in western fiction of the nineteenth century. His central character, Berrian, goes west with a mule-trading expedition, encounters an alien culture, experiences numerous perils and predicaments, and becomes romantically involved with the daughter of an influential Spanish family.

While crossing the plains, Berrian rescues Donna Martha Miguela d'Alvaro, a captive of the Comanche Indians and daughter of the powerful Conde d'Alvaro. Berrian returns her safely to Santa Fe and is invited to accompany the family to Durango, where he is to become a teacher in the conde's household.

The theme of cultural conflict, so durable in fiction of the Southwest, is evident from the beginning. Berrian encounters considerable antagonism to his own values as he lives with the family of the conde and pursues the hand of his beloved Donna Martha. Berrian is a red-blooded Anglo-American, deeply committed to republican ideals; the conde is a confirmed royalist. Respectful toward the Catholic faith of his hosts, Berrian nonetheless remains a heretic in their eyes. He also finds himself at odds with Martha's unwanted suitor, Don Pedro Guitterez, and the scheming priest who aids Don Pedro's cause. Driven from the conde's household, Berrian joins forces with the republican revolutionaries and eventually wins Donna Martha, as well as the approval of her family.

This pattern of characters and events shortly would be reduced to a trite formula, invoked repeatedly by writers whose intentions were more crassly commercial than those of Timothy Flint. The imposition of American values on an alien society; the westering hero's romantic conquest of a desirable Spanish girl; the hero's triumph over wild Indians and natural hazards; and the presence of such stock characters as the American hero, his Spanish rival, the delicate heroine, and the conniving priest — all were to become familiar to readers of adventure stories set in the Spanish borderlands.

Another widely-read romance of the Southwest was *Old Hicks the Guide; Or, Adventures in the Camanche Country in Search of a Gold Mine* (1848), by Charles Wilkins Webber. True to the tradition of Fenimore Cooper and his imitators, the story includes a wizened frontiersman, Old Hicks; a younger hero, the narrator; the hero's rival, Albert; and a delicate creature, Emilie L'Entville, who attracts the hero's affection. Emilie, who faints at moments of danger or excitement, is the epitome of a character type identified by Edwin W. Gaston, Jr., as the "frontier flower." The story proceeds through a series of wild adventures, Indian fights, miraculous rescues, and incredible coincidences, to a conclusion in which the villain gets his just desserts and the hero and his bride live happily ever after.

Vaguely located, the story follows a party of "Texan Rangers" from an emigrant colony on the Trinity River across the plains in pursuit of a legendary gold mine. The mine is said to lie in a dividing ridge "between the head waters of the Rio Puerco and those of the North Canadian" (34). This would seem to place the party's objective in the northern mountains of

New Mexico. Although the narrator indicates that the mine is "in the northwestern part of Texas proper," the likely frame of reference is a spurious claim, settled in 1850, which would have given Texas a sizable portion of New Mexico, along with parts of Oklahoma, Kansas, Colorado, and Wyoming.

Like Flint, Webber apparently had not seen much of the country in which his story is laid, so the novel is of little value as a descriptive account of the land and people. *Old Hicks* reeks of melodrama and, despite the author's protestations to the contrary, is a preposterous tale notable above all for its expression of the doctrine of primitivism. En route to the elusive gold mine, the Texan party encounters a wilderness kingdom in which Albert, a corrupt adventurer, has gained authority over a league of Indian tribes. The experience provides an opportunity for the narrator to gain insight into the "savage life," and to expound its virtues: "The savage is, most innocently, a profound master of the laws of life. He has never taken his degree at Edinburgh, or traveled to the Continental schools; yet his simple habits are so far above the *practical* wisdom of learned professors as to enable him to look down with patronizing pity upon the technical and ponderous stupidity of all the colleges of medicine and surgery in the world" (306). With nature as his teacher, the savage has learned to provide for his sustenance, to maintain health and wholeness, and to heed the guidance of a natural moral law which is superior to the tedious codes devised by civilized men.

Author Webber further declares that the character of the frontiersman, or "border ranger," comes to resemble that of the savage "when not entirely corrupted by the civilization he has left behind him." He notes, "With them the primitive virtues of a heroic manhood are all-sufficient, and they care nothing for reverences, forms, duties, &c., as civilization has them, but respect each other's rights, and recognize the awful presence of a benignant God in the still grandeur of mountain, forest, valley, plain, and river, through, among, and over which they pass" (311).

Henry Nash Smith, in *Virgin Land*, indicates that the idea of primitivism held some appeal for readers in the first half of the nineteenth century. For him, *Old Hicks* is the acknowledged high-water mark of this doctrine as expressed in western fiction. Although few writers put as much stock in the notion of primitivism as Webber apparently did, it was an idea that refused to die entirely. Writers dealing with the frontier continued to struggle with the contradictory notions of the wilderness as an ennobling influence and as a land to be conquered and civilized.

A work of greater merit was George Frederick Ruxton's *Life in the Far West* (1849). Born in 1821 in England, Ruxton traveled much of the world as a soldier and adventurer before his untimely death in St. Louis at the age of twenty-seven. Unlike so many others who were writing tales of the American West, Ruxton had traveled extensively in the West, and his observations were highly regarded. His account of the fur trade era in the Rocky Mountains, *Life in the Far West,* informed such later works as Harvey Fergusson's *Wolf Song* (1927) and remains a major source on the life and lingo of the mountain man.

Ruxton's story follows the adventures of Killbuck and LaBonté, trappers of the southern Rocky Mountains, who trade and trap, get into scrapes with Indians, and venture to California to trade for mules. After selling mules at Bent's Fort, they head to Taos to sell beaver and enjoy themselves.

In his account of the arrival of the mountain men in the village of Taos, Ruxton tells something of the relations between the trappers and the local people. The Americans are received with interest by the young women of the village, who peer from their doorways as the strangers pass by. Not everyone, however, is glad to see the mountain men:

> The men, however, seemed scarcely so well pleased; but leaned sulkily against the walls, their sarapes turned over the left shoulder, and concealing the lower part of the face, the hand appearing from its upper folds only to remove the eternal cigarro from their lips. They, from under their broad-brimmed sombreros, scowled with little affection upon the stalwart hunters, who clattered past them, scarcely deigning to glance at the sullen Pelados, but paying incomprehensible compliments to the buxom wenches who smiled at them from the doors. (195)

Ruxton describes a fandango in detail, from early preparations to the rumble into which the evening disintegrates. The Americans take the dance floor, twirling and stamping with the Mexican girls, heedless of the seething resentment of the local men: "The Mexicans have no chance in such physical force dancing; and if a dancing Pelado steps into the ring, a lead-like thump from a galloping mountaineer quickly sends him sprawling with the considerate remark — 'Quit, you darned Spaniard! you can't "shine" in this crowd'" (197). Between the insults, jealousies, and free-flowing whiskey, it's little wonder that the evening erupts in chaos, with mountain men and locals wielding knives and table legs in a display of acute cultural conflict.

In correspondence to his editor at *Blackwood's Magazine,* which first published the work in serial form, Ruxton insists that his account of the fandango is "true to the letter," adding that he and three companions once "cleared a fandango at Taos, armed only with bowie-knives — some score of Mexicans, at least, being in the room" (Ruxton, ix).

Whatever his own feelings about the conflict he described, Ruxton's accounts of life in the southern Rockies, among native peoples and the mountain men, added immeasurably to the scant and mostly dubious literature of the American West, as it was known in the middle of the nineteenth century.

Among the few who produced novels of the little-known Southwest in the years just after the American occupation of New Mexico in 1847 were two of the foremost practitioners of escapist fiction for European audiences. As Zane Grey, Louis L'Amour, and other prolific writers supplied the voracious appetites of later readers, Mayne Reid and Gustave Aimard turned out volume upon volume of fantastic adventure stories for European readers of the mid–nineteenth century. In their singleness of purpose — maximum entertainment of the reader — and in their willingness to forego authenticity for the sake of romance, the Europeans foreshadowed the coming era of the dime-novel Western and, to some extent, the entire genre of the Western as it has survived throughout the twentieth century. Exaggeration and sensationalism were raised to new heights, to the delight of readers.

Reid and Aimard had much in common, beginning with the dates of their births and deaths, 1818 and 1883. Both traveled in North America and were involved in the U.S.-Mexican War — Reid on the American side, Aimard as a naval commander on the Mexican side. Although the works of both men were highly colored, each gained some knowledge of the geography, culture, climate, and people of the southwestern borderlands.

Mayne Reid was born in Ireland and educated for the ministry. Instead of taking the cloth, he traveled to America in 1840 in pursuit of adventure. According to contemporary accounts of his life, he lived as a frontier trader and trapper prior to his Mexican War experience (Meyer). The title of "Captain" was acquired as a result of Reid's service in Mexico. He received a commission with the New York Volunteers, distinguished himself in the Battle of Chapultapec, and reportedly retired with the rank of Captain (Steele, 13).

Working as a journalist at intervals over the course of his life, Reid began producing longer works of fiction and in 1850 achieved publication of a novel for boys, *The Rifle Rangers*. Reid finally produced more than fifty novels, most of them offering accounts of hair-raising mayhem on the American frontier. Three books, *The Scalp Hunters* (1851), *The White Chief* (1855), and *The Lone Ranch* (1871), were set substantially in New Mexico.

The Scalp Hunters proved to be one of Reid's most popular tales, re-published numerous times for varied audiences. So far as plot is concerned, it follows the rutted road. Dr. Henry Haller, an Englishman traveling through New Orleans, seeks adventure in the West. He is assured that he will have all the excitement he wants if he joins with a band of traders bound for the Rocky Mountains and Mexico (12). Haller goes, investing ten thousand dollars in trade goods.

Haller arrives in Santa Fe to find it "the paradise of traders, trappers, and thieves" (36). When the caravan moves south, Haller remains in Santa Fe nursing injuries suffered in a fandango brawl, but he soon hurries on to catch up to his companions. He nearly dies of thirst when abandoned by a treacherous guide on the Jornada del Muerto, leading the author to engage in a long digression on probable scientific causes of the land's oppressive aridity. Haller is rescued and taken to the camp of Colonel Seguin and his band of scalp hunters, where he falls in love with Seguin's young daughter, Zoe. More adventures ensue, a second daughter is rescued from captivity among the Navajos, and Haller wins Zoe. The colonel forswears the life of a scalp hunter, and all principal characters repair to "the waters of the Mississippi" — probably to New Orleans — to live happily ever after (352).

We may trust that Dr. Haller has had all the adventure he desires, but he has learned some enduring lessons about New Mexico: (1) When people of varied cultures meet in the Southwest, they don't always get along. (2) The law is not a dependable refuge for aggrieved parties on the frontier. And (3) the Jornada del Muerto is vast, hot, and exceedingly dry.

A strong spirit of American nationalism, often coupled with racial slurs, marks many of the early novels. Irish by birth, Reid promoted the idea of Anglo-American dominance. In *The White Chief,* Carlos the Cibolero — the reader is not told if he has another name — takes on a corrupt Mexican military regime at the town of San Ildefonso, located vaguely between the Rio Grande and the Llano Estacado. Living in the region with his mother and sister, Carlos is an American buffalo hunter and a lone force for justice. In rising to a sporting proposition thrown down by one of the Mexican authorities, Carlos is urged on by the cry of his aged mother: "Go! Go, Carlos the Cibolero, and show the tawny cowards —

slaves that they are — what a free American can do" (42). Such strident proclamations of American superiority are not unusual in these early works.

True to the pattern of early novels of the West, Carlos woos and wins the lovely daughter of one of the Mexican aristocrats. Catalina's father and his associates are scoundrels of the worst sort, but somehow Catalina has grown up to be virtuous and a good judge of character, ready to forsake her blood kin at a moment's notice for an American who practices a smelly and disgusting profession. In his treachery, Catalina's father typifies the men of his race; in her virtue, Catalina epitomizes the women, of whom the narrator observes, "The humanity of these is in an inverse ratio to that of their lords" (55).

Sensational western romance was also the forte of Gustave Aimard (the pseudonym of Olivier Gloux). Following his involvement in the Mexican War, Aimard traveled in the Southwest, Mexico, and South America before returning permanently to his native France in the 1850s. He drew on his American experience for some thirty novels. Though Aimard wrote in French, his popularity was such that most of his works immediately were published in England, often in competing editions. Aimard's *The Trail Hunter: A Tale of the Far West* (1861) and *The Pirates of the Prairies: Adventures in the American Desert* (1862) offered views of adventure and conflict in the borderlands.

The Trail Hunter turns partly on a natural conflict of cultures along the U.S.-Mexican border, where the U.S. recently had displayed its ambition by seizing half of Mexico. "In fact," the author continues, "in Northern America two hostile races — the Anglo-Saxon and the Spanish — stand face to face. The Anglo-Saxons are devoured by an ardour for conquest, and a rage for invasion, which nothing can arrest, or even retard" (16).

Not surprisingly, the villain of Aimard's tale is a North American, a squatter known as Red Cedar. He has moved in on the estate of Don Miguel Zarate, a man "possessed of an incalculable fortune" and "beloved and respected by the Indians" (18). The two men become enemies, and Red Cedar betrays the Don to Mexican authorities; as a result, he is arrested and taken to Santa Fe.

Santa Fe is described as "a pretty town, built in the midst of a laughing and fertile plain," but the author goes on to say that the society is in such a state of decadence that "the day is at hand when it will be only an uninhabited ruin" (203–204). Don Miguel and his compatriot, General Ibáñez, are summarily convicted and sentenced to death, causing the narrator to observe, "The Mexicans, ordinarily so slow when justice has to be dealt, are the most expeditious in the world when a conspiracy has to be punished" (204).

Fortunately, Don Miguel enjoys the able assistance of Aimard's hero, Valentine Guillois, the "Trail Hunter." Guillois and other friends facilitate the escape of Don Miguel and the general from their imprisonment in Santa Fe, so that they may live to fight another day and pursue the evil Red Cedar in the promised sequel.

Laughable as they seem now, the works of Reid, Aimard, and others had far-reaching influence on popular perceptions and attitudes, as Ray Allen Billington has demonstrated. "Little known to historians of literature," Billington writes, "these best-sellers played a larger role than any other writings in shaping the European image of the American frontier" (38). Billington characterizes the distant frontier known to Europeans as a "land of savagery" and a "land of promise," but clearly it was equally a land of uncertain justice and deep-seated cultural conflict.

J. Frank Dobie observed in his *Guide to Life and Literature of the Southwest* (1943) that much fiction about the West has "betrayed rather than revealed life" (97). There was plenty of betrayal in the early reports, to be sure, but some enduring truths were revealed as well.

For better or worse, by the time Americans were caught up in the bitter conflict between North and South, the formula that would continue to guide writers of western fiction for decades to come was well established. The westering hero, representing all that was good, would tramp through countless pages to subdue the menacing red man, overcome the ravages of nature, defeat his rivals, win the heart of his beloved frontier flower, and impose his values upon an alien and presumably inferior society. But the feats he already had accomplished were as nothing compared to new highs and lows he would attain in the era to come.

DIME-NOVEL NEW MEXICO

On June 9, 1860, the New York firm of Irwin P. Beadle and Company published a modest work of fiction entitled *Malaeska: The Indian Wife of the White Hunter,* by Ann S. Stephens. This event marked the beginning of a forty-year period during which cheap paperbound novels enjoyed phenomenal popularity as a medium of entertainment for the masses. Stories of western adventure quickly took over the market, making the dime novel a powerful purveyor of images and attitudes about the West.

The initial series of "Beadle's Dime Novels" ran to some 321 biweekly issues — a mere drop in the bucket for an industry that attracted a half dozen major competitors in the U.S. alone and turned out thousands of titles and millions of copies.

The term "dime novel" is associated most closely with the firm of Beadle and Adams. The practice popularized by Irwin Beadle and his associates was to publish, for a popular mass audience, whole series of cheap, formula-driven fiction. The term eventually was applied to "any sensational detective or blood-and-thunder novel in pamphlet form," regardless of price (Johannsen, 3). In practice, such works sold at anywhere from five to twenty-five cents each during their day.

Students of literature and popular culture have been careful to distinguish between dime novels and more serious works. For Henry Nash Smith, "The unabashed and systematic use of formulas [in the dime novel] strips from the writing every vestige of interest usually sought in works of the imagination; it is entirely subliterary" (91). Generally lacking in dime novels are one or more characteristics identified by John Milton as "basic elements of good fiction": significance of theme, plausibility, a distinctive and literate style, seriousness of intent, multidimensional characterization, illumination of the human condition, and a sense of place (1980, p. 39). For all its faults, Henry Nash Smith finds the dime novel an object worthy of study for its clues to "the dream life of a vast inarticulate public" that, in the latter half of the nineteenth century, devoured huge quantities of such works (91).

Though Irwin P. Beadle and his successors may have merged the elements of formulaic writing, serial publication, and mass marketing that made the dime novel such a phenomenon in American culture, their success was made possible, in part, by timely advances in printing technology. The introduction of fast, high-volume rotary presses facilitated the production of inexpensive pocket books for a popular market.

The dime novel thus had its antecedent in various story pamphlets published sporadically in the decades preceding Beadle's emergence. One of these was *Taos: A Romance of the Massacre,* by Everpoint, a pseudonym for Joseph M. Field, published in 1847 at the Reveille Job Office in St. Louis and priced at ten cents. Originally written for the *Reveille,* Field's fictional account of the Taos Rebellion characterizes Taos as "a turbulent, rebellious quarter," and makes Padre Antonio José Martínez out to be the treacherous instigator of the 1847 revolt and massacre (14).

The massacre is also the subject of *Black Eyes; Or, The Three Captives. A Tale of the Taos Valley* (1867), the first of some one hundred Beadle issues identified by Johannsen as having a New Mexico setting. Penned by Edward Willett, a Harvard Law School graduate turned journalist and editor, *Black Eyes* actually is one of the better works from the era of "yellow-backed literature." It does, however, contain the usual elements of dime-novel fiction. Its characters include Bill Ward, an older backwoodsman of the Natty Bumppo school; Lt. Charley Bent, the young hero; Fanny Buttress, the daughter of Bent's commanding officer; and Capt. Andrew Sardis, Bent's rival.

En route from Santa Fe to the Great Salt Lake, Maj. Benjamin Buttress and his entourage are caught up in events of the rebellion. As the story opens, however, the exasperated major is involved in a debate with his impetuous young officer, Lieutenant Bent, concerning strategy in warfare with the Indians. The major defends conventional military methods, but his young lieutenant advises that these will not help the soldiers "against a savage and concealed foe who fights from behind trees and rocks, and who picks them off with deadly aim, while he keeps his own person secured from danger" (10). Bent advises that soldiers be trained in the ways of the hunter and woodsman so as to "cope with the savages in their own way, and on their own ground" (12).

Bent represents youth, vigor, and imagination, in contrast to the stodgy major, who symbolizes tradition, regimentation, and unmerited authority. It is clear enough which man the author expects his readers — many of them pawns in the hands of growing commercial and industrial organizations of the East — to identify with.

In private conversation, the major expresses his vexation with Bent and hears the opinion of his more favored junior officer, Captain Sardis: "As for this fellow's being crazy, I think he is afflicted with a species of lunacy, that is very prevalent in these times. The climate of the West is particularly favorable to the development of young America, and young America means a compound of impudence, conceit, and superficial acquirement, and boundless ambition" (19).

Indeed, Bent does represent young America, and it is just these qualities of resourcefulness and independence that make him a fitting hero. Dispatched to Santa Fe as an annoyance to the major and an unwanted temptation for his daughter, Bent, along with his two companions, passes through Taos just as the rebellion is about to commence. The three men —

Bent, Sgt. Luke Royston, and the backwoodsman, Bill Ward — are summarily imprisoned. Fanny and the major also fall into the hands of the rebels.

Following a series of improbable escapes, incredible coincidences, and the discovery of an underground temple used by sun-worshipping natives, Bent effects the rescue of Major Buttress and his daughter as troops arrive from Santa Fe to quell the revolt. The rebellion again is blamed on the village priest, Padre Abrojo, who receives a bullet in the forehead from the major's pistol. Per formula, the young American prevails and wins the heroine.

Another early entry in the annals of dime-novel New Mexico was *The Prairie Rifles; Or, The Captives of New Mexico* (1869), by Henry J. Thomas. The story's hero is Richard Hampton or "Comanche Dick," so called because of his reputation as an Indian fighter. Following an adventurous youth, he has established a sheep ranch in southeastern New Mexico, "a short distance west of the *Llano Estacado* or Staked Plain" (17). Dick employs several capable associates as sheepherders and gunmen, a practical necessity because, "in many portions of New Mexico at that day, as at the present, it is might alone which makes right, and there is no redress for grievances, except in the power of retaliation which the aggrieved party may possess" (18). Comanche Dick is able to make himself useful in such a place, contriving in the usual dime-novel ways to rescue long-lost captives, dispatch savage Indians, thwart villains, and otherwise secure the right of himself and his countrymen to dwell and prosper in the land.

The Prairie Rifles is typical of dime-novel Westerns written before 1875, in that it was set in a wilderness beyond the line of settlement. On the frontier, the hero could experience the ennobling qualities of nature and shed the restraints of society, yet act as an agent of advancing civilization by overcoming natural hazards and savage creatures. Such examples of independence, courage, and triumph apparently appealed to readers who themselves were too entangled or too timid to escape more ordinary lives, except through such vicarious adventures.

There never was much to be said for the literary properties of the dime novel, but students of the phenomenon have noted a deterioration in the quality of stories from the late 1860s to the end of the century. This deterioration is attributed, at least in part, to the emergence of a lively competition among the Beadle firm and its various rivals. One editor reportedly suggested that writers could respond simply by killing off more Indians, but the competition also led rival firms and authors to look for novel sensations and imaginative new gimmicks. Dime novelists easily made the transition from the implausible to the absurd.

In novels with New Mexico settings, this new turn is evident in such works as Frederick Whittaker's *The Black Wizard: A Tale of the Fatal Circle of Invisible Fire* (1871). In this story, Herbert Sinclair, a "conjurer," travels without fear on the Jornada del Muerto, trailing a caravan in his single wagon, with only his sister for company. His security lies in a repertoire of tricks used to frighten and amaze the Indians. He breathes fire, for instance, and camps within the encircling protection of a battery-powered fence that electrocutes intruders.

Even more ludicrous is the story of *Mountain Ned; Or, The Flying Scout* (1874), by W. J. Hamilton, a pseudonym of C. Dunning Clark. The Flying Scout is David Carter, who fled into the wilderness a madman, following an attack by Comanche Indians in which his child was killed. He effects his revenge as a parachutist bomber, jumping off high cliffs and showering his enemies with fire.

The dime novelists drew heavily on historic personages of the West for characters, mixing fact and fiction and sometimes abandoning fact entirely. Kit Carson and Billy the Kid were two New Mexicans who caught on with readers and writers, and whose mythic personae to some extent were formed and amplified through their exposure in dime novels, story papers, and other such pulp materials.

William F. "Buffalo Bill" Cody was the subject of literally hundreds of dime novels. Titles like *Buffalo Bill's Death Charm* (1895) and *Buffalo Bill's Road-Agent Round-Up* (1895), both set around "Ft. Taos, New Mexico," may have had some basis in the famous showman's life, but it is just as likely that they are total fabrications from the fertile imagination of Prentiss Ingraham, who penned no fewer than 121 Buffalo Bill stories. Other books identified as dime novels simply may be works of popular history or biography which contain so many inaccuracies and which are written in such dramatic style as to be taken for fiction. Such ambiguity characterizes *Billy the Kid, the New Mexican Outlaw; Or, The Bold Bandit of the West!* (1881), a contemporary and highly interpretive account of the Kid's life by Edmund Fable, Jr.

Kit Carson, widely admired by contemporaries but unlettered and unimpressive in physical stature, became a celebrated figure at an early age and was appropriated by the dime novelists. He appeared in numerous stories in his own lifetime and beyond, sometimes portrayed as a mature backwoodsman in the Natty Bumppo tradition, sometimes as the youthful plainsman who superseded the older hero. Stories like Albert W. Aiken's *Kit Carson, King of Guides* (1882) drew heavily on published biographies of Carson's life, while idealizing him as a great man who was honest, noble, and heroic. His actual exploits as trapper, scout, and Indian fighter typically were embellished and exaggerated, with additional feats fabricated to achieve the level of sensationalism required by editors and readers.

If some imaginative modification was required to render Carson a heroic figure of dime-novel proportions, William Bonney (Billy the Kid) proved an even more problematical subject for writers of popular fiction. Despite being a youthful folk hero to some, he was, finally, a violent lawbreaker whose deeds could not easily be justified. In an age of moral absolutes, Bonney was of limited value as a literary subject and even less as a hero. The mythic Billy would have his day in a time of greater moral relativism which was yet to come.

By the mid-1880s, the dime-novel formula had grown stale and static. In search of a more contemporary hero to replace the sadly dated backwoodsman and plainsman, Prentiss Ingraham, William G. Patten, and others hit upon the cowboy as a subject of sufficient color and animation to serve the purpose. First perceived as a hired hand of low status and little interest, the cowboy stood in need of some renovation if he was to emerge as a bona fide hero who would sell to the reading public. If the cowboy's life could only be divested of its inherent tedium and hard work — as well as the constant presence of foul-smelling animals — and be infused with excitement and moral purpose, there was hope for him as a literary subject. This was accomplished, albeit without significant effect on a formula which was wearing thin with readers.

In further efforts to modernize, publishers migrated to detective stories and offered popular western tales in briefer form — in five-cent novels, "story papers," and pulp magazines which flourished well into the twentieth century. By 1900, however, the house of Beadle and Adams had concluded its remarkable run, and the dime-novel era was all but over.

The legacy of the dime novel was the mythic Wild West, whose attributes would be celebrated, reviled, and revised without end in the national literature and in film. As a darker aspect of that legacy, dime novels propagated highly negative stereotypes of Hispanic and Native American westerners, thus nourishing the prejudices of readers who likely had few other impressions of the western country and the people who inhabited it. The dime novel also gave voice to a fervent spirit of American nationalism and expressed the nation's confidence that its heroes could overcome all obstacles that lay before them.

TOWARD THE MODERN ERA

In the waning years of the nineteenth century and the first two decades of the new century, some significant literary types appeared. These included an early example of the serious historical novel, an unusual literary projection into the region's prehistory, the first recognizable mystery novel, and the first comic novel.

These years also saw the introduction of several themes that would persist in works of fiction for decades to come. With the closing of the frontier and the settlement of the West, issues of individual freedom emerged. Increased emphasis on social organization in the western country revealed deep cultural differences concerning matters of law, order, and justice. Fiction writers also began to perceive the importance of scarce water as an issue for residents of the Southwest.

These developments gave greater breadth to a body of literature previously fixed on a tired and monotonous paradigm. Although familiar tales of the frontier would persist in works like Col. Henry Inman's *A Pioneer from Kentucky: An Idyll of the Raton Range* (1898) and Robert Ames Bennet's *A Volunteer with Pike: The True Narrative of One Dr. John Robinson and of His Love for the Fair Señorita Vallois* (1909), there was a growing market for divergent and more perceptive views of the West. The appearance of several new themes also indicated directions in which the growing body of southwestern literature would evolve.

In *Great-Grandmother's Girls in New Mexico, 1670–1680* (1888), Elizabeth Champney produced a historical novel of considerable interest, one of a dozen or so novels concerning the Pueblo Revolt of 1680. Champney introduced a theme that would become a familiar refrain — the intense rivalry of the "Two Majesties" of colonial New Mexico — the royal government and the Roman Catholic Church. In Champney's book, church and crown compete for the hearts and minds of the Pueblo Indian people of the province. There are benevolent priests among the Spanish, but the military authorities exhibit such greed and cruelty that soon "there was but one opinion, — the Spaniards, instead of being gods as the Indians had first thought them, were certainly devils" (18). Among the Indians embittered by Spanish cruelty is Popé of San Juan, who endures to exact his revenge upon the conquerors.

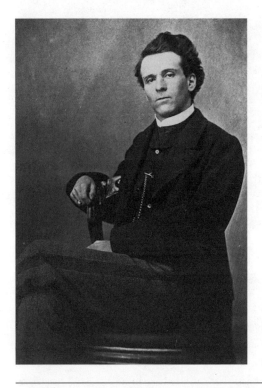

Adolf Bandelier.
*Courtesy Museum of New
Mexico, Neg. No. 9155.*

Much influence of the early western novels is evident in Champney's work. Her characters traipse back and forth across the southwestern landscape to meet countless struggles and pitfalls. When the terrible
day of reckoning arrives for the Spanish, the people of Acoma Pueblo
toss their priest off the edge of the soaring mesa. In a scene worthy of the
most preposterous fabrication of Mayne Reid or Gustave Aimard, the missionary's robe billows up to act as a parachute, and he descends safely to
the plain below. Deeply moved by the miraculous event, the Indians has-
ten to the foot of the cliff, where they are reconciled with the slightly dazed
cleric.

An effort virtually without precedent was Adolf F. Bandelier's *The
Delight Makers* (1890). The work was prompted in part by the author's desire to offer an accurate portrayal of the prehistoric Pueblo Indians to a
popular audience, and in part by Bandelier's need to make some money.

Set in Frijoles Canyon and the surrounding environs of the Pajarito
Plateau, the work draws heavily on Bandelier's archeological studies of the
area. Bandelier's story is of the prehistoric past, when Tyuonyi and other
now extinct settlements were inhabited. The tale includes some romance,
some intrigue, numerous explanations from the author's researches, and

Marah Ellis Ryan.
Courtesy of the Southwest
Museum, Los Angeles.
Photo #41902.

much speculation concerning the ways, beliefs, and eventual disappearance of the inhabitants.

The book proved, among other things, that literature was not Bandelier's forte. It did, however, win many admirers for its authoritative portrayal of a prehistoric native culture, remaining in print almost constantly until 1970.

Less durable but equally popular with contemporary readers were the novels of Marah Ellis Ryan, an Eastern-born actress and novelist who developed a keen interest in Indian cultures of the Southwest. She reportedly lived among the Navajos for a time and, according to three sources, was admitted "to the inner council of tribal chiefs." If Bandelier's novel was grounded in the bedrock of his careful research, Ryan's were born of a passion for the exotic lore of the Indians of the Southwest. Described as lyrical, poetic, and romantic, her books were among the few of her day to express sympathy and even admiration for Native American characters.

In *The Flute of the Gods* (1909), Ryan created a sprawling epic which was acclaimed for its interpretation of Indian beliefs. Set in the mid–sixteenth century, the story deals with contact between early Spanish expeditions and native peoples of the Southwest. Wary of Spanish conquerors and Spanish religion, the godlike Tahnte warns of disaster that is sure to befall the Pueblo people, should they embrace the ways of the strangers. Ryan's

The House of the Dawn (1914) again deals with Spanish-Indian conflict, this time in the context of the Pueblo Revolt.

In the works of Bandelier, Ryan, and Albert Reagan (*Don Diego; Or, The Pueblo Indian Uprising of 1680,* published in 1914), Native Americans were portrayed with unaccustomed sympathy. If the portrayals were not entirely believable, they at least expressed a growing appreciation for Indian cultures. For the literary Native American, sympathy was a vast improvement over the hostility expressed by most writers of dime novels. What remained to be attained by the nonnatives who wrote about Indian subjects was a greater degree of understanding. In the more favorable climate of twentieth-century attitudes, writers like Oliver La Farge and Frank Waters could find encouragement to explore native cultures in greater depth and develop more perceptive interpretations of Native American experience.

By the turn of the century, two other distinctive literary types had appeared. One was a mystery novel, *My Invisible Partner* (1898), by Thomas S. Denison. Though flawed by a stilted manner of expression and rendered implausible by the protagonist's eerie out-of-body experiences, the book stands as one of the first books of the Southwest to take the form of a standard murder mystery. Another new type was the "village novel," represented in Louis How's *The Penitentes of San Rafael* (1900).

In *Heart's Desire: The Story of a Contented Town, Certain Peculiar Citizens and Two Fortunate Lovers* (1905), Emerson Hough provided an element that had been lacking in most earlier works of western fiction — a sense of humor. Writing in the literary tradition of the waning "local color" movement, Hough drew on his brief experience as a young attorney residing in the rough mining camp of White Oaks, New Mexico, in the mid-1880s.

Hough's book expressed a growing change in attitudes in and about the West. As the country filled in and societies grew up, westering Anglos no longer were so concerned with civilizing a wild and lawless frontier. The frontier officially closed in 1890. Within a few years, the problem had been reframed. In building towns, schools, and churches; subduing the Indians; and instituting law and order, the westerner had gained a measure of security, but it came at the cost of his freedom. *Heart's Desire* mourns the loss of liberty and blames the recent advent of law, women, and eastern capital. Concerning the bygone era, says one bitter inhabitant in *Heart's Desire,* "We were three hundred men here, and it was Heaven" (68).

Another significant event predating the modern era was the development of the modern western novel. The cowboy hero was a product of the dime-novel tradition, a mutation in an evolutionary chain that included the backwoodsman, the trapper, and the plainsman. The prolific dime-novel author Prentiss Ingraham is widely, though not unanimously, recognized as the creator of the cowboy hero. Ingraham's Buck Taylor, reportedly modeled on one of Buffalo Bill's Wild West Show cowboys, rode through many a tale following his appearance in 1887, including at least one New Mexico title, *Buck Taylor's Boys; Or, The Red Riders of the Rio Grande* (1891). Dime-novel New Mexico also could boast cowboy characters created by "Lieutenant A. K. Sims," pseudonym of J. H. Whitson, who wrote *Prince Primrose, the Flower of the Flock; Or, The Grand Coup at Paradise Gulch* (1889); and W. G. Patten, author of the "Hurricane Hal" stories.

For Henry Nash Smith, dime novels and the pulp western magazines that lingered after them "lead in a straight line" to the popular western novels that endure to the present. This tradition includes the likes of Zane Grey, Clarence E. Mulford, and Charles Alden Seltzer and constitutes what C. L. Sonnichsen has characterized as the "low road" in western fiction. Such works generally exploit the tried and true formula, none too subtly mixing violent conflict and romance.

It was left to Owen Wister to locate the literary high road in western fiction, with his 1902 publication of *The Virginian: Horseman of the Plains.* On the high road, the author supposedly treats themes of significance, creates original and well-developed characters, exhibits a literate style, and writes with fidelity about western settings. Florence Finch Kelly could lay claim to some of these achievements in her novel of southern New Mexico, *With Hoops of Steel* (1900), which predated Wister's landmark book by two years. Kelly wrote perceptively about the ironies of law and justice, about racial attitudes in the Southwest, and about the growing influence of large commercial interests in a land that once had been the domain of rugged individuals. Among her characters were ranchers who actually worked cattle. She simply did not have all the elements required for hitting the jackpot, as Wister did, and the name "Florence" on a novel about the West probably did not help.

The early literary Western is best represented in New Mexico in the work of Eugene Manlove Rhodes, who moved with his family to southern New Mexico as an adolescent in 1881. Rhodes witnessed the last days of the open range, and he never surrendered his admiration for the independent men who worked the range or for the values they embodied. For some three decades, Rhodes hymned the virtues of his resourceful heroes in magazine stories and in several longer works, beginning with *Good Men and True* (1910). Rhodes fought the "Western" label and its automatic association with lurid works he detested. Shunned by the arbiters of literary taste, Rhodes took comfort in the assurance that his works one day would furnish fleeting glimpses of an era lost to history.

As for western writers assigned to the high road and those consigned to the low, the distinction often is a matter of personal judgment. There is little debate, however, concerning the existence of such a divide. Rhodes was insistent about his own fidelity to the times, places, and people he wrote about, and he had little patience with writers who, in his view, falsely portrayed the West and its people.

One of the few contemporaries Rhodes admired was Bertha Muzzy Bower, in whom he found a kindred spirit. In *The Phantom Herd* (1916), Bower's "Flying U" boys are camped at the foot of the Sandia Mountains, where they have been hired to work in a western movie. Fed up with the mindless shoot-'em-ups demanded by his studio, Luck Lindsay is determined to make a realistic film, but his producer has other ideas. Realism, the producer insists, won't sell to a public that demands its West "served hot and strong and reeking with the smoke of black powder" (71). In print and in film, the low road was more heavily traveled, but the high road at least had been found.

By 1920, New Mexico had gone from Spanish rule to Mexican government to American territorial status and then to statehood, and its literary stream had widened to take in new forms and new ideas. Writers like Bandelier, Hough, and Rhodes had spent time getting to know the land and the people, and they began to develop in the literature a truer and more complex sense of place.

James Maguire, in his article in *A Literary History of the American West* (1987), sets the beginning of the modern era in American fiction at 1920. This works for New Mexico, where a native son, Harvey Fergusson, was putting the finishing touches on the first of ten published novels. Tethered to the past by his place in one of the founding families of Albuquerque, and by his own interest in history, Fergusson nonetheless felt compelled to break with tradition. Put off by the rigors of cadet life, he fled New Mexico Military Institute and enrolled at Washington and Lee University.

In the East, the impressionable young westerner discovered what he later described as "a new epoch in American thought" (Fergusson, 1944,

p. 119). To be more precise, Fergusson discovered and was attracted to some ideas, newly fashionable, which would come to characterize the modernist movement. The new generation of American writers expressed society's alienation from traditional moral standards, ideals, and assumptions. Heroes were few in the newer works, and psychological dimensions were emphasized over action. On the whole, the new epoch offered a gloomier, if more perceptive, view of contemporary society, and apparently many readers and critics approved. Fergusson did not buy everything the modernists had to sell, but their repudiation of nationalistic fervor and traditional morals, as well as their dissatisfaction with the nation's intellectual life, especially appealed to him.

Fergusson was drawn to the ideas expressed by H. L. Mencken, Van Wyck Brooks, Randolph Bourne, and "all the other bright young prophets of a new day" (1944, p. 119). Determined as he was to be part of that new day, Harvey Fergusson was uniquely endowed to transcend East and West, traditional and modern, and probe the meaning of the new epoch for the society whence he came.

3 WHEN CULTURES MEET

n Thomas Hardy's *The Dynasts,* the Spirit Sinister observes that "war makes rattling good history; but peace is poor reading" (1904, Part First, Act II, Scene 5). Hardy knew, and most writers know, that this is so for fiction writers as well as for historians. Writers like the late Edward Abbey and John Nichols may rail against the forces of environmental degradation and political oppression, but the truth is, they love the fight; as writers, they live off it. Conflict is as essential to their craft as mud is to adobe bricks. No conflict, no fiction.

This may explain, in part, why New Mexico has provided such a rich body of raw material for works of fiction. New Mexicans live with a lot of conflict — conflict over scarce water, over land use, over the whole notion of "development"; conflict between tradition and change, between the frontier spirit of independence and the formidable presence of imposing federal and state bureaucracies. All these sources of conflict are evident in works of fiction set in New Mexico, but none has had a more lasting or pervasive influence on the literature than the conflict among the region's distinctive cultural groups.

Writers may like conflict, but boosters don't; it makes them nervous. According to one of the most cherished myths of the tourism industry and local chambers of commerce, New Mexico represents a blend of three distinctive peoples — Anglo, Hispanic, and Native American — all meeting in the American Southwest to form a harmonious multicultural society in which the traditions of each are enjoyed by all. This idea has been an essential tenet in the state's promotional mythology for well over half a century; as with many clichés, there is some truth in it.

Official publicists have soft-pedaled this litany in recent years, but it is still favored in some popular guidebooks. One of these tells readers that the region's tricultural heritage is among its most attractive features. Another informs visitors that "much of New Mexico's distinctiveness is owed to its tri-cultural heritage: Indian, Hispanic and Anglo populations existing together in harmony, respect, and cooperation" (DeWitt, ix).

This can hardly be the same place described by fiction writers, who portray a history of cultural relations ranging from simple misunderstandings to violent aggression and conquest. Their accounts of relationships vary, but they seldom include the words *unity, harmony,* and *cooperation.* True, there hasn't been a shooting war in some time, but neither have residents seen the multicultural lovefest that some boosters of tourism and industry like to imagine. Again, fiction thrives on conflict, and in that sense, it might be said that the fiction writer is always looking for trouble.

As to the claim that three cultures dwell in unity, writers mostly don't buy it. In Reata, a fictional representation of Gallup in Lars Lawrence's *Morning Noon and Night* (1954), the notion of interracial harmony is proclaimed loudly. Reata's newspaper sees to that, periodically trotting out a clichéd editorial for the benefit of the tourist trade: "Here, boasted the *Lariat,* three races coexisted without conflict and yet without abandoning their ancient cultures" (6). What the editorialist so delicately leaves unsaid is that the Hispanic people inhabit a squalid community two miles from town, with the blessings of Reata's Anglo majority, and that the Indians constitute an exploited population of reservation dwellers who care little for the fellowship of the townspeople.

For Frank O'Rourke, who lived all over the country and wrote more than a dozen novels out of his five-year residency in Taos, the claim makes much of nothing. Dr. Manning, the Anglo doctor of Rio Arriba in *The Springtime Fancy* (1961), has heard the familiar refrain, but he is unimpressed: "Well, and what's so unique about three cultures? In any large city you'll find ethnic groups living closely, if not contumely, speaking various tongues, publishing foreign language papers, eating native foods, continuing the excellent traditions and customs of their native lands. Do they howl about uniqueness? Hell no!" (36–37).

The whole idea of "three cultures" must leave many New Mexicans wondering where they fit. What if you don't happen to be Anglo, Hispanic or Native American, for instance? Does this mean you don't have a culture?

William Eastlake offers an answer of sorts. In *Portrait of an Artist with 26 Horses* (1963), a black man — a sight never before seen in Eastlake's Indian Country — is perceived by Navajos as "some new kind of a white man" (97). This is inferred because of the way the man acts and dresses, and because of the language he speaks. Similar logic applies in Richard Bradford's *Red Sky at Morning* (1968), as locals try explaining the system to a new arrival from Alabama. "We recognize only three kinds of people in Sagrado," the newcomer is told, "Anglos, Indians and Natives" (44). From there it gets complicated, but, one way or another, everyone is made to fit within the established categories.

Where blacks occur as residents of Hispanic New Mexico — Canuto in La Farge's *Behind the Mountains* (1956) and "El Negro Aguilar" in Ulibarrí's *My Grandma Smoked Cigars* (1977), for example — they generally appear as novel characters who evoke interest and who are well received by their neighbors. Hispanics, explains Ulibarrí, "have never had, nor do we now have, that terrible obsession the Anglo-Saxon has over the color of the skin" (73). Present in such small numbers, blacks are not perceived as a force, nor are they typically involved in social conflict. This is good, since the three official cultures manage to generate plenty of friction with no help from anyone else.

ENCOUNTERS OF AGGRESSION AND CONQUEST

As we have already seen, the earliest contacts among Indians, Hispanics, and Anglos in the Southwest were recorded by fiction writers as encounters of violence and hostility, often in response to overt acts of aggression. To be sure, history supports such an account, but conflict and violence also suited the purposes of those who wrote about the American West in the nineteenth century.

Accounts of violent conflict are found primarily in two groups of novels. These are the early novels of the Southwest, including dime novels, and historical novels written and published in the twentieth century but set in earlier times.

There is nothing subtle about the nature of race relations in the early western novels. Without shame, writers from the eastern United States and Western Europe characterized the rivals of their Anglo heroes as red savages, bad Injuns, sneaking assassins, swarthy Mexicans, and worse.

Such characterizations were driven by racial prejudice, a rampant nationalistic spirit, and the novelist's need for a menacing antagonist. The de-
monization of Native Americans by early writers may seem an instance
of gratuitous mass character assassination, but it served a purpose. According to Ray Allen Billington, the European novelists who largely were
responsible for creating the demonic savages of western myth did so because danger and action sold books. Moreover, the portrayal of Native
Americans as an incorrigible and subhuman race served to justify the aggressive exploits of the heroic frontiersmen who "civilized" the West.

The savages of Gustave Aimard, Mayne Reid, and others were a fright-
ful bunch: "Treacherous, vindictive, cruel, many of them cannibalistic,
they spent their lives scalping travelers, abducting heroines, battling with
white hunters, and devising torture techniques that would have shocked
the Marquis de Sade. Their roles in European 'Westerns' were essential,
for they provided expendable opponents for the heroes and the sensationalism demanded by the Wild West tradition from that day to this"
(Billington, 117).

Most writers of early western fiction did not have to confront their antagonists as real people, and they didn't. They simply conjured up the
bloodthirsty devils needed to charge their stories with suspense and violent action, then watched as sales soared. Social responsibility was not a
concern.

Later writers found a wealth of material for works of historical fiction.
They focused on events that evoked the color of old times and exotic cultures and that included the element of violent conflict, such a reliable
source of interest for readers. The historical novels are more rational in
their accounts of cultural conflict than are the adventure novels that preceded them; but they, too, often reflect the prejudices and nationalistic
sentiments of their authors.

New Mexico's Spanish Colonial period is celebrated in a dozen or more
novels. Focusing primarily on the Pueblo Revolt of 1680, they explore the
nature of Spanish-Indian relations and reveal that hostilities were plenti-
ful long before the Anglo-Americans began arriving in large numbers.
With a few exceptions, the Spanish are portrayed as cruel, ruthless conquerors who forced a foreign religion upon the pueblos and exploited the
meager resources of the weaker pueblo people.

The 1914 novel, *Don Diego; Or, The Pueblo Indian Uprising of 1680,* by
Albert B. Reagan, opens with the visit to Jemez Pueblo by messengers from
other pueblos of the region. Bringing news of the planned revolt, they urge

the Jemez people to join with the other pueblos. In secret council, Ojeda of Santa Ana recounts a century and a half of Spanish transgressions against the pueblos, an unbroken litany of excesses and atrocities. "The white man's rule has been nothing but oppression, flogging, imprisonment and death to my people," Ojeda says. "Not only have they compelled us to do all their labor for them, but they have taken our young women to be their wives, against their will. They have made servants and worse than servants of our wives" (40).

Les Savage, Jr., goes into greater detail concerning the colonial policies of the Spanish, explaining the *encomienda* system, in which a colonist could be granted authority to extract labor from the Pueblo people. In exchange, the *encomendero* was supposed to see to the military protection and general welfare of his wards, but the bargain seldom favored the Indians. In *The Royal City* (1956), Savage's Luis Ribera, the son of a wealthy *encomendero*, sympathizes with the Indians and foresees the likely result of the oppressive Spanish policies, but he is unable to head off the inevitable storm of Pueblo anger.

Irwin Blacker produced a popular novel of the Pueblo Revolt in *Taos* (1959), but the best fictional treatment of the revolt may be Forrester Blake's *The Franciscan* (1963). In Blake's story, Padre Lorenzo de Escalona, a Franciscan priest, is a missionary to the frontier of northern New Spain. He pours out his life in service to his vocation and to the native people of the Rio Grande pueblos, but his efforts to reform Spanish policies are thwarted by a jealous and repressive government. Banished far upriver to Chama for his sympathies, Padre Lorenzo hears of the revolt and hurries south, an anguished but hopeful peacemaker. He finds his beloved Cochiti Pueblo in chaos, the church a ruin of carnage and desecration. Padre Lorenzo is martyred at the altar, still strong in the faith.

Another event that brought forth a small eruption of historical novels was the 1846 American occupation of New Mexico. The invasion was precipitated by border conflict associated with the U.S.-Mexican War, but it followed years of Anglo-American activity in the region, dating from the days of the fur trade and the opening of the Santa Fe Trail. The occupation of New Mexico by U.S. troops under Gen. Stephen Watt Kearny increasingly has been viewed by western historians as a transparent act of aggression, the object of which was American expansion. Some fictional treatments reflect this perspective; others, particularly some of the older accounts, prefer the more palatable notion of the occupation as a mission to liberate eager natives from the clutches of a corrupt regime.

Books concerning the Pueblo Revolt and the American occupation of New Mexico have done much to promote a mythology that has been characterized by Sonnichsen as the "Black Legend of Spain" (1978, pp. 83–102). This view fosters the stereotype of Hispanic men as lazy, cruel, dishonest, dirty, treacherous, lustful, and cowardly. Some novels of the occupation reflect a countervailing interpretation that Sonnichsen calls the "Black Legend of the United States." According to this rendering of events, Anglo-Americans are an ambitious, driven, and aggressive people whose purpose is to amass as much wealth as possible, usually by taking it from native peoples.

Manifestations of the Black Legend of Spain are commonplace in novels of the American occupation. They occur in unflattering characterizations of Hispanic men, in an authorial point of view which justifies American intervention, and in the use of racially charged language. The Mexican governor, Manuel Armijo, is the stock villain in most of these works, but uncomplimentary observations often are generalized to include the male population at large. In *Jornada* (1935), by R. L. Duffus, an old frontiersman advises travelers bound for Santa Fe to be wary of the natives. "They're a rough lot, them greasers," he remarks, adding that he has no fear of the locals because "them fellows are too lazy to bear grudges" (15–16). Other writers infer that native New Mexicans prefer the rule of the conquering Americans to that of their own countrymen; under the Americans, the thinking goes, there will be justice and progress.

If novels of the occupation paint a negative picture of Hispanic society, neither are they particularly favorable to the invaders. In Duffus's *Jornada*, the Americans are perceived by local Hispanics as a greedy people who "are not happy unless they are miserable, and unless their misery is bringing them money" (157). The Americans are aggressive and determined creatures who have little time for pleasure, a fact noted by the more gregarious Mexicans. This view of the Americans is repeated in the popular *The Wind Leaves No Shadow* (1948, expanded 1951), by Ruth Laughlin. In the presence of the Americans, even the gambling *sala* is transformed into a place of joyless determination. "They are all business, business," a Santa Fe resident laments. "If our people lose they wait until good luck favors them. If the gringos lose, they are angry" (343).

Taoseños get a disturbing first impression of American justice in Frank O'Rourke's *The Far Mountains* (1959), as they witness the American takeover and its aftermath, including the trial of several Taos Indians for acts allegedly committed in the Taos Rebellion. The proceeding is seen as a

Jean Baptiste Lamy.
*Courtesy Museum of New
Mexico, Neg. No. 35878.*

sham. "This is not a trial. This is revenge," complains one of the locals. "And is it not sad and strange? The Americans take our country, then charge our people with treason for resisting" (467).

If the characterizations of Anglo-Americans in novels of the occupation did not add up to a fully developed "Black Legend of the United States," they at least made a fair beginning.

Following on the heels of the Americans came a conqueror of a different sort. He was Jean Baptiste Lamy, French-born vicar apostolic, bishop, and later archbishop of Santa Fe, immortalized as Father Jean Marie Latour in Willa Cather's *Death Comes for the Archbishop* (1927).

Writing in the *Saturday Review of Literature* in 1942, essayist Rebecca Smith declared Cather's novel "the beginning of a conscious appreciation of contemporary Southwest literature in the minds of the American public." Said Smith, "This beautiful, quiet tale of an austere French priest was the first completely successful work in Southwest fiction, and probably remains the most admired" (12).

Despite its acknowledged virtues, *Death Comes for the Archbishop* has not been universally admired, in part because of its denigration of native priests and native culture in favor of the European refinements introduced by Latour. If Smith's uncritical acceptance of Cather's work is a fair barometer, it would seem that the eastern literati were largely oblivious to the way her views struck many residents of the Southwest. Like the fictional Latour, the historical Lamy may have seen himself as the bearer of culture to an impoverished society, but in his determined imposition of Western European styles and manners, Lamy came to seem, to many natives of his desert diocese, more conqueror than servant.

ENCOUNTERS OF PERSONAL ANGUISH

Beneath a history of violent confrontation, writers have found a more subtle and persistent layer of conflict. As some writers — still mostly Anglo — began to consider cultural issues more carefully in the first half of the twentieth century, they moved away from stereotypes, and their characters increasingly took on human dimensions. Writers like N. Scott Momaday, Leslie Marmon Silko, and Rudolfo Anaya later would bring a depth of understanding and personal experience to portrayals of native characters; their works also demonstrated that, decades earlier, writers like Oliver La Farge, Frank Waters, Harvey Fergusson, and Raymond Otis had attained a grasp of some of the fundamental issues of race and culture.

Recurring in several "boarding-school stories" is the dilemma of a Native American character who is suspended agonizingly between two cultures. The character generally has been taken away as a child, taught to reject Indian ways, and indoctrinated in the values of white society. Following this treatment, the character — usually a vulnerable adolescent or young adult — remains an uncomfortable and unwelcome outsider in the white man's world and experiences dissonance and disapproval in the Indian world. The character typically suffers pain and confusion, sometimes with tragic consequences.

Oliver La Farge created such a character in his Pulitzer Prize–winning novel, *Laughing Boy* (1929), in the person of Slim Girl, a Navajo who has returned from an American school to find herself alienated from her people and their way of life. The book made La Farge a celebrated author, but he felt that readers had missed its intended indictment of U.S. government policy toward the Indians, so he retold the story at least twice more, using different characters, tuning out the lyrical quality of *Laughing Boy,* and turning up the heat. The character caught between cultures, innocent, anguished, driven toward disaster, remains at the center of these retellings. In a 1934 short story, "Higher Education," and in the 1937 novel,

The Enemy Gods, only the most insensitive reader could have ignored La Farge's bitterness over the imposition of American values and Christian religion on the native peoples.

In the same year when *The Enemy Gods* appeared, Edwin Corle produced a remarkably similar tale of woe in *People on the Earth* (1937). Like La Farge's book, Corle's novel is set on the Navajo reservation and involves the involuntary removal of a young boy to a Christian boarding school, his indoctrination in white ideas and institutions, and his ensuing struggle to regain his identity. The responsible missionary, W. R. Stratton, has devoted his life to caring for the souls of people who "were mentally children but creatures of God" (83). Red Wind's son is christened Walter Stratton and set on the Jesus Road, but his journey is mostly one of suffering; when salvation comes, it comes from his spiritual inheritance as a Navajo.

Frank Waters creates a comparable situation in *The Man Who Killed the Deer* (1942), a modern classic of southwestern literature. Martiniano, a Taos Indian, has returned to the pueblo from the white man's "away school." He sees no place for himself in the world outside the pueblo, but inside it he resists customs which no longer make sense to him, and for this he is condemned by the elders. Denied various tribal rights, he attempts to provide for his family by killing a deer out of season — the white man's season — and is plunged into the center of conflict between the values of the Pueblo people and those of the Anglo community. Martiniano's most vexing problem is not legal, but spiritual; he must find his place in a multicultural society which, for him, is anything but harmonious.

When N. Scott Momaday and Leslie Marmon Silko came along to offer Native American perspectives, they fashioned convincing portrayals informed by experience. Both writers created memorable characters who return home scarred by war and by their contacts with the Anglo world. Momaday's Abel and Silko's Tayo struggle to regain wholeness, eventually finding peace and reconciliation in the spiritual traditions of their own people.

In Momaday's *House Made of Dawn* (1968), a Pulitzer Prize–winning novel, Abel is a "relocation" Indian, an Indian who has been resettled in urban America, where presumably he can gain employment and become assimilated into the larger society. In the exile of a Los Angeles slum, Abel seeks meaning in Christianity and peyote, only to sink deeper in despair until at last he returns to Jemez Pueblo and its mysterious but proven ways.

In Silko's *Ceremony* (1977), the young man Tayo comes home sick in

N. Scott Momaday.
Photo by Cynthia Farah,
© 1986. Courtesy Center for
Southwest Research, General
Library, University of New
Mexico, Neg. 986-008-0033.

spirit. He is haunted by the war and by experiences in the strange world beyond his native Laguna Pueblo, but he is tormented more by his bitterness at the transgressions of the whites. Tayo cannot forgive whites for the shame his mother experienced as a schoolgirl, for their acts of violence against the earth, and for the incalculable loss of land, culture, and dignity; but it is he who suffers.

A variation on this theme occurs in several works involving Hispanic characters. In these novels, the character caught in the middle is a male aristocrat — heir to the proud tradition of the privileged *ricos.* The afflicted character usually is intelligent, strong, and vigorous — a young man poised to inherit the mantle of leadership. But it is his fate to be born at the wrong time, just as the Americans have overrun the territory, dominating its political and economic life and sweeping aside centuries of Spanish custom. The Americans do not appreciate the distinction of Spanish blood. To them, all non-Indian natives are "Mexicans," equally worthy of their contempt. Shunned by the Anglo elite and dispossessed of the inheritance to which he is born, the young *don* typically suffers confusion and bitterness.

A striking example of this character type occurs in the person of Ramon Delcasar in Harvey Fergusson's *The Blood of the Conquerors* (1921).

Growing up in a southwestern town (presumably Fergusson's home town of Albuquerque), Ramon is a member of an old and distinguished family. "Yet he knew of mothers who carefully guarded their daughters from the peril of falling in love with him, and most of his boyhood fights had started when someone called him a 'damned Mexican' or a 'greaser'" (8).

His family's fortune depleted, Ramon has been sent to law school in St. Louis to acquire a respectable profession. Stripped of the title, prestige, and fortune that defined his position under Spanish tradition, he is "the first of the Delcasars to face life with his bare hands" (24). Ramon attempts to maintain his position by competing on the *gringos'* terms, pursuing a desirable Anglo girl and engaging in the pragmatic scramble for wealth and influence; but his effort proves futile. Disillusioned and dispirited, Ramon gives up the struggle and retreats to the solitude of a small ranch to live quietly with his common-law wife, a young Hispanic woman of common origins.

The character type is drawn even more sharply in the case of Lorenzo de Baca in Raymond Otis's *Fire in the Night* (1934). Well born and well educated, Lorenzo is aware of his problem — that the old order has disintegrated before the onrushing *gringos:* "Americans appropriated not only the land, but the culture also, substituting democracy for feudalism, automobiles for coaches, even breaking the hold of the Church upon the people. They substituted efficiency for charm, ugliness for beauty, wherever beauty was tender and yielded to the remorseless power of this new race among them" (18–19). Worse, the Americans filled the heads of the peasantry with ideas of democracy and equality, "until the last generation was beginning to believe it, and the teaching and training of centuries was undone" (19).

Deprived of his identity as an aristocrat, Lorenzo agonizes over a detestable choice: to remain among his people and accept his diminished status or attain success on the *gringos'* terms. Ramon Delcasar's dilemma is Lorenzo's dilemma, too: he must choose a path, but neither alternative leads to a satisfactory future.

Though embodied in lesser characters, the diminished aristocrat also appears in Mary Austin's *Starry Adventure* (1931) and in Paul Horgan's story, "The Hacienda," in *The Return of the Weed* (1936). Don Elizario in "The Hacienda" is a superannuated relic of the old aristocracy, inspiring pathos by his pretense of elegance while drinking his way into oblivion in the dingy confines of the local Elks' Club.

In these stories, it is apparent that the suffering of a conquered people is not momentary, but rather is experienced time and again as alien ways and values are imposed upon one's native culture. They also show that the virtues of the great American nation are not universally appreciated — particularly by those who unwillingly fall under the influence of a society viewed by the vanquished as aggressive, heavy-handed, and self-righteous.

LIVING WITH DIFFERENCES

In works produced in the last half of the twentieth century, cultural conflict remains a prominent feature, sometimes in the plot and some-times in portrayals of time and place. The more contemporary explo-rations of cultural conflict tend to focus not on violence and aggression, but on the subtleties of racial prejudice.

As a meeting place of cultures for centuries, a place of distinctive and vocal factions and a history of turbulence, Taos invites observation of re-lations among its diverse peoples. From the time of the American occupa-tion, writers passing through Taos have had a good deal to say on the sub-ject. Mostly they tell of a local populace under siege by a succession of conquerors bent on converting, colonizing, and owning them.

Edwin Shrake's *Blessed McGill* (1968) is the chronicle of a former buf-falo hunter, gold seeker, brawler, and frontier gambler who lives on the Valdez Rim above Taos. A friend to the people of Taos Pueblo, Peter Hermano McGill urges restraint on the missionary priests who seek his help in evangelizing the Indians. "These people don't need the word of the Lord," he tells them. "They need for you to let them alone. They were do-ing better before you priests came than they are now" (228).

Undeterred, Father Higgins seeks to convince McGill, a man respected by the Pueblo people, of his logic. "Once the Conquistadores landed on this continent, the Indians were finished," Higgins contends. "The In-dians now have to choose whether to perish or be absorbed. Being ab-sorbed is better" (228). McGill does not agree that being absorbed is bet-ter and goes to his death despairing of the intent and actions of the meddling priests.

In the 1951 mystery, *The Far Cry,* Fredric Brown provides a contempo-rary view of racial tensions in the Taos Valley, as experienced by an out-sider. Brown's main character, George Weaver, a businessman suffering from exhaustion, is in town for the summer to relax and regain his bal-ance. His neighbors are friendly enough, but Weaver senses a general-ized hostility toward Anglos. His neighbor, the local newspaper editor, explains: "[Arroyo Seco] is one of the last strongholds of the old-line Spanish-Americans that hate Anglo ways and everything about Anglos. Especially ones like us who try to live out here among them — taking over their land, buying it when they have to sell — and then fixing it so they can never get it back" (65). Newcomers bring money and improve the homes they have acquired, driving real estate prices higher and leaving many natives unable to afford property. "We're changing this country, their way of life," the editor concedes. "We're interlopers" (66).

The degradation of native cultures is examined further in John Nichols's trilogy, set in and around the Taos Valley. In *The Milagro Beanfield War* (1974), Nichols tried to draw attention to the displacement of native Hispanics by development-minded Anglos, but apparently many readers relished the book's comic quality while missing its more serious point. So Nichols did as Oliver La Farge had done following his experience with *Laughing Boy*; he wrote a second novel reprising the theme in a more biting manner. In *The Magic Journey* (1978), Nichols shows Anglo promoters enticing residents of the Indian pueblo to buy electrical gadgets and bring power lines to the pueblo, thus setting off a chain of events that makes the natives dependent on credit and turns them into virtual serfs of the Anglo capitalists. Meanwhile, the nearby town of Chamisaville (Taos) is being made over as a heavily promoted mecca for tourists.

Cultural differences are again compounded by economic differences in Richard Martin Stern's *The Big Bridge* (1982). Hired to build a bridge spanning the perilous Tano Gorge (based on the Rio Grande Gorge near Taos), a San Francisco contractor sees the community's diversity as a problem to be managed. In a clumsy beginning, the company fails to hire locals, a fact soon reported in Santa Fe. "Why, hell's bells," the politically sensitive governor fumes, "that's Tano County! Everybody up there is either Spanish or Indian! You take as many Anglos as you can round up, ranchers, businessmen, those artists and writers and the like, and even the *touristas* just passing through, and you still wouldn't have enough to invite to a fair-sized barbecue!" (27). New management consults the local political boss and hires accordingly, but this does not quell fears that the bridge will change the town, to the detriment of its indigenous peoples.

School is a place of pain for young Hispanics in Joseph Foster's *Stephana* (1959) and Rudolfo Anaya's *Bless Me, Ultima* (1972). Attending high school in Albuquerque, Foster's Stephana finds an uncomfortable atmosphere of tension, politeness, and "subtle, subtle reservations about

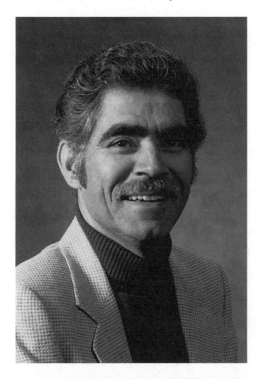

Rudolfo Anaya.
Courtesy University Archives,
University of New Mexico.

you that you couldn't overcome" (52). Eight year old Antonio Marez endures a humiliating first day of school in Anaya's *Bless Me, Ultima,* as
much for his rural origins as for his race. A lunch of hot beans, chile, and
tortillas, lovingly packed by his mother, brings laughter and derision from
the town kids, who taunt Antonio with their sandwiches. Alone in a
strange new world, the boy experiences la *tristeza de la vida,* a deep sadness
of the soul.

In *Heart of Aztlán* (1976), Anaya examines the plight of Hispanic people
who have been uprooted from the sacred land and deposited in the urban
barrio. The old people remember with pleasure and sadness how it used to
be when they lived on the land, when each person was supported by the
concern and labor of all. They lament that the young know nothing of
their culture. "In the city we have forgotten the old ways," says one of the
men, "and we have changed until we have become like the gringos" (103).

Prejudice sometimes is experienced not as overt hostility, but as a
subtle negation of one's personhood. In *Mother Tongue* (1994), Demetria
Martínez explains to a Nicaraguan refugee how this works in Albuquerque. If a brown-skinned person is quoted in the local paper, the refugee

Demetria Martínez.
Photo by Jeff Smith. Courtesy
Demetria Martínez.

is told, "what you say will be followed by words like *Romero claimed.* Whereas if you were white, it would read, *Romero said.* That is how they disappear people here" (21).

In these works and others, it is apparent that much of the conflict suffered by members of minority cultures is internal, experienced as anguish and bitterness at the loss of land and culture, status and control.

While Hispanic New Mexicans share many common social, cultural, and political institutions with their Anglo neighbors, the state's Native American communities tend to stand apart, maintaining a healthy distance between themselves and the dominant Anglo society. The reservation system, the principle of tribal sovereignty, traditional religious beliefs, and a natural resistance to assimilation all work in the direction of such a separation, but the distance also is the result of a conscious effort to preserve the privacy and integrity of native cultures. Thus the relationship between Native Americans and Anglos has been very different from that between Hispanic New Mexicans and Anglos. Despite the Indians' resistance to assimilation, or perhaps because of it, Native Americans have been subjected to intense, systematic efforts to dismantle their cultures and replace them with the values, beliefs, and institutions of the whites. In literature, this is most evident in the novels and early short stories of Oliver La Farge, who described the personal chaos that came in the wake of Navajo contacts with white society.

The Indian's preference for cultural autonomy is illustrated in numerous works, including La Farge's stories of the fictional San Leandro Pueblo — a community based on one of the Rio Grande pueblos near Santa Fe. The elders of San Leandro maintain cordial relations with their white neighbors, but they keep their fences high and in good repair, and this seems to account for the relative health and wholeness they enjoy as a people. The tribe initially is grateful to a local white boy who helps locate and return a stolen ceremonial object in "The Little Stone Man" (1960), but when he lets privileged information slip to a university professor and it ends up in a published article, gratitude turns to hostility, and he is banned from the pueblo. In "The Ancient Strength" (1963), the tribal council considers the request of an anthropologist who wants to dig in the pueblo's trash heap in order to help the Indians prove an old land claim. The elders very much would like to regain lost pueblo lands, and they appreciate the scientist's efforts, but in the end they conclude that it is more important to forego the excavation and keep everything whole.

William Eastlake's Checkerboard Navajos — encountered in *Go in Beauty* (1956) and other works — are quietly superior to their Anglo neighbors. Anglos seem to assume that everyone should embrace their ways of thinking and acting, but the Navajos think otherwise. While letting noisy Anglo tourists go their way, the Navajos cannot help but wonder at the lack of common sense the whites display in their attitudes toward the earth, time, and other people. The Indians find little to envy in the white man's world and even less to emulate.

It may be fine to live apart from the white man and keep faith with tribal traditions, but when the world apart consists of a poverty-stricken reservation, one has to wonder, are old myths worth maintaining? This is the quandary weighed by Buddy Red Bird in David Seals's *The Powwow Highway* (1979). It is not only the squalor and hopelessness of reservation life, but also the pathetic cultural poverty of his people that depresses Red Bird. Futility floods in on Buddy, the cynical bystander at a powwow at Pine Ridge: "He hated stupid-ass powwows. They were idiotic family affairs. Kids and old ladies crawled all over their previous Indian heritage like it was some goddam Indian blanket. They acted like a few lousy beads and some smelly feathers were a big deal, a culture. It was pitiful, that's what it was, pitiful. Look at 'em, traipsing around on a basketball court in a dying town like it was something alive, like they were something alive" (156–57).

Buddy may be worldly-wise and jaded, but his friend, Philbert Bono, displays a childlike faith in his heritage. Overweight, out of work, lightly regarded on the reservation, Philbert nonetheless senses that there is power in the ways of the old ones. En route to Santa Fe with Buddy to aid Buddy's sister, Philbert steers his heap to the Black Hills for a quick pilgrimage to the sacred Bear Butte. Armed with the medicine of a Cheyenne warrior, he heads south again. Like Momaday's Abel in *House Made of Dawn* and Silko's Tayo in *Ceremony*, Philbert finds strength not in the ways of the white man, but in the traditions and beliefs of his own people. Life remains a struggle for Philbert and the Cheyenne people, but the effect of Seals's novel is to affirm the power of native cultures in contemporary society.

Reinforcing Seals's dismal portrait of reservation life — and offering fewer rays of hope — are Dan McCall's *Messenger Bird* (1993) and Ron Querry's *The Death of Bernadette Lefthand* (1993). McCall portrays violence, despair, and tragedy on the Mescalero Apache reservation in a time of unrest at the height of the American Indian Movement. Querry's story, involving the demons of alcohol and witchcraft, takes place farther north, on Navajo and Jicarilla Apache reservation lands.

Tony Hillerman's Navajo police officers, Joe Leaphorn and Jim Chee, are Native American characters who successfully reconcile their cultural heritage with the realities of the modern world in which they live. Both have attended universities away from the reservation, and both are accustomed to dealing with non-Indian law-enforcement officers; but they differ in their attitudes toward Navajo culture. Leaphorn pays minimal homage to Navajo beliefs, while Chee aspires to be a Singer, performing the various rituals of Navajo religion. Although able to transcend cultural differences and function in white as well as Navajo society, the two men experience some dissonance in their relationships with whites. Periodically they must endure the superior attitudes of FBI agents who assume they know everything. Chee's relationship with Mary Landon in *The Ghostway* (1984) is also a casualty of irreconcilable cultural differences. Chee and Mary have a genuine affinity for one another and might have had a life together, but it boiled down to this: "Either he stayed Navajo or he turned white" (8).

Tony Hillerman.
Photo by Michael Mouchette.
Courtesy University Archives,
University of New Mexico.

TO BE CONTINUED

Contemporary fiction reflects some improvement in relations among New Mexico's cultural groups, evident in a moderating of both language and attitudes. Writers no longer feel free to generalize, as did Harvey Fergusson, that "all Mexican women love to be stared at" or that "the Mexicans all liked their women plump, soft and sweet" (1954, p. 102). Neither is it likely that any contemporary writer would think to describe a Hispanic character as Fergusson did Ramon Delcasar, "sitting on the sunny side of his house with his heels under him and his back against the wall — a position any Mexican can hold for hours" (1921, p. 266).

Cross-cultural friendships and romantic relationships now are relatively common in novels and stories; where cultural conflict occurs, it is more likely to be rooted in issues and values than in the overt prejudice found in many earlier works. Higher values occasionally are expressed in works like the bilingual stories of Sabine Ulibarrí — tales of triumphant human spirits transcending differences of color, culture, and language.

Sabine Ulibarrí.
Photo by Cynthia Farah,
© 1986. Courtesy Center for
Southwest Research, General
Library, University of New
Mexico, Neg. 988-030-0011.

In truth, there probably is at least as much harmony, conciliation, and mutual enjoyment as conflict among cultural groups; but harmonious relationships do not serve the fiction writer's purposes nearly so well as do relationships involving tension and conflict — relationships which evoke personal responses on the part of the reader. As long as serious differences remain to create oppositions among characters and groups, they are likely to command the attention of writers.

One writer in 1972 suggested that a synthesis was in the making — that the cultural forces of Indian, Hispanic, and Anglo-American peoples were "today working toward a genuinely unique culture in New Mexico." Postulated Paige Christiansen, "The Indian gods of air, earth, and sky and the white man's gods of morality and science do not differ a great deal in their aspirations for their chosen people, and perhaps they will decree a splendid and unique synthesis from the cultural mosaic" (15).

If there was any chance of this in 1975, William Eastlake did not see it. Born in Brooklyn and reared in New Jersey, Eastlake sought the West as an unexplored frontier for serious writers and settled on a ranch near Cuba, New Mexico, in 1955. He adopted as his literary domain the "Checkerboard" area — where reservation lands and private holdings lie

William Eastlake.
Photo by Larry Ketchum.
Courtesy the Bisbee Observer.

in alternate sections, bringing Navajos into close contact with people of other cultures.

In *Dancers in the Scalp House* (1975), Eastlake's Checkerboard Navajos fight off as many of the white man's encroachments as they can, taking out unsightly neon signs, sabotaging a "coyote shoot," and smuggling a bomb into the Four Corners Power Plant. In the end, however, they forego plans to blow up a dam that will flood their homeland, opting instead to leave this troubled world. They steer their red canoe into the depths of the new lake in search of the "undiscovered country": a place free of human turmoil, a place of love, compassion, wonder, and fulfillment (244–45).

After centuries of invasion, conquest, social interaction, and intermarriage, cultural differences are alive and well in New Mexico, as is revealed almost daily in incidents reported in the state's news media.

In 1997, five young Native Americans made news when they quit the Laguna-Acoma High School football team, which had qualified for the state playoffs, in order to go deer hunting. Two of the boys explained that the decision was an easy one, citing the fun of hunting and their family's need for the meat; but their young coach, who grew up in Ohio, was perplexed. "I've never seen anything like this," he admitted. "I know it's different here, but this is the playoffs. They have the rest of their lives to go hunting." When confronted about the decision, the students had little to say. "They're very quiet boys," the coach observed. "They just looked at me, shrugged their shoulders and walked off" (Mark Smith, A1).

As 1998 began, many New Mexicans were preparing to celebrate the four hundredth anniversary of the arrival, in 1598, of the first Spanish settlers and their leader, Don Juan de Oñate. The commemoration at first seemed like a good idea, but then things got complicated. Plans for a monument recalling the arrival of the Spanish drew mixed reactions in Albuquerque. Some thought the monument should focus on the settlers, some thought it should honor Oñate, and some didn't care for the idea at all. Then the state was shocked to learn that an unknown person or persons had cut off the right foot of a statue of a mounted Juan de Oñate at the Oñate Monument and Visitors Center near Española. According to a note sent to the *Albuquerque Journal,* the gesture was meant to remind New Mexicans of the punishment dealt to twenty-four men of Acoma Pueblo who resisted the Spanish incursion; each had a foot cut off, apparently on Oñate's orders. The note further indicated that the bronze foot was to be melted down and made into medallions "to be sold to those who are historically ignorant" (Díaz, A1).

An incident no more profound than these caught Frank Waters's attention and set him ruminating on the greater meaning of Indian-white relations, ultimately inspiring *The Man Who Killed the Deer.* Such encounters of opposing assumptions, interests, values, and world views have been happening for centuries. They feed the writer's insatiable appetite for conflict and continually test the compassion and understanding of those who live in the land of sun and adobe, where cultures meet.

4 FREEDOM AND RESTRAINT

Having traversed the Santa Fe Trail and ventured into the southern Rocky Mountains in 1831–32, Albert Pike considered the lives of men he had encountered there and found them reasonably congruent with the characters of James Fenimore Cooper and others, in this respect: there was freedom to be enjoyed on the frontier.

There is so much independence and self-dependence in the lonely hunter's life — so much freedom from law and restraint, from form and ceremony, that one who commences the life is almost certain to continue in it. With but few wants, and those easily supplied, man feels none of the enthrallments which surround him when connected with society. His gun and his own industry supply him with fire, food and clothing. He eats his simple meal, and has no one to thank for it but his Maker. He travels where he pleases, and sleeps whenever he feels inclined. If there is danger about, it comes from enemies, and not from friends; and when he enters a settlement, his former life in the woods renders it doubly tedious to him. (58)

Cooper's heroes were but the first of many fictional characters of the nineteenth century who found that the blessings of life and liberty were best pursued not within the confines of a society regulated by the American government and the several states, but beyond the reach of established settlements and political institutions. Natty Bumppo was followed by Timothy Flint's Francis Berrian, the dime-novel personifications of Kit Carson and Buffalo Bill, and, in time, the cowboy heroes who carried the ideal of frontier freedom into a new century. These characters were ideally suited to capture the interest of eastern readers who were tied to farms, factories, families, and mortgages: they enjoyed an enviable measure of freedom from such encumbrances, and they faced danger.

Inspired by Frederick Jackson Turner's celebrated thesis, "The Significance of the Frontier in American History," read before the American Historical Association in 1893, historians have examined and reexamined phenomena of the nineteenth-century West and their influence on the destiny of the nation and on the shared values of its people. Inspired by the works of Henry Nash Smith and others, cultural historians have hastened to study objects of popular culture — most notably, art and literature — in light of Turner's ideas.

The resulting analyses concerning young America's pursuit of freedom and its self-contradictory pursuit of civilization and order are revealing. Theories concerning the "frontier experience" and its influence on the national character attempt to bring motive, image, and effect together in an elegant, logical synthesis. They are helpful in interpreting much of the history and early fiction literature dealing with New Mexico and the West.

These analyses, it should be noted, are premised upon a migration of mostly English-speaking peoples, who started from the Atlantic coast of North America and proceeded westward across a continent which was largely devoid of permanent settlements. Indians and Spanish-speaking residents of the Rio Grande were not considered to be people, but rather were viewed as obstacles to westward expansion, much like the dry desert, extremes of climate, and the imposing barrier of the Rocky Mountains. These works leave something to be desired as explanations of activity and motive in New Mexico.

New Mexico confounds the conventional explanation of American frontier settlement. In the orthodoxy established by Turner and others, westering Americans and immigrants venture forth from the Atlantic states, bringing civilization to the unsettled margins of the nation. In successive waves, they move across a wilderness continent, overcoming obstacles and claiming the land for civilized habitation. In New Mexico, however, permanent settlements and cultural traditions existed long before the great westward migration began, and before the earlier migration of the Spanish out of Mexico. Says Patricia Nelson Limerick, a western historian of the new school, "The old concept of the frontier — that bipolar opening-and-closing operation — never looked sillier than it did when applied to New Mexico" (1991b, p. 76).

In New Mexico, the advance of civilization based on European traditions did not entail simply conquest of the wilderness and displacement of nomadic dwellers of the forests and plains. It meant subjugating an established people, taking their land and labor, and foreclosing their capacity for self-determination. This was first accomplished by the Spanish, who colonized New Mexico in 1598, reconquered it following the Pueblo Revolt, and exerted varying degrees of domination over the Pueblo Indians in more than two centuries of colonial rule. Anglo-Americans repeated the process, superseding the Spanish and fashioning political, economic, and cultural structures according to their own assumptions. These events, largely ignored in conventional studies of the American frontier, have begun to receive the attention they deserve, in such works as David J. Weber's on the northern frontiers of Spain and Mexico.

Such deficiencies in the national memory have led Richard Slotkin to conclude that a new mythology is needed. He says, in *Gunfighter Nation: The Myth of the Frontier in Twentieth Century America* (1992):

> Even in its liberal form, the traditional Myth of the Frontier was exclusionist in its premises, idealizing the white male adventurer as the hero of national history. A new myth will have to respond to the demographic transformation of the United States and speak to and for a polyglot nationality. Historical memory will have to be revised, not to invent an imaginary role for supposedly marginal minorities, but to register the fact that our history in the West and in the East, was shaped from the beginning by the meeting, conversation, and mutual adaptation of different cultures. (655)

Even as Professor Slotkin wrote these words, like-minded historians were already at work hatching a new paradigm to explain events in the American West in the nineteenth and twentieth centuries. The new credo was christened the "New Western History," and its assumptions added up to a repudiation of much that Turner had postulated.

According to Limerick, ostensible leader of the movement, New Western Historians reject the familiar notion of an American "frontier" as essentially nationalistic and racist. They see the West as a region, whole and continuous, altered and influenced by a variety of cultural encounters, political actions, and economic activities. To describe the encounters of diverse peoples, Limerick says, "New Western Historians have available a number of terms — invasion, conquest, colonization, exploitation, development, expansion of the world market" (1991a, p. 86).

From this it may appear that the New Western Historians are planning an industrial-strength guilt trip for much of white America, but Limerick specifically disclaims any such intent. The point, she says, is "to make it clear that in western American history, heroism and villainy, virtue and vice, and nobility and shoddiness appear in roughly the same proportions as they appear in any other subject of human history (and with the same relativity of definition and judgment)" (1991a, p. 86). Much of the emphasis in New Western History seems to be on recognizing diverse viewpoints and experiences — both male and female, and encompassing varied cultural groups — and who can argue with that?

In attempting to turn the herd from the precipice of faulty Turnerian logic, Limerick and her fellow drovers have much to overcome. Their peskiest adversaries and their most articulate allies may turn out to be not historians but fiction writers. Howard Roberts Lamar attributes the continuing popularity of Turner's ideas at least in part to "the presence of a generation of famous novelists, poets, folklorists and journalists, whose careers paralleled those of the academicians, and who also embraced Turner's ideas and incorporated them into their writings" (233). To be sure, the Myth of the Frontier, so repugnant to the New Western Historians, is much in evidence in the fiction literature of New Mexico and the West.

Limerick and like-minded historians argue effectively against the existence of a frontier as Turner conceived it, and against the notion of the frontier as a useful concept for describing events in the American West. At the least, it probably must be conceded that the concept of "frontier," as commonly applied to the American West, represents an ethnocentric point of view. It has to do largely with the westward movement of Anglo-Americans intent on overcoming natural and human obstacles to make the western country serve their purposes. Hispanic and Native American writers do not often mention the frontier, and certainly do not speak of it in the same approving terms so many Anglo writers use. As an instrument of history, the idea of the frontier may be of limited value; as a construct that helps explain how many European and American readers and writers have viewed the West, however, the concept is indispensable.

Fiction writers, especially serious writers, often are inclined to challenge rather than parrot conventional views; not all have adopted the Turnerian perspective. The New Western Historians will find many instances in which fiction writers have been out front in recognizing the experiences of indigenous peoples and exposing instances of greed, social injustice, and environmental degradation in the West.

FREEDOM AND RESTRAINT IN THE FRONTIER WEST

While fictional accounts of repression and resistance depict Spanish aggression against the Pueblo Indians and Anglo-American aggression against the Indians and Spanish, little is said of individual liberty as a major concern of either the Indians or the Spanish. There are several possible reasons for this. One is that the Anglo writers who produced most of the works concerning these events lacked the insight to comprehend and interpret Indian or Spanish motives. Another is that neither group was conditioned by culture to pursue individual freedom in the way that the Anglo-American frontiersman and settler did. Tribal culture did not encourage individual self-determination, and neither did the aristocratic social structures of Spanish Colonial society. So, while it may be stipulated that a great many New Mexicans have suffered loss of freedom as a result of the aggression of one culture against another, and while such losses are duly recorded in the fiction literature, the obsession with individual freedom is associated primarily with the ideology of the upstart Americans. It is their own freedom that they are most concerned about, and the struggle they wage over freedom is one that they have with themselves.

Frontier freedom carried the seeds of its own destruction. The woodsman or trapper of American frontier mythology went into the wilderness seeking to cast off the bonds of society, find untapped wealth, and experience the exhilaration of adventure in the wild. But no sooner did he go than he began transforming the wilderness. Daryl Jones explains it this way:

> Within the historical context established by the frontier setting, the Western hero of the early dime novel typically functions as an agent of civilization. A fiercely independent man, he is neither suited to nor comfortable amid the laws and properties of the settlement. Instead, he lives a perilous but free life on the frontier. Here he contends with the forces of ignorance and savagery. Always triumphant, he slowly but surely pushes back the wilderness, blazing a trail which his

more civilized brothers may follow to a golden age in which a free and equal citizenry, physically invigorated and spiritually purified by close and continual contact with Nature, will someday live in perfect harmony. (26)

In other words, the frontiersman, by his labors and his fortitude, unwittingly helped to recreate something resembling the society he had fled.

This cycle is evident in Harvey Fergusson's *Grant of Kingdom* (1950), based on the history of the Maxwell Land Grant in northern New Mexico. Jean Ballard successfully builds an empire in the wilderness, only to see it slip from his grasp. Expert in dealing with Indians, facing hazards and making the land safe and profitable, he lacks the business sense to comprehend matters of high finance and fend off the high rollers his domain attracts.

Early New Mexico fiction has its share of heroes who risk comfort and safety to live the free life on the great frontier. One of the earliest and most articulate statements in praise of frontier life comes from an unexpected source — a woman of Mexico, Adela Miranda, in Mayne Reid's *The Lone Ranch, a Tale of the "Staked Plain"* (1871). Exiled to the Llano Estacado with her brother, Adela Miranda takes a liking to the place, turning aside her brother's apology for the primitive circumstances she must endure: "You know I never cared a straw for what the world calls 'society.' I've always liked better being free from its restraint and conventionalities. Give me nature for my companion — Nature in her wildest moods" (210). These lines written for Adela Miranda no doubt had greater appeal for the author and his likely readers than they did for a Mexican aristocrat driven to the parched solitude of the Staked Plain.

Most of those who reveled in the wilderness life, though, were Anglo males and, increasingly, Anglo-American males. In Karen Osborn's *Between Earth and Sky* (1996), Abigail Conklin is a strong woman of the frontier, guiding her family through hard years in southern New Mexico and better years on a farm on the upper Rio Grande; notwithstanding Reid's Adela Miranda, the early writers were all but incapable of visualizing such a character. The sturdy male adventurer had his way throughout much of the dime-novel era, overcoming all opposition, persisting in the face of natural hazards, building, civilizing, and foisting the values of American ideology on an unwilling native populace. When his quest for freedom finally ran into trouble, it came not from Indian or Hispanic rivals but from the civilization he had created. Freedom became an issue of serious literary interest only when the freedom of the frontier began to erode.

One of the first to speak up was Florence Finch Kelly, in a novel of range life, *With Hoops of Steel* (1900). Kelly's southern New Mexico country is full of small independent ranchers, but they are being crowded hard by the Fillmore Cattle Company, a big outfit owned by a corporation. The Fillmore's manager, recently spared a painful death by the daring action of one of the local cowmen, does not allow sentiment to cloud his business sense. Faced with the reluctance of the small brands to accept the inevitable trend toward larger ranches and corporate control, he delivers himself as follows:

> The most distinctive commercial feature of this period is the constant growth of the big interests at the expense of smaller ones. It is something that the individual members of a big concern can't help, because it is bigger than they are. Our stockholders will undoubtedly wish to enlarge their holdings and increase their profits, and I, being only one of a number, can have no right to put my personal feelings above their interests. You ought to see that the result is going to be inevitable in your case, just as it is everywhere else. (193)

It comes as no surprise that the speaker wins no converts among the range-hardened cattlemen, who would rather fight than surrender their autonomy to a corporation.

Another early work to mark the passing of the free man's West was Emerson Hough's *Heart's Desire* (1905), based on the author's brief residency in the New Mexico mining camp of White Oaks. In a whimsical story with a serious point, Hough describes a utopian paradise, where each man could do exactly as he pleased, even fire off his pistols on Main Street to express his joy in living, without fear of reproach. A newcomer is shocked to find the town in such a state: "No organization — no government — Good God! what kind of a place *is* this?" (225). But the season of contentment in Heart's Desire comes to a screeching halt with the arrival first of law and then of ladies.

The decline of personal freedom was also noted by Thomas Janvier, an eastern journalist and writer who traveled the American West and Mexico in the 1880s. In the comic novel, *Santa Fe's Partner* (1907), Janvier describes the antics of a pair of con artists in a track-end town on the Rio Grande, where law is absent and people run wild. By the end of the book, the townspeople have concluded that law and order must come to Palo-

Eugene Manlove Rhodes.
*Courtesy Rio Grande
Historical Collections, New
Mexico State University
Library, Neg. Ms 82.13.*

mas, but the decision is made with some regret. They realize that freedom will be diminished and, along with it, the colorful characters and free spirits who have brightened their lives.

But the undisputed champion of rugged individualism was Eugene Manlove Rhodes, who accompanied his father to Engle, New Mexico, at the age of twelve in 1881. He witnessed the last days of the open range in a land characterized by C. L. Sonnichsen as the "last of the frontier West," and he formed vivid impressions of a time and place not to be forgotten. Rhodes cherished those remembrances and incorporated them into the little world he created in his novels and stories.

Rhodes took as his literary stomping ground a vast area of southern New Mexico and Arizona. In a land dismissed by others as hot, dusty, and uninteresting, he found infinite variety and character. In the montage of mountain, plain, and desert, white sands and forbidding *malpais,* he found a frontier of the imagination.

The Rhodes country is as much a state of mind as a place. For, although it is based on places, people, and cultural phenomena which were well known to the author, Rhodes was writing about it mainly from memory, having quit the country in 1906 for reasons which may have included avoidance of legal difficulties, preservation of his fragile health, and pursuit of domestic tranquillity. A man of emphatic philosophical preferences, Rhodes endowed the country and its people disproportionately with qualities he admired. As beauty is in the eye of the beholder, so Rhodes's country is best appreciated by those who prefer solitude and independence, and who are not averse to putting up with hardships incidental to primitive living.

For Rhodes, the country from which he was exiled remained a powerful symbol of freedom and independence, the marshaling of physical and mental resources to overcome challenges, and triumph of the right and true in an arena where courage frequently was the deciding factor. It was a proper stage for his tales of stout-hearted men maintaining decency in a land not broken to the rule of law and etiquette. If the author was troubled by the fact that his independent characters were dependent largely upon the availability of free public range and liberal provisions for mining on the public lands, he never said so.

Rhodes really had but one heroic character, whether his name was Jeff Bransford, John Wesley Pringle, or Steve "Wildcat" Thompson. The Rhodes man is a clever conversationalist in the western idiom of exaggeration and understatement. He is fair to all but takes no guff off anyone. He is not to be found among the wealthy and powerful, but among those who use their hands and their minds. Rhodes's hero occasionally may stray outside the law, but he lives by a code of honor and follows it consistently. If employed, he gives his best to the work at hand, out of loyalty to ranch, brand, and comrades and out of pride in his profession.

Rhodes saw the threats to the freedom enjoyed by the men he admired. They came by way of lawyers, bankers, barons of enterprise, and government officials, and these were the stock antagonists in his stories. Rhodes was well aware that the way of life he held dear had all but vanished, but he held fast to the ideal; his free and resourceful men never lost. Rhodes knew all about the realities of contemporary life, but he kept his stories free of its wearisome tribulations. It was his preference to pay tribute to the men of his youth and the principles they stood for, rather than to heed modern literary trends that he considered decadent and defeatist.

Rhodes was but one of the most passionate among the many who held the cowboy up as a symbol of freedom. The cowboy's independence was a cardinal feature wherever he appeared. He couldn't be bought or bluffed, brought to heel on command, or tied to a plow. Most fictional cowboys eschew entangling alliances and reject town life except for short periods on special occasions. Tom Outland, a New Mexico cowboy who travels to Washington in Willa Cather's *The Professor's House* (1925), takes pity on the clerks he sees streaming out of huge government buildings. "They seemed like people in slavery, who ought to be free," he observes (234).

If the notion of an invincible American nation, moving westward behind an advancing frontier, found credence among historians in the years following Turner's exposition of his famous thesis, one of its most enthusiastic expositors in fiction was Conrad Richter. Richter was thirty-eight years old and already an accomplished writer when, in 1928, he moved from his native Pennsylvania to New Mexico for an extended sojourn.

In New Mexico, Richter talked with old-timers who related tales of early days in the territory, and he developed an appreciation for what he called "That Early American Quality" (1950). It was not the native peoples of New Mexico but the Anglo-American pioneers who caught his interest, first expressed in an anthology, *Early Americana and Other Stories* (1936). In 1950, Richter wrote in admiration, "What these early Americans had that so many of us today do not have are a sense of sovereignty, a rank vitality, and a deep unswerving belief in the dignity of man, beginning with themselves" (28).

When Emerson Hough and Thomas Janvier wrote about increasing restraint brought to bear in the frontier settlements, theirs was a good-humored response to what they saw as a natural evolutionary process. It was fun while it lasted, that rollicking frontier society where boys could be boys and damn the consequences; but it always was part of the plan that the West would be settled and tamed. Paul Horgan could muster little regret when he wrote, in a story of pioneer merchants in *Figures in a Landscape* (1940), "The frontiersman who did what he liked faded away slowly, and the general good governed in place of the solo wildcat law which has left so many funny and so many tragic stories behind it" (160–61).

FREEDOM AND ITS ADVERSARIES IN THE NEW WEST

By the time Edward Abbey began taking soundings on the state of affairs in the West, it was clear that some virulent forces had been loosed. Hough and Janvier had observed a reining in of the worst excesses of frontier freedom, in their eyes an acceptable consequence of progress. By Abbey's time, the forces of law and order had spawned a massive government bureaucracy, impersonal in its deliberations and awesome in its power; Abbey, the writer, set out to do something about it. Reflecting on

Edward Abbey.
Photo by Cynthia Farah,
© 1986. Courtesy Center for
Southwest Research, General
Library, University of New
Mexico, Neg. 986-008-0001.

his work, he observed, "Most of my writing has been in the field of the novel, explorations of certain aspects of the human comedy, especially the traditional conflict between our instinctive urge toward fraternity, community, and freedom, and the opposing demands of discipline and the state" (1984, p. ix).

A self-proclaimed anarchist, Abbey honed his writing skills as a student at the University of New Mexico and as editor, for a few brief months, of the Taos weekly, *El Crepúsculo.* By the time he wrote *The Brave Cowboy: An Old Tale in a New Time* (1956), he was well practiced in the creation of prose which was politically charged, passionate, and purposely offensive to those he considered enemies of freedom.

Jack Burns, the brave cowboy, actually is a sheepherder whose only crime is his refusal — perhaps his inability — to fit himself into the modern world. Burns rides into Duke City (Albuquerque), where he and his frightened horse encounter angry motorists. He carries no identification — inconceivable to the bureaucratic authorities. Burns hopes to rescue his one-time college friend, Paul Bondi, jailed for refusing the military draft. Following his own ethical code, Bondi is protesting within the system. Burns does not even recognize the system, much less make any effort to act in conformity with it. Acting on his own impulses, Burns embarks on a course of action which is intended to help his friend but actually leads only to his own destruction.

Burns is not a hostile or menacing character; in fact, he is a person of well-considered principles, which happen not to conform to those upon which contemporary society is ordered. Lacking the adaptive gene, he does not survive. Jack Burns gets in the way of the system, and for that he is destroyed. As Rhodes's Jeff Bransford remarks, "There ain't no sympathies to machinery. Your intentions may be strictly honorable, but if you get your hand caught in the cogs, off it goes, regardless of how handy it is for flankin' calves, holdin' nails, and such things" (1914, p. 10). Burns is a man caught in the cogs of postindustrial, bureaucratic society, recently arrived in the West.

The situation had not improved by the time Abbey wrote *Fire on the Mountain* (1962). If anything, it had become worse. It was the Brave Cowboy's misfortune to wander into the path of a bureaucratic machine that, in Abbey's view, was inimical to the notion of individual freedom. John Vogelin, owner of the hardscrabble Box V Ranch, is strictly minding his own business, trying to survive the double whammy of drought and Depression, when trouble comes knocking on his door. Its agents are not jackbooted storm troopers, but they might as well be. The Air Force sends a colonel and a U.S. marshal, who proffer various compromises, moral arguments, and appeals to Vogelin's patriotism. The old rancher won't dicker, however, so his cattle are confiscated, and finally he is brought to his knees by a fusillade of tear-gas canisters. Vogelin is every inch the equal of Rhodes's fearless men, but he is no match for the U.S. government, its law enforcement officers, military forces, and attorneys.

There was little to cheer defenders of freedom in either of Abbey's New Mexico novels, but he was still around to take part in a popular uprising that appeared in the literature in the mid-1970s. Its precursor was a strange four-volume work by Phillip Stevenson, a Marxist who wrote under the pseudonym Lars Lawrence. Stevenson lived in Santa Fe for a time and learned about New Mexico's labor problems and the labor struggle and riot that rocked Gallup in the mid-1930s. These events formed the basis of his novels, published between 1954 and 1961, which were set in the fictional town of Reata but included as characters numerous people known to contemporary residents of Gallup (Fellin to Caffey). Framed as a conflict between workers and capitalists, Stevenson's novels depict the struggle of ordinary people to reassert their rights through collective action.

By the mid-1970s, fiction had begun to reflect social upheaval that included the civil rights movement, the environmental movement, and the era of vehement popular protest against the war in Vietnam. These events had demonstrated that ordinary people, acting in concert and committed to a common cause, sometimes could prevail against the forces of wealth and governmental authority. Banding together and sometimes resorting to subversive methods, people long oppressed by those with political and economic power began to win some battles.

In fiction, the first notable instance of this resurgence occurs in Richard Bradford's *So Far from Heaven* (1973). Primo Rael, a character perhaps inspired by land-grant activist Reies Lopez Tijerina, leads La Compañía de Tierra y Libertad [the Company of Earth and Freedom], a group bent on recovering grants stolen from Hispanic New Mexicans. A prime target is the upper Juan Tafoya Grant, taken from the Tafoyas through a crooked survey and a tax scam. Rael's group scares off one owner and reveals that a group of Texans is planning to build a sprawling residential development which would deplete the area's groundwater. His illegal plans exposed, C. C. Cotton sells the upper grant — some 380 sections — to the State of New Mexico, and it is turned over to La Compañía, to be settled by families who will work the land.

A similar rebellion occurs in Nichols's *The Milagro Beanfield War* (1974), when residents of the village of Milagro reassert their lost water rights and thwart the efforts of developer Ladd Devine III to consolidate the small landholdings and build his beloved Miracle Valley Recreation Area. The villagers cannot match the legal and political forces available to Devine, so they employ guerrilla tactics, burning his new sign to the ground, disabling company equipment, and providing omens of doom for Devine and his lackeys to contemplate.

Subversive resistance again is the strategy of choice in Edward Abbey's *The Monkey Wrench Gang* and William Eastlake's *Dancers in the Scalp House,* both published in 1975. Abbey's eco-warriors and Eastlake's environmentally threatened Navajos devise creative ways of sabotaging the road builders, strip miners, dam builders, coyote shooters, power plant polluters, and others who would despoil the West. Their efforts meet with mixed results, but they at least have mustered the temerity to fight back, and unlike Paul Bondi and John Vogelin, they do not feel constrained by notions of law or civil behavior.

FREEDOM FROM WHAT?

More than a century after the announced closing of the frontier, New Mexico remains a place where restless young Anglo-Americans come seeking something. In contrast to the men and women of the old frontier,

Natalie Goldberg.
Photo by Ritch Davidson,
© 1995. Courtesy Bantam
Books and Natalie Goldberg.

their struggles are with their own feelings and anxieties, rather than any external antagonist. The new Anglo freedom seekers are, for the most part, physically and financially secure, but they suffer various forms of middle-class angst.

Natalie Goldberg's *Banana Rose* (1995) provides a fine portrayal of the "hippie" era in northern New Mexico, when young people fled society as they knew it, to pursue more harmonious lives in communes near Taos. Goldberg's Nell Schwartz — Banana Rose — has come to the Elephant House in Talpa following some uneventful years in which she conformed to her family's wishes, earning a degree in education and teaching in Ann Arbor, Michigan. Finding her life not fulfilling, she "moved to Taos and broke free" (15). Liberated from the constraints of her conservative Jewish upbringing, Nell paints and pursues a variety of personal and sexual relationships. All is not pure light and harmony at Elephant House and beyond, but Nell at least knows what it is to be alive and to accept responsibility for her life.

Others seek freedom from a variety of ghosts and maladies. Tormented by his Vietnam War experience, Michael Smith makes his way to northern New Mexico in John Nichols's *American Blood* (1987). Using and abusing the women in his life, he struggles to break free of the violence that fouls his relationships and diminishes his capacity to live productively.

Kevin McIlvoy.
*Photo by Matt Gray. Courtesy
News and Publications, New
Mexico State University.*

In Robert Cohen's *The Organ Builder* (1988), Herschel Freeman seeks to exorcise the ghosts that remain from his childhood, when his father, a wartime Los Alamos scientist, deserted the family, leaving Hesh and his mother to fend for themselves. Hesh has to know the what and the why of his father's disappearance before he can get on with his own life.

Kevin McIlvoy's *The Fifth Station* (1988) and *Little Peg* (1990) involve characters engaged in introspective journeys in the southern New Mexico city of Las Almas, a thinly disguised Las Cruces. In *The Fifth Station,* Michael and Luke McWelt are in need of spiritual healing following the death of a third brother, Matthew, in an industrial accident in the Midwest—a tragedy for which they feel responsible. In *Little Peg,* Peg O'Crerieh, a writing instructor at the Las Almas Branch Community College, struggles to be free of her addiction to alcohol and a bad marriage.

Numerous other works of the 1980s and 1990s have to do with painful relationships and a protagonist's struggle to be free of the feelings of failure, self-doubt, anger, and guilt that typically accompany such experi-

Elizabeth Tallent.
Photo by Cynthia Farah,
© 1986. Courtesy Center for
Southwest Research, General
Library, University of New
Mexico, Neg. 988-030-0009.

ences. Such personal crises are at the heart of works by Lee K. Abbott, Cathryn Alpert, Mary Cable, Eddie Lewis, Bradford Morrow, and Elizabeth Tallent. And what better place to live through one's season of discontent than Santa Fe, Taos, or, like Jo-Ann Mapson's Maggie Yearwood in the 1994 novel *Blue Rodeo,* in Blue Dog, New Mexico?

Clearly, middle-class Anglos of the 1990s, at least as portrayed in numerous works of fiction, have little in common with the men and women who sought the frontier a century and more ago. The contemporary immigrant, unlike the pioneer described by Albert Pike at the beginning of this chapter, faces danger not from enemies but from friends and lovers. He suffers not from the spears and arrows of a hostile people, or from exposure to hazards of climate and wild animals, but from his own neuroses. The objects of his quest are not conquest, fortune, and adventure, but identity, self-esteem, and inner peace. He is not looking to tame a wilderness or take on an antagonistic rival, or even necessarily to commune with nature. He would be satisfied just to get himself centered.

5 ATTITUDES TOWARD THE LAW

I n *Heart's Desire* (1905), Emerson Hough creates a utopian frontier society in which each man does as he pleases, unimpeded by law or feminine influence. There is some ambivalence concerning the lack of female companionship, but the law is not missed at all until two attorneys take up residence in the remote mining camp. In their efforts to scare up an adjudicable dispute, the nearest the lawyers can come is an incident involving the accidental shooting of a pig. The pig's owner and the shootist want to settle amicably, but the lawyers won't have it. They insist upon a trial.

The hastily organized trial generates some excitement in Heart's Desire, but its greater significance does not escape notice. As Dan Anderson, counsel for the defense, warms to his oration, the import of the occasion is driven home to all: "There came a swift, sudden chill, a gripping as of iron, a darkening, a shrinking of the heart of each man in that little room. It was the coming of the Law! Ah! Dan Anderson, you ruined our little paradise; and now its walls are down forever, even the walls of our city of content" (46–47).

The law never has been warmly received in New Mexico — not by the hardy souls of the frontier West and certainly not by natives, for whom American law was an alien and inimical force. But there were those who were willing to force the issue, men whose fortune and influence were at stake. In their forefront were lawyers. Echoing the sentiments of John Locke, Hough's Dan Anderson argues passionately on behalf of the law.

Emerson Hough.
*Courtesy Special Collections
Department, University of
Iowa Libraries.*

"Without law there could be nothing but anarchy," he declares. As anarchy is the enemy of progress, right-minded citizens of Heart's Desire must give up a measure of individual liberty and embrace the law, "that beneficent agency of progress, that indispensable factor, that inseparable attendant upon civilization" (47–48).

This may be fine for the creatures Eugene Manlove Rhodes called the "tumblebug people" — timid souls who require leaders and crave security — and finer still for those who plan to profit by the law. For the independent men and women of the frontier, however, the coming of law represents a call to give up precious freedom. Therein lies the prickly heart of the matter, for some of them may not want to. Even among those who are willing to go along, there likely will be differences of opinion as to how much liberty is to be surrendered, to whom, and under what circumstances.

Jean Jacques Rousseau wrote in his *Social Contract* (1762), "All justice comes from God, who is its sole source." Governments would like for their laws to be thought of in the same way, as sacred writs divinely conceived and bestowed upon a grateful people from on high. This is one reason why judges wear black robes instead of Bermuda shorts and why an archaic manner of expression persists in court proceedings. With respect to its laws, the state desires that they be regarded with reverent obedience, but that idea never has quite taken hold in New Mexico.

Law is seldom discussed in isolation from other, more value-laden concepts. If it were, it might be all too apparent that laws are only rules and that they are subject to debate. It would not do to teach children that the law is subject to political manipulation in pursuit of selfish ends. Instead, we usually hear about "law and order," or law as an instrument of justice. These linkages express the altruistic intent of many citizens concerning the purposes of law, and they are part of the window dressing in which all kinds of laws are clothed.

New Mexico fiction has a good deal to say about law, order, and justice and about the prevailing attitudes toward them in a pluralistic society which has been profoundly influenced by its frontier heritage.

THE LAWLESS FRONTIER

In Mayne Reid's *The Scalp Hunters* (1851), Dr. Henry Haller declines to seek redress for ill-treatment at the hands of a fandango crowd in Santa Fe, explaining, "I know too well the lawlessness of the place to apply for justice" (55). Cutting short his recuperation from injuries sustained in the brawl, he hastens south toward Chihuahua but again is victimized when a crooked guide makes off with his pack mule. Once more, Dr. Haller is persuaded that it would be folly for him to seek justice in the villages of the lower Rio Grande; they, too, are lawless places.

Haller's experience typifies that of adventurers heading west in the pages of novels and stories written in the mid–nineteenth century. They find no law on the frontier, whether among hostile tribes, Hispanic settlements of the Southwest, or unruly Americans who have fled the bonds of law and society. The absence of law reinforced the image of the West as a "land of savagery" and provided an abundance of opportunities for violent conflict.

Dime novelists of the 1860s and 1870s thrived on images of lawlessness on the frontier. In many of the early dime novels, the protagonist goes west expressly to escape the restraint of law. The heroes of the backwoods place little faith in the formal apparatus of law and courts, and they do not seem to mind applying their own judgment to resolve such conflicts as may arise. It is a small price to pay for the freedom they enjoy.

Toward the end of the century, the writers of western fiction placed even greater emphasis on frontier lawlessness, often focusing on conflict between the emerging forces of "law and order" and the lawless element that stood in the way of civilized society.

Twentieth-century writers have continued to emphasize lawlessness as a defining characteristic of the frontier West. Rhodes acknowledged a lack of formality in matters of law and justice in the old West he portrayed, but he was neither ashamed nor alarmed about it. In fact, he took pride in the capacity for self-government exhibited by the men he knew and admired. In *Pasó Por Aquí* (1927), he places Jay Hollister, a young nurse, among a group of men who while away the afternoon swapping stories on the steps of the Alamogordo hospital. There is general hilarity at the report of a bungled bank heist, but Jay is outraged. "Now isn't that New Mexico for you?" she raves, "A man commits a barefaced robbery, and you make a joke of it" (166). The outburst is received with amusement, but no attempt is made to refute the indictment. On the contrary, the men feel complimented on the self-sufficiency they enjoy in a remote frontier society.

The absence of law is remarked on both the high road of western fiction and the low. No group of writers has done more to promote the reputation for lawlessness than the creators of popular "adventure westerns." In Cort Martin's *Bolt No. 4: The Guns of Taos* (1981), a self-proclaimed "adult western," the hero makes it with a saloon singer, an heiress, and a beautiful girl from the nearby pueblo. But he has to spend his spare time running down murderers, because there is no law in Taos except that imposed by the local boss — which is to say, there is no law at all.

By 1996, nineteenth-century New Mexico still was defined by its propensity for lawlessness. When Abigail Conklin comes west in Karen Osborn's *Between Earth and Sky*, she begins a long correspondence with her sister in Virginia, relating the hardships of the country. "There is little law here, and I don't believe many of the criminals ever get to court," she writes. "If they are caught they might go straight to the end of the rope, but most of them head south into Mexico and are never apprehended" (53). A decade later, the situation has not improved. Resettled in the north near Santa Fe, Abigail learns of the shocking rituals of the Penitentes. "In Virginia they would be arrested for it and should be here," she writes, "except that we have no law to prevent barbarity and no one to enforce such laws if they did exist" (123).

When Anglo-American pioneers complain about a lack of law, what they usually have in mind is a lack of order. They mean that there is too much violence and treachery, too little peace and decency. But law and order do not equate for the likes of Emerson Hough — who briefly worked as a frontier attorney in the mining camp of White Oaks — and Eugene Manlove Rhodes. They concede that there is not much law in the western country, but for them its absence is among the country's virtues. Their capable heroes can impose such order as may be needed without ceremony, curbing the excesses that must be expected in such a state of freedom.

THE COMING OF THE LAW

A surprising number of fiction writers have pondered the advent of law in the frontier society of territorial New Mexico. Their views may be summarized as follows: The establishment of law is a necessary and inevitable development, but it also implies loss of cherished freedoms and raises apprehensions concerning possible corruption among the authorities chosen to enforce laws.

Matthew Garth, pioneer rancher in David Thompson's *Silver Light* (1990), does much as he pleases but welcomes the law, which he says represents "the enactment of reasonable order" and so makes possible "the preservation of life and property." Both life and property are of considerable interest to him. Law, he declares, is as useful to polite society as "a good map and a horse [are] in the wilderness" (121). True, concedes a wistful companion, but law takes away the wildness that brought men to such a country in the first place.

Most profoundly affected by the coming of the law are those fictional characters who have helped to tame the wilderness and evict the natives. Peaceful settlement has been made possible by their willingness to risk all, and they do not suffer curtailment of their freedom graciously.

One who is reluctant to let the old ways go is Buell Wood, former sheriff of Harding, New Mexico, in Glendon Swarthout's *Skeletons* (1979), a book based in part on the Villista murder trials of 1916–21, held in Deming (see Baxter). Upon hearing of his wife's tragic death, in an accident caused by the thoughtless actions of three rowdy men, Wood has taken down his pistols and killed all three. On trial for murder in 1910, Wood is upbraided by the prosecutor as a throwback to gun law. "New Mexico is no longer a frontier — it will soon be a state. And this very building attests to the determination of the citizens of New Mexico to take the law out of the hands of individuals and repose it in the collective conscience of that state. Like Buell Wood and his weapons, the justice of the Old West is obsolete. Justice must henceforth be dispensed equally to all, under law which applies equally to all" (105). Wood may be an anachronism in the eyes of the prosecutor, but he is acquitted by a jury of his neighbors in Harding.

Another transitional figure is Jean Ballard, a fictional representation of Lucien Bonaparte Maxwell in Harvey Fergusson's *Grant of Kingdom* (1950), a book based on the famed Maxwell Land Grant. Says the book's narrator, "When society is unorganized, personal allegiance always takes the place of law, and the force of individual personality is the only thing that can hold men together and create order" (97). Ballard possesses the courage and personal strength needed to keep the peace and build an empire of ranching, mining, timber, and trading interests; but he runs his business casually, allowing small ranchers to settle on the grant. Transactions are consummated informally, leaving settlers without documentation to support their claims of ownership. When the ailing Ballard sells out to a syndicate, the law becomes an instrument of injustice, allowing the syndicate to evict settlers ruled to be without valid titles to the land they occupy.

LAW AND ORDER ... AND JUSTICE

Once established in New Mexico, American law lived up to the expectations of many skeptics by failing to produce a just and orderly society. It became clear, at least to several fiction writers, that law, order, and justice were three different constructs and that they did not magically converge in the presence of the American legal system.

In *Skeletons,* a southern New Mexico judge expatiates on the differences among these concepts, relating his father's views on the evolution of civilized society on the frontier: "First you must have order. You get it however you can, usually with a gun and a rope. Then you need law. You write that and try to live by it. Order and law — these come first, even among animals. When you have them, you can take time to think about wallpaper and a choir for the church and sunsets and indoor privies. Oh yes, and justice" (68).

Rhodes never confused the ideas of law and justice. His men of the frontier West were bound by an unwritten code of honor which demanded the pursuit of justice but regarded the law and its official machinery with suspicion.

Numerous Rhodes heroes, including Jeff Bransford, Pres Lewis, and Steve "Wildcat" Thompson, make clear both their skepticism concerning the law and their allegiance to higher values. In *The Proud Sheriff* (1935), Spinal Maginnis, the wily sheriff of Hillsboro, finds it necessary to smoke out a murderer by allowing suspicion to fall on an innocent boy. He sees nothing wrong with this, but the strategy draws a mild rebuke from Andy

Hinkle. "But to keep back vital evidence?" implores Andy. "You are supposed to be a servant of the law, ain't you?"

"Supposed is right," the sheriff responds. "Me, I sort of aim to deal out justice — which isn't exactly the same thing" (76).

Jim Chee takes much the same attitude a century later, in Tony Hillerman's *Sacred Clowns* (1993), opting to let a hit-and-run driver go free when it becomes clear that the man is making recompense to the victim's family in accord with Navajo custom.

In the twentieth-century West described by Edward Abbey, individuals no longer are free to pursue justice by direct action; instead, they are largely at the mercy of a legal system which is fixated upon process rather than product, and which is highly vulnerable to manipulation. The law is a blunt instrument of government authority in Abbey's *Fire on the Mountain* (1962), as law-abiding John Vogelin is pushed off his southern New Mexico ranch by means he can only regard as "legal thievery."

Steve Thompson lives the dream of many an ordinary citizen in Rhodes's *West Is West* (1917), bringing the government to its knees and imposing his own form of justice. Informed by officials of Saragossa County that he cannot offset taxes owed with bounties offered by the county on the scalps of designated predators, Steve dispenses with technicalities: "'Very pretty,' said Steve. 'As it happens, I've seen the scrip you issue. The law is printed on the back of it. No bounty is paid to men owing back taxes. Likewise, I pay no taxes to counties owing me back bounty. I hereby unanimously repeal your laws and offer you a perfectly just settlement, man to county, without no law'" (175).

Wildcat Thompson makes good his bluff, holding indignant county officials at bay with a pipe concealed in his coat pocket so as to resemble the muzzle of a loaded pistol, and forcing acceptance of his proposal. Unfortunately, for John Vogelin and most other decent mortals there is no such fantasy to be conjured up.

TWO COMPLAINTS

It is small wonder that American law held little appeal for Native American and Hispanic New Mexicans following the American occupation of New Mexico. American law was rooted in ideals about individual worth, private property, and personal liberty — premises which did not necessarily arouse the same passion in many native New Mexicans as in the self-aggrandizing Americans. Likewise, the invading Anglo-Americans assumed the desirability of law which was written, codified,

and applied consistently to all, without regard for circumstances extrane-
ous to the issue at hand. Such a system was flawed in the eyes of many natives; it was overly rigid and intentionally blind to many of the facts that
had to be considered when determining right and wrong, guilt or innocence, or liability for injury to one's neighbor. Hispanic New Mexicans
could hardly lay claim to a system free of corruption, but the old regime
was corrupt in a different way, a way that they understood.

In the eyes of several fiction writers, American law quickly became an
alienating influence among the native peoples, riding roughshod over
long-standing customs and disregarding deeply held cultural values. Such
judgments are expressed in numerous works, but most of the cultural
differences concerning the law are summed up in two complaints, one
against the native peoples and one against the conquering Anglos, that appear time and again in the fiction of New Mexico.

The indictment against Hispanic and Native American people alleges a
permissive attitude that gives rise to lawlessness. Hispanics, especially, often are portrayed as condoning violent crimes and disregarding laws
propagated for the public good. It is further implied that their disregard
for the law discourages outside investment and impedes progress.

An opposing view holds that the *gringo* cares little about justice, but
uses the law to further his selfish interests. According to this view,
American law is not an instrument of justice but, in fact, a self-serving
mechanism by which the rich and clever may manipulate circumstances
to their own advantage, to the detriment of those who may be unlettered
in the English language or unfamiliar with the American legal system.

The indictment against Hispanics goes back to the earliest examples of
English-language fiction about the West. The two complaints are found
together in Florence Finch Kelly's *The Delafield Affair* (1909) and again in
Harvey Fergusson's *The Blood of the Conquerors* (1921), and they have ap-
peared individually or in tandem many times since, contributing to the
Black Legends of both Spain and the United States.

In Kelly's novel, an Anglo ranch manager complains that the territory's
Hispanic justices of the peace consistently "make justice look like a bob-
tailed horse" and that they do not take lawbreaking seriously. Says the
rancher, Curt Conrad, "Up north last week one of 'em fined a man five
dollars for committing murder and warned him not to do it again or he'd
have to make it ten next time" (67).

In Fergusson's book, set in Albuquerque, emotions are excited by an
editorial on the unsolved murder of a prominent citizen. The editor, late

Harvey Fergusson.
Photo by Cedric Wright.
Courtesy The Bancroft Library,
Neg. 1905.2 Por 4 ff ALB.

of New York, moralizes on the deplorable state of law enforcement in the community: "He cited statistics to show that the percentage of convictions in that State was exceedingly small. Daringly, he asked how the citizens could expect to attract to the State the capital needed for its development, when assassination for personal and political purposes was there tolerated much as it had been in Europe in the Middle Ages" (91). The editorial appears to blame the state's Hispanic population, a fact noted by a rival paper which decries the editorial as "a covert attack on the Mexican people" (92).

Rural Hispanics are again shown to be soft on crime in Robert Bright's *The Life and Death of Little Jo* (1944), a novel set in the village of Talpa, near Taos. When law officers come from town in search of a killer, they learn little or nothing in the village; in the eyes of the villagers, the victim was a bad man who deserved what he got. Among the lawmen, there is one who has little enthusiasm for the investigation: "He really loathed chasing criminals, especially those of his own people, the Spanish-Americans of New Mexico" (40). The officer's sympathy, like those of the villagers, is for the wife and child of the accused man.

Residents of the northern village of Rociada, as described in Oliver La Farge's *Behind the Mountains* (1956), also might have been accused of inordinate permissiveness. There, La Farge relates, several men had served time in the state penitentiary, but only one was considered truly criminal.

Oliver La Farge.
Photo by Wyatt Davis.
Courtesy John Pendaries
La Farge.

As for the others, he says, "the feeling is best expressed in the literal meaning of our expression, 'He fell foul of the law'" (82).

Martiniano, a Taos Indian, falls foul of the law in Frank Waters's *The Man Who Killed the Deer* (1942), when he kills a deer out of season in the national forest reserve. For his transgression, Martiniano is fined by the white man's court and punished by his own tribal council. To him, the law is senseless. "What is the difference between killing a deer on Tuesday or Thursday?" he laments. "Would I not have killed it anyway?" (22). Joe Mondragon displays a similar contempt for hunting laws in Nichols's *The Milagro Beanfield War* (1974). Along with most of his neighbors, he regards them as "so much bullshit" and takes his rifle into the woods whenever he feels like it, without troubling to buy a hunting license (20–21).

Such contempt for American law usually is depicted in characters with whom the author sympathizes. They are decent people caught in a clash of cultures, grappling with differences in language and custom, set against a powerful legal system predicated on values they do not comprehend.

In Larry McMurtry's *Dead Man's Walk* (1995), Bigfoot Wallace takes a stab at explaining the indifference of a renegade Apache toward the prevailing legal authority. Informed that Gomez "knows no law," Wallace allows that the man may know plenty of law, "but it ain't his law and he don't mind breaking it" (320). The same might be said of many other fictional lawbreakers who feel no ownership of an alien law imposed by outsiders.

An early instance of the accusation against *gringos*— that they manipulate the law to gratify their own appetites — occurs in Kelly's *The Delafield Affair,* when a young woman lately arrived from the East is introduced to the business practices of certain Anglo businessmen. They accumulate land and property, she learns, by loaning money to local Hispanics in the expectation of an eventual foreclosure. Lucy Bancroft proclaims the practice "a shameful piece of business" but is reminded by her father, no saint himself, that the mortgage loan business enjoys "the full sanction of law and custom." "I can't help it, daddy," she rejoins, "if all the Congressmen and lawyers and business men, and preachers too, in the United States are engaged in it — that doesn't make it right" (102–103).

In Fergusson's book, the indictment of Anglos is implicit in the character of an Anglo lawyer who has designs on a fertile valley in northern New Mexico. His plan is to open a store and lend money to unwary residents: "Whenever there was a birth, a funeral or a marriage among them, Mexicans needed money, and could be persuaded to sign mortgages, which they generally could not read. In each Mexican family there would be either a birth, a marriage or a death once in three years on average. Three such events would enable the lender to gain possession of a ranch" (109).

In *People of the Valley* (1941), Frank Waters views a similar ploy by *gringo* outsiders philosophically, but real bitterness over loss of land and culture is expressed in several works by Native American and Hispanic authors. In Rudolfo Anaya's *Heart of Aztlán* (1976), men exiled to an Albuquerque barrio brood upon the injustices suffered by their people. With longing, they recall the glorious history of the Spanish in New Mexico; but their reminiscence ends in grief, as they recall the coming of the *Americanos* and a ruinous era in which "men of power using the new laws for selfish gain encroached upon the land and finally wrenched it away" (103–104). In David Seals's *Sweet Medicine* (1992), Buddy Red Bird, a Cheyenne Indian from Montana, responds to a frame-up perpetrated against his sister with outrage rather than grief, orchestrating a seizure of the Taos Ski Valley Road and venting his anger to newsmen. In his view, the American legal system is a manifestation of the corruption and injustice of the dominant society and is unworthy of obedience or respect.

In works like Richard Bradford's *So Far from Heaven* (1973), William Eastlake's *Dancers in the Scalp House* (1975), and Nichols's *The Magic Journey* (1978), wealthy *gringos* again are seen to use the law as a tool of capitalist greed, to the detriment of native peoples.

The continuing relevance of the two complaints in present-day New Mexico is evident in routine news items. In debates over drunken driving, Indian gaming, Indian sovereignty, mandatory auto insurance, economic development, zoning laws, and other matters, there is often an undercurrent of racial tension. Whatever its merits, a familiar refrain emerges from the chorus of opposing grievances: Hispanic and Native American people stand accused of inflicting moral degradation on the society through their disregard of the law, while domineering outsiders are accused of imposing their own alien values and using the law to line their pockets.

A MATTER OF PERSPECTIVE

To be sure, New Mexico could not have continued forever relying on the *ad hoc* justice system favored by Rhodes and his bold frontier characters. For all its faults and imperfections, its cultural myopia, and the abuses to which it has been subjected by men and women of dishonorable intentions, American law has provided a framework for social order and the peaceful resolution of disputes; presumably, a goodly portion of justice has been dispensed along the way. What has interested writers, however, is the amoral character of the legal process, its dependence upon human judgment and character, and its vulnerability to manipulation.

"A good law is as handy as a good pocketbook," allows Rhodes's Jeff Bransford. "But law, simply as such, independent of its merits, rouses no enthusiasm in my manly bosom, no more than a signboard the day after Halloween" (1914, p. 5). The free-thinking Bransford goes on to say that his policy is to obey good laws and ignore bad ones. Questioned as to who is to determine which are the good laws, Jeff cheerfully accepts that responsibility, explaining his logic to those assembled: "If I let some other man make up my mind I've got to use my judgment — picking the man I follow. By organizing myself into a Permanent Committee of One to do my own thinking I take my one chance of mistakes instead of two" (6).

If, as charged by Bransford, the law is not a reliable authority in matters of truth and right and justice, what is it? In the eyes of a good many fiction writers, the law is an instrument of political and social control, serving the interests of those who are most skilled in its use.

This seems to have been the conclusion of Padre Antonio José Martínez, whose famous advice to his seminary students following the American occupation of New Mexico is repeated in Elliott Arnold's novel, *The Time of the Gringo* (1953). In explaining the defining features of the new government, the priest advises his pupils, "You might say, my son, that the American government is like a burro, but on this burro jog along lawyers and not clergy" (612). According to Pedro Sánchez, this observation prompted several of the padre's more ambitious pupils to pursue a different vocation, abandoning their training for the priesthood and devoting themselves instead to the study of law.

6 SKY DETERMINES

n 1934, an Episcopal clergyman transplanted to the Southwest wrote, "In New Mexico whatever is both old and peculiar appears upon examination to have a connection with the arid climate." The clergyman was Ross Calvin. He was living in Silver City for his health, and his observation became the thesis of a classic work of regional interpretation, *Sky Determines* (vii). Calvin maintained that the climate — specifically, the scarcity of precipitation — was responsible not only for the pattern of flora and fauna, but also for much of what could be observed of human activity in the Southwest. The author elaborated upon this premise, applying it to many types of natural and cultural phenomena. He might have added that climate has had an equally pervasive effect upon the region's literature.

Encompassing everything from Sonoran desert to Alpine mountains, the southwestern climate is one of extremes. As characterized by John Sinclair in *In Time of Harvest,* his novel of Estancia Valley bean farmers, "the sky and air down here don't dribble: drouth or moisture, heat or cold, — they do business only in wholesale lots" (108). There is plenty of perfectly nice weather, of course, but that rarely enters into a writer's plans in an active way, as destructive, oppressive, or threatening events do. Writers have used a variety of climatic events to make their points. Most literary references to climate have to do with water, its scarcity in the Southwest, and the essential necessity for water in order to sustain life. Desert heat, violent winds, and winter blizzards also inspire comment, as writers portray a continuing struggle of men and women against the elements in a vast and unforgiving landscape.

LITERARY USES OF WEATHER AND CLIMATE

Climatic events sometimes are useful as sources of immediate danger for characters. Floods, tornadoes, winter storms, and high winds can be used to create acute dramatic situations, while showing how characters respond in a crisis. No character in New Mexico fiction has enjoyed a more spectacular demise than Florence Gresham, Myron Brinig's fictional Mabel Dodge Luhan in a biting satirical novel, *All of Their Lives* (1941). Daring and defiant in the face of a fierce lightning storm in the Taos Mountains, Florence refuses to abandon what had begun as a pleasant horseback outing to the Indians' sacred ceremonial lake. Bolting ahead of her companions, she dashes across the exposed ridge, where woman and horse are consumed in a sudden bolt of white fire. But this was Florence. Her reckless disregard of the rules, her flare for the dramatic, and her willful pursuit of life allowed neither retreat nor compromise.

Chronic conditions, such as drought and incessant winds, are adversities against which characters must struggle. Seeing the westerner through a drought, chapter after chapter, is a little like watching paint dry, but it does allow the reader to observe significant traits and values that help establish character — determination, perseverance, or trepidation in the face of adversity, for example. The classic literary treatments of drought and wind are Texas books — Elmer Kelton's *The Time It Never Rained* (1973) and Dorothy Scarborough's *The Wind* (1925). In Kelton's book, stubborn Charlie Flagg is the last holdout among ranchers besieged by a long drought; while neighbors all around him are reduced to accepting government assistance, Charlie suffers greatly but does not give in. In *The Wind*, a fragile flower of Virginia, living on the Texas prairie with her rancher husband, is driven mad by the incessant howling of the wind. New Mexico fiction has nothing to match these two examples, but drought and wind enter into a good many New Mexico novels, with significant, if less dramatic, consequences.

There are indications in some works of fiction that climate helps make people what they are. In a story called "Old Bum" in his *Spinning Sun, Grinning Moon* (1995), Max Evans talks about the wind around Hi Lo, a fictitious cowtown in northeastern New Mexico, indicating that it blows about two-thirds of the time and has a tendency to make folks tense. The

Judith Van Gieson.
Photo by Robert R. White,
© 1998. Courtesy Robert R.
White.

place is prone to sudden outbreaks of fistfighting, he says, because "the people are all on edge from bucking this infernal wind" (239).

Neil Hamel, the Albuquerque-based lawyer of Judith Van Gieson's popular mystery series, also finds wind an unavoidable but unsettling fact of life in New Mexico. Approaching by air in *North of the Border* (1988), Neil observes that spring has arrived in the city. Its sure sign is a cloud of dust that swirls over Albuquerque, obscuring familiar landmarks: "Spring in New Mexico means wind — not breezes, *wind.* Wind that smashes tumbleweeds into your car and dust into your eyes, that whips your hair around, that howls and rips at the windows until it unsettles your brain" (108).

At Shiprock, Tony Hillerman's tribal policeman, Jim Chee, acquires habits natural to one reared in the high desert of the Navajo reservation; but some of his ways jangle the sensibilities of his Anglo girlfriend. When Chee finishes a cup of coffee, he swishes water around to rinse the cup, then swills the brown water. To Chee, this is second nature; in a country where water must be hauled, you grow up learning not to waste it (1986a).

Of all things in nature that men have sought to control, weather has proven one of the least tractable and least understood. Humor and superstition are time-honored responses to perplexities that must be endured. Thus, in *Mother Tongue* (1994), by Demetria Martínez, old men gather on Albuquerque's Old Town plaza to endure the sweltering summer days; lacking any other explanation for the oppressive heat, they speculate that it is a punishment from God "for having sold so much land to the gringos" (34).

In some cases, climate accounts for the presence of particular characters in New Mexico. This is most often the case in novels involving characters who have sought the dry desert air for their health, like eastern composer Edmund Abbey in Paul Horgan's *No Quarter Given* (1935) and the Sitwell family in Mary Austin's *Starry Adventure* (1931). Such characters frequently bring more than an infirmity to their new home. The respiratory sufferer often comes with a foreign perspective that makes it possible to see the country through inquiring eyes, to point out peculiarities that may not occur to those who are already accustomed to the local scene. The patient also may bring a heightened sense of the fragility of life. He may be more acutely aware of sights and sounds and more appreciative of precious time.

Fiction needs conflict, and the arid climate plays a role in generating conflict, as opposing interests compete for control of scarce water. Contemporary New Mexicans need look no farther than the daily newspaper to be reminded that water is and always has been a source of conflict. Almost always, New Mexico has at least one row going with its neighbor to the east over water. When lucrative but thirsty industrial prospects consider locating in Albuquerque, the forces of environmental protection and economic development are likely to clash. They clash in fiction, too.

The weather, then, is not just an inert attribute of setting or local color. Climate often plays an important part in characterization, plot, and the creation of suspense. Climatic events sometimes shape character and sometimes reveal character. Climate also provides objects for characters to struggle against and to fight over.

MAN AGAINST THE ELEMENTS

In early works of fiction, the weather was added to other hazards to portray the West as a land of dangers, toils, and snares. Heroes of highly imaginative picaresque adventures had to live through a lot in a three-hundred-page novel. They fought off vicious jaguars (sometimes more than one at a time), grappled with villainous rivals, were set awash in raging floods, and got trampled in buffalo stampedes. Tame by contrast but nonetheless worthy of mention were climatic hazards that threatened to do in the heroes. In Reid's *The Scalp Hunters* (1851), for example,

Dr. Henry Haller is thrown down by a pack of wild cyclones, "vast towers of sand — blown up by the whirlblast," as he traverses the Jornada del Muerto (63). Then his pack mule runs off, leaving him many miles from water, with a powerful thirst.

On the parched Jornada, the traveler risks all in a struggle with the elements: "Water is his chief care; his ever present solicitude. Water the divinity he worships." In his delirium, Haller stumbles off a cliff, where he would plummet to his death but for the lucky accident of becoming entangled in his *lazo*, still tethered to his horse. Thus does Dr. Haller learn of the great western desert and the *"thirst that kills!"* (65).

Willa Cather's prose is several shades lighter than the vivid purple preferred by Capt. Mayne Reid, but in her admiring treatment of Jean Baptiste Lamy and the early missionaries of the Southwest in *Death Comes for the Archbishop,* she also employs climatic events to make a point. The refined, almost delicate French priest, Father Jean Marie Latour, follows his vocation to Santa Fe in the mid–nineteenth century. Grace and dignity surround him at all times; but, as he persists in the face of high winds, sandstorms, and a horrendous blizzard, it is apparent that he has the mettle needed to contend with the difficulties and build an enduring legacy.

That his determination transcends such hazards is a tribute to the character of Father Latour. This is surely the author's intent in *Death Comes for the Archbishop,* and it is likely the intent of authors who use climate in a similar manner in other novels celebrating the triumphant Anglo male hero. It is curious that such admiration does not normally accrue to the countless natives who are exposed to the elements on a daily basis and whose people have survived centuries in the same harsh land. This disparity lends some credence to the complaint that native peoples and women have been largely invisible to the outsiders who have produced most of the published literature of the frontier West.

"God damn the goddam weather," exclaims Tom Foote in Harvey Fergusson's *In Those Days: An Impression of Change* (1929), a fictional chronicle of early Albuquerque (79). Foote speaks emphatically, because he is seeing the profits of a successful trading trip blown away in an early winter blizzard. Loss of goods is a certainty and loss of life a real possibility, as the party faces five days' snow from a purple sky, while crossing the mountains on the return trip from Arizona. Exhausted, the men are reduced to eating horse flesh to stay alive. Still, it's all in the bargain for Foote and his partner, Robert Jayson, who risk much to profit much in a land where there are opportunities to match the hazards. Jayson rationally concludes that he will probably die in the wilderness, but in the end the experience is simply one more measure of his fitness to prevail in a hard land.

Larry McMurtry wants to show the same qualities of determination and resourcefulness in his two storied Texas Rangers, Woodrow Call and Gus McCrae, who, in *Dead Man's Walk* (1995), join the ill-fated Texan–Santa Fe Expedition as naïve young adventurers. Poorly equipped and poorly led, they stumble across Texas to face unmitigated disaster. New Mexico was supposed to have been easy pickings, but the country is full of hazards.

"I hate New Mexico," says Gus, "If it ain't bears, it's Indians" (368). Much of the men's misery, however, is due to the harshness of the arid land. Sustained by brackish water holes and found bits of dead game, they traverse the Llano Estacado en route to the Mexican settlements. Traveling southward across the Jornada del Muerto — the "big dry" — as captives of the Mexican army, it's worse. They shiver through freezing desert nights and are lucky to find the makings for wolf and coyote soup to nourish them across the wasteland. The last impression of the country is no better than the first, as the survivors are herded toward El Paso in a howling sandstorm. "I guess they call it the Pass of the North because all this dern wind out of New Mexico blows through it," observes Bigfoot Wallace. "If it gets much stronger it'll be blowing pigs at us" (400). Call and McCrae suffer much, but they return to Texas better, stronger, more wary men, prepared to survive all the rigors and calamities of primitive life in the borderlands.

In Richard Martin Stern's *The Big Bridge* (1982), wind is an obstacle against which engineers and builders must struggle to span the breathtaking Tano Gorge north of Santa Fe. Ross Associates of San Francisco has built engineering marvels the world over, but the company never has had to contend with the wicked and unpredictable gales of the great gorge of the Rio Largo. Luckless construction workers plunge to their deaths, and the company learns to respect the powerful wind. In the book's climactic scene, it's man against nature, as a violent storm threatens to send the great steel skeleton crashing into the gorge. Heroes on bulldozers fight it out to hold the nearly completed structure in place.

Wind is just one aspect of the culture shock that defines second-year teacher Birdy Stone's life in out-of-the-way Pinetop, New Mexico, in Antonya Nelson's *Nobody's Girl* (1998). Birdy had learned to cope with the gales for which her native Chicago is famous, but here she is unnerved not

Antonya Nelson.
Photo by Shale Aaron.
Courtesy News and
Publications, New Mexico
State University.

only by the wind, but by her neighbors' attitudes. "Here, people pretended the wind was not incessant. They walked out of their houses with tentative grips on their possessions, their hats and umbrellas and trash sacks. Their skirts flew up and their television antennas snapped, laundry defied the line. Both this year and last, everyone assured Birdy it was highly unusual, all this wind. They went around being astonished by it, exclaiming. She was suspicious of their wonder" (17).

Another character who battles it out with the wind is Louis Figman, a California expatriate who hits the road hoping to learn something before he dies of a suspected brain tumor, in Cathryn Alpert's *Rocket City* (1995). By sheer happenstance, Figman lands in Artesia, where he rents a house and falls for a checker at the local E-Z Mart. Figman has planned to take up painting, but, having just cleaned his new abode, he soon finds himself under siege by a howling dust storm. The experience is unnerving to Figman but routine to his landlady, who explains that such winds commonly put out the furnace and blow shingles off the roof. No big deal. Driving through the blowing dust with his new lady love, fearful of plowing into another vehicle in the brown haze, Figman's only consoling thought is of a crash so fiery that "his ashes would mix with hers and blow forever over the plains of New Mexico" (225).

THE LONG DRY

Floods, winter storms, and gale-force winds may be terrifying and deadly, and heroic characters typically respond with determination and

Cathryn Alpert.
Photo by Marco Alpert.
Courtesy MacMurray
& Beck, Inc.

courage. They act swiftly, boldly, and with good effect. This is what makes them heroes.

Drought, though, withers the spirit by degrees, testing the limits of patience, draining hope, fraying nerves, and nourishing seeds of self-doubt. This is a different sort of pestilence, and it calls for a different kind of courage. Its essence is not action, but long suffering. Paul Horgan, in *A Lamp on the Plains* (1937), expresses the anxious thoughts of ranch people waiting out a drought on the plains of central New Mexico. They wonder when they will be able to sleep again, "without this waiting, waiting, for something, for delivery, for the completion of an act of life, nourishment where it is needed, and the seed wetted, so that it may grow" (232).

For Joanna Davis in Conrad Richter's story "Long Drouth," in *Early Americana and Other Stories* (1936), the drought is a test of faith; her planned marriage to a young rancher depends on a break in the weather, hence better times for stockmen. While she waits, her world is slowly transformed: "She was seeing blue sky, once the most uplifting thing she knew, turn hideous in front of her eyes. Even the warm sun had become a malevolent, staring eye, watching without compassion the slow death of every living thing" (127–28).

Paul Horgan.
Photo by William Van Saun,
© 1979. Courtesy Office
of Public Information and
Publications, Wesleyan
University.

On the Laguna reservation, an oppressive drought after World War II evokes not only haunting memories of past dry spells, but a familiar pattern of loss. Tayo, a troubled veteran returning home in Leslie Marmon Silko's *Ceremony* (1977), finds the land parched and the livestock gaunt, reminiscent of the 1930s, "when buyers came from Albuquerque and Gallup and bought the cattle and sheep for almost nothing" (25). Like the withered land, Tayo's own despairing spirit awaits the gentle rain that will restore life and health.

The western hero can fight back against a jaguar, wage war against his rivals, and battle his way to safety through a winter storm. In a drought, though, there is not much to do but suffer and wait, and that is what most literary characters do.

Crusty rancher John Vogelin in Edward Abbey's *Fire on the Mountain* (1962) has battled many a drought by the summer of his discontent, when forces of the government come to take his sandy, hardscrabble ranch in order to expand the White Sands Proving Grounds. He has been through the cycle many times — feeding cactus, buying commercial feed, selling animals off too cheap when the money is gone, hoping for rain in time to hold his creditors off a little longer. To his grandson, he is a man to be admired: "My Grandfather Vogelin was one of the few independent ranchers who somehow had survived the wheel of drouth and depression. He seldom broke even but he didn't break" (36). Just being there, year after year, is an achievement in Vogelin's desert country.

It would be unlike any character of Eugene Manlove Rhodes to stand around and wring his hands. In the story, "Aforesaid Bates" (1928), Rhodes shows how his men respond in a drought. They respond by attacking a hillside with axes, hacking down the tall sotol plants and feeding their fleshy hearts to the cattle. They also feed prickly pear with the spines burned off. Having held back better grass against the certainty of an eventual dry spell, they have some decent pasture available. These measures, along with assorted shenanigans designed to frustrate the opportunistic plans of the local business sharp, enable the Little World cowmen to get by. Says the practical Andrew Jackson "Aforesaid" Bates, "The way to take care of cattle durin' a drought is to begin while it is rainin' hard" (154).

A FIGHTING MATTER

Rhodes was also one of the first to make use of a conflict over water for literary purposes, and he did so in several stories. Rhodes knew well the seriousness of such controversies, having grown to manhood in southern New Mexico and having himself tried ranching in the Tularosa Basin. In *The Trusty Knaves* (1933), a local conspiracy comes to light when a crooked rancher attempts to charge for watering of livestock crossing his range — an outrage, according to the ways of the time and place. Here, as elsewhere on the open range, the government owned most of the land. Where private ownership could be established by homestead or otherwise, cowmen naturally filed on the few scattered water holes. Through control of water, they gained de facto control over large sections of the open range.

In this case, George Carmody is attempting to move cattle from his drought-stricken range to better grass in Arizona. Erie Patterson's assessment for watering is judged unneighborly at best, and it is Elmer Farr's considered opinion that the real intent is to provoke violence and relieve Carmody of his cattle. Farr reasons that this minor affront is but one instance in a general epidemic of treachery around Target, involving an assortment of corrupt men. It is the business of an opposing band of "trusty knaves" — Farr and his friends — to impose swift and effective remedies.

A similar confrontation occurs in William Eastlake's *The Bronc People* (1958), when a rider from the Circle Heart Ranch drives his cattle through the red bluff country to "the only active water hole in thirty miles" and ends up in a shoot-out with the owner of the water hole (9). The owner of the water is a black man whose ranch house is full of books and records, and the encounter is observed by two Indians who follow the events with detached curiosity from a perch in the nearby rocks. In Eastlake's other-worldly Indian Country near Coyote, there is much to ponder.

Fighting over water is not the exclusive privilege of ranchers. The farmers do it, too. They fight each other, and they fight the ranchers. In Raymond Otis's *Little Valley* (1937), a novel of Hispanic village life, an old feud between neighbors erupts in a dispute over water rights. In Vallecito, as in other mountain villages, water is distributed to the small farms by means of an *acequia,* a ditch governed by a local committee and administered by the *mayordomo.* Deprived of his rightful turn at the water, Juliano Trujillo confronts his rival, who also happens to be the *mayordomo.* The dispute is resolved when the two men discharge their ancient weapons in anger and fall to the ground "in a dead embrace that looked grotesquely amiable" (273).

Such violence is not an anomaly, but an accepted part of the riparian system in New Mexico, according to rancher Cruz Tafoya in Richard Bradford's *So Far From Heaven* (1973): "You buy your water rights on a ditch. Somebody upstream diverts it. You ride up there and tell him to stop it. If he doesn't, you ride up there again and shoot him" (206). In Karen Osborn's *Between Earth and Sky* (1996), Anglo immigrants Clayton and Abigail Conklin watch their alfalfa wither in a summer drought along the Rio Grande, suffering silently in the knowledge that influential neighbors likely are stealing their share of water from the community ditch. "Only our second summer," Clayton tells his wife, "and I see already how a man could kill for water" (108).

Water is at issue in some of New Mexico's most celebrated works. A classic confrontation occurs in Richter's *The Sea of Grass* (1937) and another in Nichols's *The Milagro Beanfield War* (1974). In Richter's novel, hard-nosed cattle baron Jim Brewton knows that his land is cattle country, with water enough to support livestock but not near enough to grow healthy crops year in and year out. He knows this with certainty, but he cannot convince or overcome the eager sodbusters who covet the vast tall grass prairie he occupies. Brewton stews in righteous anger as the farmers go bust and retreat, leaving the once-beautiful sea of grass a scarred, wind-blown waste.

In Nichols's book, the opposing forces are Hispanic villagers and high-rolling developers. Nichols frames the conflict as a struggle among social classes and among cultures, but the center of the dispute is, again, scarce water. The villagers want only to continue tilling their hillside plots and eking out a living on the land of their parents and grandparents. But Ladd Devine III is bent on elevating the land and water to their highest and best use, supporting a posh resort that will justly reward those with the fore-sight and gumption to bring the project to fruition.

The strife over water could go on forever; from all indications, it will.

'NEATH THE WESTERN SKIES

According to Henry Nash Smith, the westward movement of Anglo frontiersmen was stymied for several decades by the belief that the land beyond the one-hundredth meridian never would support agriculture. In other words, it would not support civilization as the Americans knew it. But a westward surge after the Civil War carried farmers far out onto the plains. In many cases, they found that they could not count on sufficient rainfall to support crops year after year. In some places, farmland reverted to ranch country, as in Max Evans's account (1961) of the transformation of the fictional Hi Lo, a place on the hard edge of the Dust Bowl.

Determined farmers and ranchers have plied the frontier with irriga-tion techniques, drought-resistant crops, hearty breeds of livestock, and other measures designed to make the most of scant precipitation. For all their efforts, which in many cases have yielded impressive rewards, the Southwest remains an arid land in which farmers and stockraisers almost constantly are at some degree of risk. For whatever water exists, they must contend not only with one another, but also with industrial users, munic-ipal users, recreational users, and developers. It's likely, then, that the cli-mate will continue to be a force to be reckoned with, and water an object of contention.

As for the more acute threats, it's hard to make a case that New Mexi-cans suffer any greater distress from wind and weather than do folks living in northern Minnesota; or along the Gulf Coast, where hurricanes play; or in sunny California, where brush fires and mudslides plague the rich and famous. Still, it's hard to ignore the elements, and in the interest of retain-ing an identity with the old frontier, some of us like to claim credit for any and all the hardships that we cheerfully endure. It is plausible, then, that the weather should remain a notable presence in our conversation and in our literature.

In a time before *Lonesome Dove* (1985), Texas literary oracle Larry Mc-Murtry was urging writers to move beyond the myths of the Old West and attend to the urban experience that more nearly expresses the reality of contemporary westerners. He followed this advice himself, for a while. In more recent excursions revisiting significant events of western history and in some cases recasting the myths, McMurtry confirms what Ross Calvin observed: in New Mexico and in much of the West, "history has not taken place under a roof" (2). It can also be said that the shift of population and economic activity from rural to urban settings has not served to insulate New Mexicans from all effects of weather and climate. It was perhaps more true in days of yore, but it is still true today, that southwesterners cannot begin to understand who they are and why they behave as they do without taking into account the climate that exerts so profound an influence on their lives and fortunes.

7 VILLAGE NOVELS

I t has been said of Max Evans's *The One-Eyed Sky*, that Evans reveals "the whole world in a sandy arroyo," meaning that birth, death, self-confrontation, and all the sad and funny truths of life are to be found in an ecosystem consisting of a cow and her calf, a family of coyotes, an old cowboy, and the windswept draw in which they meet. Evans's piece may be the extreme example of a time-honored approach in literature — seeking to reveal truths of universal significance in the small and ordinary events of life.

It is possible to point to another dozen or so novels written about New Mexico places and subjects, in which the authors have attempted to reveal the world in the microcosmic society of a rural village. The village novels celebrate an appealing phenomenon of New Mexico's Hispanic cultural heritage, examining patterns of life in isolated rural communities. Sometimes these works reveal harsh realities unsuspected by the casual visitor, and sometimes they betray the prejudices of writers and readers. In the best village novels, the author teaches readers about continuity and change, social and personal conflict, hope and despair, joy and pain — about life as we know it, in Tokyo or in Truchas.

Even as they evoke a vanishing lifestyle of rural New Mexico, many of these novels also reveal the vulnerability of traditional villages to transformations wrought by changing times and the dominant Anglo-American society. Some such works recall a history of exploitation and dominance of indigenous residents by outsiders. Others reveal again the ambivalence of inquisitive newcomers who are drawn to the western country and its rural communities by the beauty and splendid isolation they offer, but who immediately set about remaking their new environs according to their own values and sensibilities. In a smaller number of novels and stories, villages are portrayed according to the recollections of native writers who grew up in rural New Mexico. For them, the culture of village life has an entirely different meaning.

MOUNTAIN VILLAGES

The Hispanic villages of New Mexico, particularly those of the northern mountains, long have been recognized as scenic and cultural attractions — each one a cluster of houses, sheds, and stables; a few stores; a post office; and an abandoned school, perhaps; all clustered around an old adobe church. Such villages frequently are set amid landscapes of incredible beauty — in narrow valleys and along winding streams; or, like Truchas, perched on jutting tablelands before shining mountains.

The land around the village normally supplies all the basic requirements of primitive living: water for household use and irrigation; tillable acreage for crops, gardens, and orchards; grazing lands for livestock; forest for timber, fuel, and game. Irrigation water is distributed by means of a system of *acequias,* ditches controlled by the opening and closing of gates, governed by a local committee and managed by the *mayordomo.*

The villages are artifacts of Hispanic settlement on the northern frontier of New Spain, and many vestiges of Spanish culture remain. Spanish is commonly spoken among older residents, and the Catholic Church is the most prominent feature in many villages. For many years, buildings were fashioned entirely of native materials — adobe, stone, and timber. Planning and zoning are notably, agreeably absent. Houses, barns, and sheds often cling to hillsides or huddle close together to allow maximum use of arable lands of the valley floor. For all their pastoral beauty, these are places where winter lies long and heavy, as is indicated by the sharply pitched roofs and towering woodpiles of many of the dwellings.

The village is an important social institution, founded on closeness of family and community. Communal labor and mutual aid have been critical to the survival of the villages. In the absence of higher institutional authority, the villages of old governed themselves. "Neglected by both church and state," writes Nancie L. Gonzalez, "each village developed a relatively autonomous system for maintaining law and order, socializing the children, perpetuating the faith and their culture in general" (41).

In earlier times, the villages were virtually self-contained, supported by a pastoral economy that required little in the way of cash trade or social interaction with the outside world. But in recent decades, the villages have suffered crippling economic losses, accompanied by inevitable changes in social structure. Cut off from natural resources by new game laws and federal forest-management practices, village residents no longer are able to rely on the land alone. Unable to wring a living from their small plots, many natives have fled to seek employment in nearby towns or mining jobs in the Mountain West, leaving fewer able-bodied adults to carry on the work of replastering communal structures and cleaning the *acequias,* and fewer people to maintain the cultural traditions of the villages.

Artists and writers long have found the villages places of extraordinary interest and visual appeal. The record left by painters and photographers who captured images of village life before World War II is priceless, especially in light of changes wrought by the automobile, the mechanization of farming, the growth of manufacturing, and the development of a cash-driven market economy. Much also has been written about the villages — by historians, anthropologists, sociologists, travel writers, journalists, and students of the village arts.

These writers have had plenty to say concerning the origins of the villages, and about the observable phenomena of material culture, economic and social conditions, patterns of settlement, religious practices, and the like. They have not said much, however, about the joy and pain of family relationships, or about the seething anger of villagers wronged by neighbors or dispossessed by strangers. They have had little to say about the anguish and ecstasy of romantic love, or the satisfaction of seeing crops grow from the earth, or about the hopes and disappointments of living. They are all but silent regarding the secret yearnings of the people who inhabit these hidden places. They have missed much, but fiction writers exist to probe just such matters.

In fact, the villages have inspired a good many novels and stories. The early novels, written mostly in the 1930s and 1940s by Anglo males, offer remarkably similar portrayals of lifestyle, culture, social structure, and relations between the village and the wider world. It is likely that some of the novels provide reliable insights, while others appear merely to capitalize on sensational or exotic aspects of culture, sometimes reinforcing negative stereotypes of Hispanic and rural people. All of the works offer clues to the responses of outsiders to a unique cultural phenomenon that so many have "discovered" along the byways of rural New Mexico. Later novels of village life, including works by Hispanic writers whose roots are in the village culture, provide a useful diversity of perspectives.

WINDS OF CHANGE

The first work typical of the New Mexico village novels, ironically, is set not in New Mexico but just over the state line in the San Luis Valley of southern Colorado, in a village possibly based on the tiny community of San Pedro y San Rafael. The area is one which shares with New Mexico a common cultural heritage attributable to Hispanic settlement in the region of the Sangre de Cristo Mountains. *The Penitentes of San Rafael: A Tale of the San Luis Valley,* by Louis How, was published in 1900 and is, in every important respect, representative of the typical New Mexico village novel as it appeared in the first half of the twentieth century.

The pattern established in How's book holds for most of the village novels that followed it. The author portrays an insular community hidden away in the seldom-visited foothills of the Sangre de Cristos. The people of San Rafael have little contact with the outside world and little reason or opportunity for trade or social interaction. Most of the residents are poor, uneducated, and superstitious. In the simple lives they lead, they are guided by tradition, the Catholic faith, and a few powerful individuals who govern the village, usually to their own advantage.

In a plot or subplot common to the early village novels, the village and its people are profoundly disturbed by a threat from the outside. Its rhythms uninterrupted through long years of isolation, the village suddenly finds itself buffeted by forces the people can neither comprehend nor resist. Not only are time-honored customs and routines shaken, but also fundamental beliefs that have held for generations. In *The Penitentes of San Rafael,* danger arrives in the person of a nosy stranger — a self-righteous *gringo* who has stumbled onto the village while on a fishing holiday. Appalled at the barbaric rites of the Penitentes, he sends word to church and military authorities, who descend upon the village to stop the outrage and punish the offenders.

The people of San Bartolo face a similar menace in D. J. Hall's 1937 novel, *Perilous Sanctuary,* when a fugitive *gringo* wanders in from the wilderness, raising fears that he will disclose the secret rites of the Penitentes. When found wandering in the desert near San Bartolo, Hick Bowles has nothing more in mind than staying ahead of the law, but his appearance in the village is greeted with suspicion and hostility by the local patrón.

The introduction of paved roads threatens the peace and privacy of villages in Raymond Otis's *Miguel of the Bright Mountain* (1936) and O'Kane Foster's *In the Night Did I Sing* (1942). As villagers in both books go about their daily lives, they become increasingly aware of the approach of great fire-belching machines working their way toward the villages — Hormiga, assumed to represent Truchas; and Sangre de Cristo, a fictional representation of Ranchos de Taos. The new blacktop roads may signify progress to the *gringos* who have ordered them built, but the prospect of increased scrutiny by outsiders alarms the wary village people.

Although the villagers of Otis's book do not want the new road, they are powerless to stop the road builders: "Like a small army they moved over the countryside by day, leaving a straight scar behind them in the land, gnawing their way forward with their machines like an earth-eating monster. They obeyed a remote will which commanded them to advance and stop for nothing" (248).

In Foster's Sangre de Cristo, villagers sense that their world is being invaded and transformed by forces they can neither see nor understand: "From somewhere came all this flattening activity, this dumping, crunching, crashing of their landscape — of their lives" (186). The storekeeper alone finds reason to rejoice in the new road, and that only after he has been assured that the road will run past his store.

Changing economic conditions threaten accustomed ways in other traditional novels of village life. The Great Depression and new government policies bring shattering changes to the village of Vallecito in Otis's *Little Valley* (1937). Cut off from the public forest by new laws, the village men no longer can raise cash by selling firewood in town. Even if they could sell wood from the forest reserve, the men would find the market diminished, as more of the townspeople use gas to heat their homes. Flattened by the collapsed economy, the people of Vallecito are thrown on the mercy of the new welfare system. Some adapt readily, but the process is hard on proud men who are accustomed to providing for their families through honest labor.

In Frank Waters's *People of the Valley* (1941), denizens of the Blue Valley — the valley surrounding the village of Mora — are victims of capitalist greed, finally surrendering their homes and farms to two Irishmen who have used their mercantile business to generate debt and financial ruin among the villagers. The men want to build a great dam and flood the valley, in order to develop the area and enrich themselves. Introducing themselves as "Los Mofres," the Murphy brothers, industrious Irishmen, have ambitious plans for the valley and little regard for its native people.

There is no immediate or tangible villain in the demise of the old way of life in Rociada in *Behind the Mountains* (1956), Oliver La Farge's fictionalized memoir of the sheep-ranching Baca family, in-laws of the author. The traditional lifestyle instead is done in by the cumulative effect of economic tremors in distant places like Wall Street and Australia. "It was not quite clear to Consuelo why the low price of wool in Boston should affect them so directly in New Mexico, but it did," La Farge writes of his eventual wife's reaction to the confusing transformation that effectively ended her girlhood in the pastoral ranching community (167).

The military draft disrupts the lives of villagers in two novels of the Taos Valley, Robert Bright's *The Life and Death of Little Jo* (1944), set in Talpa; and Joseph Krumgold's . . . *And Now Miguel* (1953), a story depicting life on the Blas Chavez family sheep ranch near Los Cordovas. The conscription of local men brings a distant rumbling of war home to the people of Talpa in *The Life and Death of Little Jo*.

In Krumgold's book, a call to military service deprives ten-year-old Miguel Chavez of the companionship of his older brother, Gabriel, and introduces the possibility that external events can disturb the peaceful life Miguel has known in Los Cordovas. Gabriel Chavez views the call to service as an acknowledgment of his readiness to assume an adult role. He goes to meet the world, an eager and confident young man.

In this, Gabriel differs from Bright's Jo Sandovilla and many characters in other village novels. Villagers more commonly are portrayed as backward people who can function only in the cloistered environment of the village. Perplexed by forces he cannot understand, the typical villager feels powerless to resist the tides of change and fearful of their impact on the customary lifestyle. So it is that Little Jo, who has nothing against the German people, leaves the village and goes to war, a pawn in the hands of men more resourceful and determined than he.

VILLAGE CHARACTERS

Familiar characters populate the village novels, among them the patrón, the storekeeper, the village priest, the outsider, and a character who, though lacking power, wealth, and position, serves the people as a paragon of wisdom and common sense. Most residents of the fictional villages are poor, ignorant, and passive, easily led and manipulated by those more clever or ambitious than they.

In the traditional villages, economic and political power usually are vested in a *patrón,* who is sophisticated in matters of business, law, and politics, and who has some knowledge of the outside world. The *patrón,* personified in Don Santiago Salvador Ramos of D. J. Hall's *Perilous Sanctuary* and Don Augustín Vierra of Harvey Fergusson's *The Conquest of Don Pedro* (1954), is born to wealth and status, trained to rule and direct others. If he is any good, the *patrón* is a responsible and benevolent patriarch, advising the people in legal and financial matters and rendering aid in time of trouble. Alternatively, the *patrón* may function as a feudal tyrant, living by the sweat of the poor man's brow, exercising absolute control over the people, and practicing a highly developed form of corruption.

In the absence of a traditional *patrón,* the village storekeeper fulfills many of the *patrón's* functions, serving as banker, personal advisor, and land baron while maintaining his own favored status and providing guidance to his more submissive neighbors. He also may serve as an intermediary between the villagers and the outside world. Such surrogate *patrones* appear in O'Kane Foster's *In the Night Did I Sing,* Bright's *The Life and Death of Little Jo,* and the village novels of Raymond Otis.

Foster's Señor López is brutally pragmatic, his customers hopelessly gullible. They rarely pay for their purchases in cash, nor does Señor López wish them to do so. He much prefers providing immediate gratification for the small needs of the people in exchange for deferred benefits to himself. "When you settled with Señor López you went into his little pine board office and sat patiently under the stuffed puma head until Señor López added and re-added your account incorrectly. Then you gave Señor López a hundred dollars or a deed to your house and land. With your deed went your self-respect — and it was not long before you spent the whole day in the Plaza laughing and talking with the blind man" (18). In this manner, the storekeeper comes to own much of the village, while alienating most of his neighbors.

Another familiar figure is the village priest, whose influence derives from his education and the sanction of the Church. There is considerable variation in degree of piety among fictional priests. Father María de Jesús, appearing in How's *The Penitentes of San Rafael,* is an outlaw priest in league with the Penitentes; he not only tolerates the unsanctified rituals of the brotherhood, but encourages them. An unnamed priest in Waters's *People of the Valley* is a more objectionable agent of corruption, rebuffing the request of two villagers for the sacrament of marriage but taking the coins they have saved to pay for the ceremony. Father Vigil, the pastor of

Sangre de Cristo in *In the Night Did I Sing,* is merely irrelevant; he is widely ignored among his parishioners, most of whom prefer the more passionate and personally satisfying worship of the Penitentes.

At best, the priest may serve the people as a friend, father confessor, confidante, and moral authority. Father Aloysius is such a sympathetic character in Otis's *Miguel of the Bright Mountain,* guiding Miguel through a time of torment and confusion with wisdom and a gentle spirit. Likewise, in *The Conquest of Don Pedro,* Father Orlando comes to the aid of a troubled couple, handling a delicate situation with understanding and discretion.

In some village novels, one among the common people emerges as a repository of traditional wisdom — a person who, through selflessness and understanding, wins the trust of the people. The oracle is possessed of neither wealth, nor power, nor position, but stands apart as one who is immune to corruption. Maria del Valle, the onetime "goat girl," becomes the true leader of the community in *People of the Valley;* hers is "the wisdom of the people who do not think, but feel" (96). Old Cornelio, the village musician, serves a similar function in *The Life and Death of Little Jo,* ensuring that the poor and powerless at least are supplied with wisdom, truth, and love.

The outsider in a village novel almost always brings trouble. This is true of Deloss Devlin, an outdoorsman who stumbles upon San Rafael and upsets the old ways in *The Penitentes of San Rafael;* and of the Murphy brothers, who dispossess unwary residents of the Blue Valley in *People of the Valley.* Other outsiders invade villages to enforce alien laws, conscript local boys for military service, and otherwise pursue interests which are at odds with the settled order of village life.

The villagers generally value tradition, community, land, and family, but the values of the outsider exalt progress, mobility, individualism, profit, and the rule of law. These differences point to many of the serious concerns that are at issue in village novels, including control and use of scarce water, the loss of Hispanic property to greedy Anglos, and the imposition of American law.

TOLD IN THE HILLS

Writers, both outsiders and those with roots in the rural villages, have made heavy use of exotic cultural materials in works of fiction depicting village life. Subjects of interest include the Penitentes, witchcraft, ghosts, and supernatural healing.

The fictional ordeal of the Penitentes often seems as tortuous and painful as the storied rituals of the self-flagellating brotherhood. Almost every work dealing with the Penitentes emphasizes the gore and mysticism of conventional lore, while foregoing any attempt to comprehend and interpret the traditions, beliefs, and practices upon which the brotherhood is based. Sensational accounts of Penitente rituals appear in Harvey Fergusson's *The Blood of the Conquerors* (1921), a novel set partly in the northern villages; Hall's *Perilous Sanctuary;* Foster's *In the Night Did I Sing;* and Waters's *People of the Valley.*

All these works contribute to a stereotype of rural Hispanic people as backward, superstitious, and inclined to violent behavior. In Fergusson's novel, a Hispanic aristocrat undergoes painful rites of initiation in an attempt to ingratiate himself with the village people for pragmatic reasons. He is given to understand that betrayal of Penitente secrets will cause him to be buried alive with his head exposed above ground, so that ants may eat his face. In *People of the Valley,* a villager endures crucifixion and dies the death of Christ; according to tradition, his shoes are placed at the door of his house, a sign to the family that a loved one will not return.

The sin of such works is not so much that they disseminate untruth — Waters insisted that his portrayal was based on events he witnessed in the Mora Valley — but that they emphasize the most lurid aspects of the brotherhood, without examining fully its role and function in village life or its significance in the lives of its adherents.

More thoughtful fiction portrayals of the Penitentes appear in the writings of Fray Angelico Chavez and Raymond Otis. Both writers took pains to convey something of the importance of the brotherhood as an institution of communal life, one that provided spiritual guidance and discipline to people who did not have regular contact with clergy or who could not find fulfillment in the orthodox rituals of the Church. Chavez's benevolent attitude toward the Penitentes was formed in a boyhood spent in Wagon Mound, New Mexico, and nearby villages of the northern mountains. In "The Penitente Thief," a story in *New Mexico Triptych* (1940), Chavez deals with penance, piety, and God's judgment in a fabulist treatment of Holy Week in a New Mexico village.

Otis, an easterner who moved to Santa Fe in 1927 and spent the remaining eleven years of his life there, developed an affinity for the rural Hispanic people of New Mexico. In "Medievalism in America" (1936), an essay on the Penitentes, he wrote, "To pass judgment on these people without first attempting to understand them, is an injustice too often

Fray Angelico Chavez.
Photo by Cynthia Farah,
© 1986. Courtesy Center for
Southwest Research, General
Library, University of New
Mexico, Neg. 986-008-0007.

committed. They are good and kindly and hospitable, and their crowning virtue is integrity" (90).

In *Miguel of the Bright Mountain*, Miguel López ventures into the world beyond the village and returns guilt-ridden over having wronged a lover. Previously scornful of the backward ways and beliefs of the Penitentes, Miguel can find peace only in suffering as Christ suffered, as the men of his village suffer in their traditional rituals of repentance and devotion. Otis provides a sensitive portrayal of the Penitentes of Hormiga, conveying the meaning of penance for Miguel and other men of the village.

New Mexico has long been a reputed hotbed of belief in supernatural phenomena, including witchcraft, ghosts, and the healing arts, which may involve the use of natural remedies as well as practices rooted in faith or superstition. It is difficult to determine the extent to which such beliefs permeate New Mexico's varied cultures or to gauge the degree to which such phenomena are taken seriously. It is apparent, however, that tales of witchcraft *(brujería)*, ghosts *(fantasmas)*, and healing *(curandismo)* have persisted in the rural villages of Hispanic New Mexico for generations. It is not surprising, then, that this subject matter commonly is encountered in novels and stories laid in the villages.

Raymond Otis.
Courtesy Emily Otis Barnes.

Among beliefs commonly attributed to village residents in works of fiction are the idea that evil spirits reside in animal forms and the notion that a witch can appear in the form of an animal or a ball of fire. These and similar notions appear in several novels, including Fergusson's *The Conquest of Don Pedro,* in which the Jewish pack peddler, Leo Mendes, travels among the villages of the Rio Abajo and hears many tales of supernatural phenomena; he concludes that such beliefs are powerful and widely held.

In *Behind the Mountains,* such notions are familiar to the villagers, but it is not clear that they are taken seriously by all members of the community. A strange noise or inexplicable happening may be blamed on witches in jest. The threat of ghastly supernatural hazards also is raised as a way of frightening children into behaving as their parents wish.

In some instances, witchcraft figures in a plot or subplot, as forces of good and evil clash in a battle of spiritual powers. In *The Life and Death of Little Jo,* for example, a witch induces painful swelling in a woman's feet by throwing a shoe at her, but a healer removes the curse by sprinkling herbs in a foot bath, laying a cross of sticks at the afflicted woman's door, and rubbing a paste of bread and water on the door. Similar spiritual confrontations occur in Frank O'Rourke's *The Man Who Found His Way* (1957) and Rudolfo Anaya's *Bless Me, Ultima* (1972).

Healing more often is a matter of folk medicine than witchery, as

demonstrated in Chicago native Ana Castillo's contemporary novel of
Tomé, *So Far from God* (1993). Included are the natural *remedios* favored
by Tomé's renowned *curandera*, Doña Felicia, for *empacho* (gastrointes-
tinal obstruction), *aigre* (internal draft), and the dreaded *mal de ojo*, or
evil eye.

THE CONTEMPORARY VILLAGE NOVEL

Although the formulaic quality of village novels produced in the 1930s,
1940s, and 1950s is not evident in more recent works, the village has continued to interest fiction writers as a primary setting. In the 1970s, John
Nichols used *The Milagro Beanfield War* (1974) as an instrument of political and social protest, and Rudolfo Anaya evoked the experiences of his
childhood to produce the moving story of a young boy's loss of innocence
in *Bless Me, Ultima*.

Contemporary views of traditional village life also appear in the bilingual *cuentos* of Sabine Ulibarrí and Jim Sagel. Ulibarrí has drawn on recollections of his youth in the Tierra Amarilla area to create delightful stories, many containing edifying object lessons, published in the 1970s,
1980s, and 1990s. Sagel takes as his literary province the Española Valley
and the Hispanic heartland stretching north to Colorado. He celebrates
the ordinary experiences of village life but also evokes some of the significant events and personalities of his *tierra encantada;* "El Santo Queso,"
the title story of a 1990 collection, brings to mind the remarkable career of
Rio Arriba political boss Emilio Naranjo. Echoes of the traditional village
novel are evident in *Stone Horses* (1996), by Sallie Gallegos; here Eduardo
Montez grows up in Los Torbellinas, his childhood rudely ended by the
disruption of World War II.

While works by native writers deal with much the same subject matter as earlier village novels, the perspective clearly reflects the insider's
experience. Born in 1937, Anaya's earliest memories were of the village
of Pastura, near Santa Rosa, New Mexico. In "Short Autobiography of
Rudolfo Anaya" (1972), he recalls that place: "I have haunting memories
of the small pueblito: bright sun and limitless sky, herds of cattle grazing
in the grass of the llano, beautiful ancianos who hobbled over dusty
streets, the train forever creating dreams and fantasy of where? Why?,
brilliant blood-red sunsets, and immense nights that brooded over the
pocket of life the village affirmed with farole-lit windows. It seemed as if
we were an old people, as old as the earth, one with the llano" (4).

If loss of land was a comical matter in the eyes of some of the earlier

Ana Castillo.
Photo by Tom Maday.
Courtesy Tom Maday.

Anglo writers, it is a source of deep and lasting sadness to the families of Anaya's fictional Las Pasturas and Guadalupe. Likewise, for all the faith and optimism of Ulibarrí's stories, he reserves harsh words for Archbishop Jean Baptiste Lamy and Lamy's suppression of the Penitentes. Such personally informed views of village life are not always pretty; as testimonials of Hispanic experience in New Mexico, however, their value is immeasurable.

More recently, Ana Castillo has expressed a view of village life which emphatically contradicts the denigrating attitudes implicit in many earlier works. Hers is a village novel with some contemporary twists. Tomé's people observe the ritual Way of the Cross at Easter, but the traditional liturgy is replaced with prayers lamenting Hispanic and Indian poverty, uranium contamination on the Navajo reservation, AIDS, nuclear power plants, pesticides, and other such plagues. *So Far from God* (1993) celebrates the strength and dignity of women, but the author delivers a stinging indictment of men and, to a lesser extent, of Anglo society.

In contemporary works of fiction, the village no longer appears as an organism whole unto itself. Its vital communal life has been withered by overpowering change, and the village that remains is a weathered artifact of times past, a quaint pocket of poverty. It is increasingly likely to appear as a sanctuary for those fleeing the Anglo mainstream — hippies in Talpa in Natalie Goldberg's *Banana Rose* (1995), radical feminists near Arroyo Seco in Steve Brewer's *Witchy Woman* (1996), yuppies living the country life in the stories of Elizabeth Tallent.

Rick Collignon.
Photo by Jennifer Ammann.
Courtesy MacMurray &
Beck, Inc.

In the village novel of the 1990s, an interesting transformation is evident in the attitudes expressed by Anglo writers. Once viewed with condescension and sometimes exploited as a place of quaint and colorful customs or as a source of comic relief, the village has become, for harried fictional characters of the 1990s, a place to get in touch with one's lost humanity. In three of the latest novels of village life, Rick Collignon's *The Journal of Antonio Montoya* (1996), Lesley Poling-Kempes's *Canyon of Remembering* (1996), and Dorothy Cave's *Go Find the Mountain* (1996), world-weary characters seek refuge from the frenzied pace and inane values of modern society. In the villages to which they retreat, the puzzle of life is reduced to simpler terms. The village offers hope of regeneration through a simpler lifestyle, honest relationships, renewal of family and cultural ties, and greater harmony with the natural earth.

Although portrayals of the village have evolved over the many years since its appropriation as a subject of fiction, its appeal for writers remains much the same as in times past. It is a setting rich in exotic cultural materials, a pool of life apart from the mainstream, a microcosm within which ordinary lives take on extraordinary significance.

Some of the village novels have been recognized as meritorious works of fiction; many have not. Among the varied portrayals of village life are judgmental works reflecting harsh prejudices, sympathetic treatments by outsiders, and revealing works by writers whose roots are in the rural villages. Taken as a group, all these novels are of interest because they evoke a unique social and cultural phenomenon — one which, despite the remarkable durability of the villages, seems eminently vulnerable to the ravages of political, economic, and social change.

8 LIVES AND LEGENDS

Summing up present-day perceptions of his subject, land grant entrepreneur Lucien Bonaparte Maxwell, Lawrence R. Murphy says this: "There are in reality two Lucien Maxwells. The first is the frontiersman described from contemporary sources in the preceding chapters. A second has been created by the generations of amateur writers, novelists, and historians who have written about Maxwell in the decades since his death." So detached from reality is the creature of legend, says Murphy, that "a new and mythical person has been created" (210). As Murphy goes on to demonstrate, the historic Maxwell is hard pressed to compete with the legendary figure for the hearts and minds of contemporary readers.

The same might be said for any number of historic persons whose lives and legends are celebrated in works of fiction. In some four and a half centuries of recorded history, New Mexico has produced a good many personalities whose stories live on through countless retellings in schoolrooms, history books, and works of the imagination. Fiction writers have helped to create many legendary figures, sometimes contributing invented notions that then have been incorporated into the popular images of historic persons, and sometimes popularizing ideas gleaned from more obscure sources. Some historic figures are well established in legend, while others, like Georgia O'Keeffe, subject of Alan Cheuse's *The Light Possessed* (1990), are only beginning to be recast as fictional characters.

It would be handy to assume that historical and biographical works reveal the real person, while the mythic or legendary figure appears only in creative works, but this is hardly the case. On the contrary, inaccuracies and misconceptions which have become part of the legendary persona frequently are attributed to defective "nonfiction" accounts. In the case of Lucien Maxwell, Murphy identifies Col. Henry Inman's *The Old Santa Fe Trail: The Story of a Great Highway* (1897) as the source of many unsubstantiated and questionable notions. According to Murphy, the image of the Maxwell Land Grant as a feudal kingdom ruled by a quirky owner with a penchant for lavish hospitality and high-stakes gambling is largely Inman's doing. Incorporated into Harvey Fergusson's popular *Grant of Kingdom,* erroneous or exaggerated notions gleaned from Inman's account reached and presumably influenced a wide audience. In Murphy's estimation, Fergusson's book "was certainly read by more people throughout the United States than all other books about Maxwell combined" (224).

Fergusson was attentive to the history that engaged his imagination, but he was not bound by it. In the estimation of Tom Pilkington, he was a "philosophical novelist," meaning that "he developed a coherent and consistent system of beliefs, both practical and metaphysical, and then designed a series of characters and incidents to illustrate those beliefs" (143). Thus Jean Ballard, the fictional Lucien Maxwell, is portrayed in accord with Fergusson's notion of "destiny." In his ascendancy, Ballard possesses all the requisite skills and traits of character to ensure his success as a builder and entrepreneur. He enjoys his turn at center stage, then passes from the scene, eclipsed by men better equipped to function in a more competitive legal and business environment.

If Lucien Maxwell's popular image is attributable largely to exaggeration and Fergusson's philosophical casting of him, such was not the case with respect to Maxwell's friend and business associate, Kit Carson. Much of Carson's fame in the latter half of the nineteenth century rested not upon embellishments of the truth, but upon tales made up out of whole cloth by the writers of cheap dime novels. Had these writers not taken it upon themselves to improve upon history, it is doubtful that Carson could have attained the notoriety he did, for the historic Carson, by all reliable accounts, was a quiet and unassuming person who lacked formal education, a plainspoken man of simple convictions. Portrayed by some writers as a gallant and athletic youth and by others as a refined gentleman of the frontier, the dime-novel Carson was shaped and reshaped to suit popular whims.

To be sure, Carson was a man of remarkable deeds, but these were not the basis of his appeal as a character of popular fiction, and many historical figures of equal stature never attained the recognition accorded the legendary Carson. Jessie Benton Frémont, wife of John C. Frémont, is widely recognized for her artful editing of the reports of her husband's explorations of the 1840s — documents which helped to establish Carson as a popular figure of the frontier West (Henry Nash Smith, 84). Inspired by Frémont's accounts of Carson's exploits as a scout and guide, writers seized upon him as a character of heroic stature. By 1849, Carson had made his debut as a fictional character, appearing in Emerson Bennett's *The Prairie Flower; Or, Adventures in the Far West;* and, more prominently, in Charles Averill's *Kit Carson, the Prince of the Gold Hunters; Or, The Adventures of the Sacramento.*

Carson's arrival as a figure of popular literature preceded by some years the emergence of the dime novel. As the market for tales of western adventure grew, the Carson legend provided a ready source of raw material. By Daryl Jones's count, Carson appeared in some seventy dime novels, performing feats of derring-do that must have stupefied and sometimes embarrassed the living hero — a man still very much engaged with the realities of frontier life. One cover illustration reportedly had Carson killing seven Indians with one hand while supporting a swooning maiden with the other. Such exploits quickly became passé in the dime-novel era, inspiring writers to even more stunning and original portrayals. Mercifully, Carson did not live to see all that the creators of sensational fiction would dream up for him.

Several of Carson's early biographers also led readers astray, gilding the historical frontiersman to present a figure of noble manner and refinement. By 1996, scholars concerned with the historic Carson were hard at work trying to unravel the tangled strands of truth and falsehood, as is demonstrated by a collection of essays, *Kit Carson: Indian Fighter or Indian Killer,* edited by R. C. Gordon-McCutchan.

Carson appears as a character in several fictional works produced after the dime-novel era, including two novels by Dane Coolidge, *Under the Sun* (1926) and *Comanche Chaser* (1938), and Willa Cather's *Death Comes for the Archbishop* (1927).

There has been little demand for Carson as a fictional character in recent years, perhaps in part because of an uncomplicated persona that seems to neutralize and deflect curiosity and in part because of scrutiny brought to bear on Carson as a symbol of the white man's transgressions against the Indians. Norman Zollinger's *Meridian* (1997), a novel of Carson's life in the years preceding the American occupation of New Mexico in 1847, represents an attempt to restore some of the frontiersman's lost honor. Zollinger says (1998) that he approached the subject with an open mind but became convinced that the negative portrayal of Carson by contemporary apologists was as bogus as the heroic persona invented by dime novelists. Identifying anthropologist Shirley Hill Witt as the chief architect of Carson's downfall, Zollinger acknowledges his own effort to counter what he saw as a systematic dismantling of Carson's reputation. Ray Hogan offers another admiring portrayal in a recent novel, *Soldier in Buckskin* (1996).

THE BLACK LEGEND

As we have already seen, the literature of the American West is replete with unpleasant racial stereotypes. Whatever its merits, the Black Legend of Spain, a negative stereotype based in part on early reports of Spanish cruelty to Indians in the New World, has persisted since the sixteenth century. C. L. Sonnichsen has shown how the Black Legend found a haven in western fiction (1978, pp. 83–102). The legend also is evident in historical fiction of the 1940s, 1950s, and 1960s, particularly in negative portrayals of notable Hispanic and Native American figures of New Mexico.

If the Americans needed a villain, Gen. Manuel Armijo, thrice governor during the brief period of Mexican rule, was an easy target. Armijo is commonly portrayed as a cruel and cowardly despot who plunders the public treasury and diverts the government's levy on the Santa Fe trade to his own accounts.

One of the earliest indictments of Armijo appears in the western adventure novel, *The Lone Ranch, a Tale of the "Staked Plain"* (1871), by Capt. Mayne Reid, a tale brimming with racist and American nationalist sentiments. Citing narratives of the Santa Fe traders as his sources, the author denounces Armijo as a despot "guilty of every act that could disgrace humanity" and accuses him of conspiring with the Indians to kill and plunder his own people.

Such sentiments are expressed time and again in fictional accounts of the American occupation of New Mexico, virtually all of them by Anglo authors whose sympathies lie with the victorious Americans. In the 1935 novel, *Jornada*, by R. L. Duffus, Armijo is judged a sheep stealer, a card cheat, and a taker of bribes — charges which appear in numerous tales of the occupation. Says an American detractor in Clarence E. Mulford's *Bring Me His Ears* (1922), "His whole career is built on treachery, sheep-stealin', double dealin' and assassination" (303). Judging from available historical accounts, Manuel Armijo well may have been a scoundrel, but he also made a convenient scapegoat for the political and literary champions of Manifest Destiny.

The conventional portrayal of Armijo as a corrupt despot is disputed by Ray John de Aragón, who contends in *Padre Martínez and Bishop Lamy* (1978) that the negative image was promoted by American military officials who were eager to discredit the deposed Mexican governor for political reasons. In de Aragón's estimation, Armijo was a military genius, falsely maligned by Americans who feared that he would return to incite a popular rebellion against them.

More difficult to justify are several highly negative portrayals of Padre Antonio José Martínez of Taos, as much a man of his epoch as was the more celebrated Archbishop Lamy of Santa Fe. Like Lamy, Martínez was a bringer of civilization and culture. The printing press purchased by Martínez in 1835, possibly the first in New Mexico, was used in the production of schoolbooks, prayer books, and pamphlets, the first volumes published in the region. Padre Martínez established a seminary in Taos and carried on an energetic ministry among the people of the valley. Following the American occupation, he participated in efforts to organize the new territorial government and adopt a constitution. He was a member of the first territorial legislature and was selected as its president.

Very little of this makes it into fictional portrayals of Padre Martínez, in part because Martínez was not an agent of the advancing Anglo-Saxon society; he was, rather, a defender of native peoples and traditional practices. Martínez typically functions not as a heroic character but as an agent of a morally and intellectually inferior culture that must be overcome by the Anglo-American hero. Therefore, a negative portrayal is indicated. Padre Martínez is portrayed variously as an autocrat, a hater of *gringos,* a greedy manipulator, the sire of illegitimate children, and the instigator of the 1847 Taos Rebellion. By Willa Cather's account in *Death Comes for the Archbishop,* Martínez not only incited the rebellion but also "managed to profit considerably by the affair," taking possession of lands belonging to men convicted of crimes committed during the rebellion and then deserting them as they were led to their deaths (140).

Cather also endows the priest with a grotesque appearance. His shoulders are said to resemble those of a buffalo, and atop a thick neck sits the defiant padre's big head. In addition, "his mouth was the very assertion of violent, uncurbed passions and tyrannical self-will; the full lips thrust out and taut, like the flesh of animals distended by fear or desire" (141).

Willa Cather.
Courtesy Museum of New Mexico, Neg. No. 7112.

The charges against Padre Martínez are disputed by Fray Angelico Chavez, who offers considerable evidence of the priest's acceptance of the new regime and attributes the accusations against him to racial and political scandal-mongering: "It all went back to the deliberately malicious lies and libels peculiar to politics, and no less to the combined ethnic and religious bigotry of certain ones among the newcomers — like those first newspaper editors who still looked down on their fellow citizens of Hispanic or Mexican descent, and most especially on their clergy, as low-down Catholic Mexicans" (1981, p. 90).

With respect to the literary merits of *Death Comes for the Archbishop*, Fray Chavez freely gives Cather her due, characterizing her portrayal of Lamy as "a fine romantic picture of a great and good man upon the strange beauty of a land that she appreciates." On a personal level, he finds the book disheartening for its gratuitous vilification of Padre Martínez: "It is indeed a masterful painting of my Penitente land," he writes, "but with penitential strokes that hurt" (1974, p. 258).

A female contemporary of Armijo and Martínez, Doña Maria Gertrudis Barceló, fares somewhat better in fiction, most notably in Ruth Laughlin's *The Wind Leaves No Shadow* (1948, 1951) and Blanche Grant's *Doña Lona: A Story of Old Taos and Santa Fe* (1941). These are largely admiring portrayals of a strong woman who rose from poverty to own and operate popular gambling establishments in Taos and Santa Fe, winning the friendship and respect of the influential men of her era. In *Doña Lona*, Grant intended to counteract negative historical portrayals of Doña Tules that she believed were unfounded: "Not a man ever said that he really *knew* her. Seemingly these early commentators felt that she must conform to the type with which they were familiar, the disreputable frontier gambling woman. My own research through many years convinces me that they have maligned her" (viii). Grant was not the first or last writer to engage in purposeful efforts to influence public perceptions of a historic person through literature.

Given the aversion of Pueblo Indian cultures to the celebration of individual personalities, it is not surprising that few Native Americans appear as major characters in works of fiction. One who does is Popé, a San Juan Indian recognized as the mastermind of the Pueblo Revolt of 1680. Popé is indispensable to virtually every account of the revolt, including several fictional treatments.

In the absence of authoritative accounts, writers are left to conjure up many of the specifics of Popé's character and personality. As a youth in Elizabeth Champney's *Great-Grandmother's Girls in New Mexico, 1670– 1680* (1888), Popé responds to the kindness of the missionary priest at San Juan but is radicalized when his father is robbed and murdered by Spanish military authorities. In Albert Reagan's *Don Diego; Or, The Pueblo Indian Uprising of 1680* (1914), he leads the pueblos to victory; but his arrogance alienates many allies, and the pueblos fall back into their previous state of disunity. Popé again is cast in a negative light in *The Royal City* (1956), by Les Savage, Jr., summarily ordering the death of a young Spaniard who has sought justice for the Indians. A good deal of speculation is involved in these and other such portrayals.

From the turbulent Mexican period, Taos native José Gonzales emerges as a minor legend, leading the pueblos and dissident Mexican forces in an 1837 uprising, disposing of the Mexican governor and seizing the office for himself. Sometimes portrayed as a Taos Indian, Gonzales was, according to Fray Chavez, a *genízaro* — a man of mixed ancestry, raised outside the pueblo (1981, pp. 54–55).

Like Popé, the fictional Gonzales is a mystic and a man of power. In this he recalls the ideal of the "noble savage," but Gonzales lacks sufficient political acumen to maintain himself in authority over more determined and better prepared Hispanic rivals. In Laughlin's *The Wind Leaves No Shadow* and Elliott Arnold's *The Time of the Gringo* (1953), Gonzales is swept to power on the strength of the Pueblo warriors, but the spectacle of an "ig-norant, superstitious savage" in the governor's palace is too much for the Mexican aristocracy to stomach. The jealous Armijo overpowers Gonza-les's inferior forces, then wastes no time in dispatching his former ally.

The partisan character of so many portrayals of native New Mexicans recalls the popular wisdom which holds that "history is written by the vic-tors." Certainly much of New Mexico's history has been written by Anglo-Americans, and much of that has been based on the observations of some highly biased participants. It might be added that many of the impres-sions formed in this manner move into the realm of legend through the medium of creative literature, crafted from available sources by the literati of the dominant society.

The approaching cuatrocentennial observance of the arrival of Juan de Oñate and the first Spanish settlers in 1598 brought about a resurgence of interest in the colonial period of New Mexico's history — an interest reflected in new works of historical fiction and new portrayals of historic characters. Two recent works provide divergent views of the Spanish con-querors and demonstrate the importance of a literature that includes var-ied cultural perspectives. The novels provide very different portrayals of Oñate, leaving the reader to make such further investigations as he or she may choose, and to draw conclusions accordingly.

Lana Harrigan's *Ácoma* (1997) is apparently well researched, but is crafted as an appealing work of fiction with well-developed fictional char-acters, explicit sexual scenes, and a forbidden romantic liaison between the wife of a Spanish officer and her Acoma slave. The novel reinforces notions of the Black Legend of Spain, as Oñate and his officers are cruel to women and natives, but Indian characters are admirable and Spanish women are portrayed sympathetically. Oñate is a peripheral character in Harrigan's novel, but he is perceived primarily as an agent of Spanish con-quest and repression.

Miguel Encinias's *Two Lives for Oñate* (1997) treats the same period and many of the same events, but with much greater sympathy for Don Juan. Encinias, a writer deeply interested in his own cultural roots in New Mex-ico, provides far more historical detail than is usually found in compa-rable historical novels dealing with this period. He displays relatively little interest in the literary possibilities of his subject; in this case, the medium of fiction serves the purpose of liberating the author from the exacting de-mands of history, allowing him to fill in gaps in the historical record, create dialogue, and adopt a fluent narrative style. Encinias presents his subject, Juan de Oñate, as a complex character, revealing the conqueror as a devoted family man and inviting readers to sympathize as Oñate endures financial troubles and agonizing delays in getting his expedition approved by royal authorities. In a departure from other accounts depicting Spanish cruelty to the Pueblo Indians, Encinias portrays Oñate as a thoughtful and responsible governor. Faced with multiple and sometimes conflicting considerations, he metes out punishment to Spanish and Indian subjects alike and attempts to establish and maintain order in the province he has come to claim. Encinias's Oñate brings an army upriver, to be sure, but the expedition's professed purpose is not conquest, but "only to take possession peacefully and spread the faith" (47).

LOOKING FOR BILLY THE KID

The legendary figures of New Mexico have included rich, famous, and powerful personages of religion, commerce, and politics, but it was left to a young outlaw to transcend history and legend and soar headlong into the realm of myth. No character from New Mexico's past has so captivated generations of readers and motion picture audiences as has Henry McCarty, also known as Henry Antrim, William Bonney, and Billy the Kid. The Kid generated considerable notoriety during his lifetime, owing mainly to his involvement in the Lincoln County War. But upon his death, the meager facts of his brief personal history immediately were transformed into an imaginative construct which took on a life of its own, regenerating and sometimes recreating itself, fascinating millions and enduring in popular culture for well over a century, with no end in sight.

The legend began even before the Kid's death, with sensational and, according to his most reliable biographers, overblown newspaper accounts of his exploits. In addition, he was celebrated in numerous dime novels, including a handful published just before and after his death in 1881. In keeping with the tradition of cheap popular fiction, the authors played fast and loose with the truth, borrowing from inaccurate newspaper stories, coloring the known facts, and relying on imagination for the kinds of dramatic elements that would attract readers.

Much of the blame for the young outlaw's distorted image belongs not to works of fiction, but to a narrative purporting to be factual: Pat Garrett's *The Authentic Life of Billy the Kid, Noted Desperado of the Southwest* (1882). Although not credited on the title page, Marshall Ashmun Upson is widely acknowledged as Garrett's collaborator and the source of many distortions concerning the Kid. A sometime newspaper writer with a penchant for colorful prose, Upson fluffed up Garrett's account and added some ideas of his own. "More than any other influence," says Robert M. Utley, "the Garrett-Upson book fed the legend of Billy the Kid" (199). Picked up by writers consulting a source presumed to be reliable, the book's falsehoods found their way into numerous nonfiction accounts, as well as into works of fiction.

In particular, Utley argues, Upson is responsible for the contradictory images — boy hero and cold-blooded killer — that have made the Kid an inscrutable character of enduring appeal. It is just this element of contradiction, says Jon Tuska, that endows the mortal Billy with the quality of legend; he is a Janus figure who can be portrayed as "all bad, all good, or part good and part bad" (204).

In *The Saga of Billy the Kid* (1926), a book widely regarded as fiction, Walter Noble Burns capitalized on the contradictions in character to portray the Kid as a social bandit who challenged the political and economic powers while enjoying the adulation of common folk. As portrayed by Burns, says Robert Utley, "He is a symbolic transition between the old and new, driven to violence by injustice, his guns blazing in protest against corruption and greed, and at last his life an essential sacrifice in the rise of the human condition" (200).

Burns's widely circulated work popularized notions gleaned from the Garrett-Upson portrayal of the Kid. "Masquerading as history but singing with the vivid writing of a novel," writes Utley, "Burns's *Saga* ranked a close second to the *Authentic Life* in its decisive impact on the legend of Billy the Kid" (200).

The literature of Billy the Kid includes some twenty-one titles identified by Tom Lewis as works of fiction with New Mexico settings. These include numerous adventure westerns, like Nelson Nye's *Pistols for Hire* (1941) and Frank O'Rourke's *Legend in the Dust* (1957). A few Kid novels, like Amelia Bean's *A Time for Outrage* (1967), may fairly be classified as historical fiction.

Despite the general decline of popular western fiction, the Kid remains a powerful symbol. Elizabeth Fackler's 1995 novel, *Billy the Kid: The Legend of El Chivato*, is frankly dedicated to the notion of the Kid as a heroic freedom fighter who was "sacrificed because he refused to submit to the political and social order of his time" (512). Rudolfo Anaya's 1995 play, *Billy the Kid*, explores the myth from a Hispanic perspective; among older Hispanics of Anaya's youth, "Bilito" was admired as a sympathetic figure who shared many of their grievances against the Anglo-American establishment.

Factor in all the dime novels, pulp western stories, comic book appearances, movies, television shows, popular histories, and other such nonsense celebrating the legend of Billy the Kid, and you have a cultural icon of major proportions. It has taken a small army of professional nitpickers to sift the facts from the mass of distorted, misinformed, and fabricated accounts of the Kid's life. To his credit, Billy has attracted some of the best, beginning with Col. Maurice Garland Fulton and including Jeff Dykes, Robert Utley, Jon Tuska, Ramon Adams, and Frederick Nolan.

To be sure, the legend of Billy the Kid has inspired a great deal of pulp fiction. The canon, if it could be called that, includes poorly crafted historical novels which repeat earlier inaccuracies, as well as sensational and sometimes fabricated stories bearing little relation to the Kid's life. At the same time, the subject has attracted serious writers whose interest is not so much in the history as in the literary possibilities of an enigmatic character whose legend transcends time and place. Michael Ondaatje explores the legend in *The Collected Works of Billy the Kid* (1970), a work that defies easy classification, but proceeds as a series of prose poems and vignettes, many of them written as first-person narratives from Billy's point of view. Here the author is interested in the ambiguous characters of Billy and his foil, Pat Garrett, and in the questions of life and death and fate and destiny that are inherent in the legend of Billy the Kid.

It is notable that two Pulitzer Prize–winning novelists have found the legend worthy of examination in works produced in the last decade. N. Scott Momaday is mindful of the historical facts concerning Billy the Kid, while Larry McMurtry couldn't care less, but it is the myth that interests both writers.

The story of Billy Bone, told in McMurtry's *Anything for Billy* (1988), is something of a fable, loosely fashioned around the legend of Billy the Kid. Mostly, McMurtry has fun with it, creating a menagerie of improbable, outlandish characters who range across a surrealistic landscape. Billy Bone is a complex personality, lacking confidence and self-esteem; suffering severe headaches, mood swings, and depression — a volatile character who is prone to fits of sudden violence. In his depressive state, Billy sometimes sees the "death dog," harbinger of a tragic end. Billy feels no remorse for his deadly outbursts, but in his better moods he remains a naïve and affable youth who retains the loyalty of companions eminently more sensible and decent than himself.

In Momaday's *The Ancient Child* (1989), Billy is the imaginary lover of Grey, a young Kiowa-Navajo woman who lives on dreams while awaiting the arrival of her real-life love. Having read *The Saga of Billy the Kid,* Grey relives the defining moments of Billy's life in her mind's eye. She is haunted by his death. Grey's imagined Billy is attractive but unassuming, gregarious and likable. Billy's eyes sometimes convey an expression of sorrow; at other times Grey can discern no expression at all. Appearing in visions, Billy fills a void in Grey's life until she meets Locke Setman, a man who draws her to him as Billy did, but who, unlike Billy, can be saved for a life together.

New Mexico lawman Pat Garrett became a legend, too, by virtue of his association with the Kid. A man of mortal proportions, Garrett is subject to interpretations that vary according to the author's disposition toward the Kid. In response to an unfavorable portrayal of Garrett in Burns's *Saga,* Eugene Manlove Rhodes countered with an admiring portrayal in his own story, *Pasó Por Aquí* (1927). Rhodes's characterization reveals Garrett as a man of competence, justice, and compassion.

The traditional western formula requires agents of good and agents of evil. Shades of gray are rarely tolerated. Billy the Kid, forever young in legend, refuses to fit the familiar stereotypes of hero and villain. He remains, instead, a figure of simple circumstances and complex virtues, at once naïve and impulsive, vulnerable and violent, affable and deadly — a youthful enigma moved by unfathomable forces. Billy is a puzzle that will not resolve, which may explain why those who search for meaning in the frontier experience cannot be done with him.

MABEL

Equally conflicted is the legacy of Mabel Dodge Luhan, Taos socialite, writer, patron of the arts, and philanthropist, a figure whose fame best may be explained by an enduring public fascination with the lives of the rich and famous. Mabel was both, and she surrounded herself with personalities of note — artists, writers, musicians, and other movers and shakers.

Mabel Luhan was not a desperado in the same sense as Billy the Kid, but she was a social outlaw who delighted in doing the unexpected. When she fled New York, relocated in Taos, and later made a Taos Indian her

Mabel Dodge Luhan.
Courtesy The Harwood
Museum, University of
New Mexico, Neg. 98.81.

fourth husband, it was clear that she did not intend to be bound by the sensibilities of others.

According to Lois Palken Rudnick, Mabel actively sought to be depicted as a fictional character, in hopes that her writer friends could reveal the true identity that had eluded her (viii). The resulting portrayals were generally unflattering and seemed to convey varying degrees of hostility. Having reviewed several such characterizations, Rudnick observed, "By now it must be apparent that Mabel Dodge Luhan has been imagined dead in a greater variety of ways than any other woman in American literary history. She has been disposed of by gang rape and suicide, had her heart torn out in an Indian sacrificial ritual, been squeezed to death by a snake and blinded by a vulture" (302).

Mabel's sacrifice at the hands of a savage tribe in Mexico in a story, "The Woman Who Rode Away" (1928), came courtesy of D. H. Lawrence, with whom she carried on a mutually stimulating, if conflicted, relationship. If, as Lawrence wrote of another Mabel-inspired character in *St. Mawr* (1925), Mabel's great dread was "to die an empty, barren death," she well may have reveled in the stunning exits written for her by intellectually gifted men who, if they did not exactly admire her, found it impossible to ignore her (135). She hardly could have relished other, nonlethal portrayals which reveal a personality characterized by vanity, pettiness, and vindictiveness.

Carl Van Vechten's Edith Dale, a character developed in *Peter Whiffle: His Life and Works* (1922) and referred to in *Spider Boy* (1928), is more moderate in tone. Van Vechten's portrayal evokes Mabel's life in New York, where, between an extended residence in Europe and her eventual removal to Taos, she brought together leading intellectuals and artists for encounters she hoped would be lively and stimulating. A woman of exquisite taste, Edith Dale has made her apartment a place of beauty and grace, European in style. She is easily bored, acquiring and discarding acquaintances according to whim. If Edith is something of a parody of Mabel, most of the humor is well intentioned. As first-person narrator in *Peter Whiffle,* however, Van Vechten cannot resist noting that he has neither seen nor heard from Edith Dale in five years, "owing to a slight misunderstanding" — a reference to Mabel's penchant for turbulence in close relationships (237).

Little admiration is displayed in Harvey Fergusson's *Footloose McGarnigal* (1930), as Alec McGarnigal, a young easterner, surveys the eccentricities of Taos's artistic community. At a party, Alec's host points out Mrs. White Horse, a wealthy woman who has shocked the town by marrying a Taos Indian. Mrs. White Horse is described as "a squat middle-aged person with an expression at once imperious and a little worried" (119). Fergusson also pokes fun at Mabel's husband, Tony Lujan, who appears in the novel as Tony White Horse. Fergusson later reported that the reference had cost him whatever good will Lujan formerly might have felt toward him (1971, p. 40).

Mabel is disparaged further in the Oliver La Farge story, "Hard Winter" (1933); in a Frances Crane mystery, *The Turquoise Shop* (1941); and in Paul Horgan's short story, "So Little Freedom" (1942). In these works, characters based on Mabel are portrayed as vain, shallow, manipulative creatures who require constant stimulation and who need to control others.

One of the most thoughtful and thorough portrayals appears in Myron Brinig's *All of Their Lives* (1941). Brinig was a frequent visitor to Taos in the 1930s, owing largely to Mabel's solicitations. The relationship was predictably unstable, but Brinig probably knew Mabel as well as anyone who tried to write about her. Brinig's character is Florence Gresham, a woman born to wealth and educated in exclusive schools. As a young woman, Flo-

Myron Brinig.
*Courtesy The Harwood
Museum, University of
New Mexico, Neg. 4.80.*

rence romps through a series of marriages and affairs. She lives in Europe for a time, returning to New York to preside over a coterie of artists and intellectuals before forsaking the metropolis for a remote village in the mountains of New Mexico. Florence enjoys the stimulation of lively conversation, but she cannot stand dull people. A mercurial sense of social responsibility propels her into various causes, most of which are quickly forgotten.

Florence embodies the best and worst of Mabel as Brinig knew her. She is a vibrant woman with a sense of mission, conscious of her self-defined role in the world, a rebellious visionary capable of remarkable charm and incredible pettiness.

Not all writers have been so harsh in their judgments. Mabel and her husband, Antonio Lujan, were honored by Frank Waters and Max Evans with book dedications. Claire Morrill notes in *A Taos Mosaic: Portrait of a New Mexico Village* (1973) that Mabel freely disclosed her faults while concealing her virtues. Among the latter were generosity, a sense of civic responsibility, and an active concern for people in distress (113).

Mabel's four-volume autobiography reveals much concerning her values, aspirations, prejudices, and shortcomings. Clearly she was a woman of contradictions, one who elicited mixed reactions from those who knew her. Whatever her influence, whatever the true nature of her character, it is apparent from the various fictional portrayals that, for literary purposes, writers have much preferred the vibrant and volatile Mabel to the generous and public-spirited citizen of Taos.

MEN OF SCIENCE, MEN OF WAR

The novels of wartime Los Alamos tell of men who under duress of war came together to pursue common ends, but who clashed in matters of philosophy and approach.

Chief among the legends of Los Alamos are J. Robert Oppenheimer, director of the scientific work, and Gen. Leslie Groves, military overlord of the Manhattan Project. Yoked by destiny with a world hanging in the balance, they represent competing majesties and exhibit contrasting physical characteristics and philosophies. Together, they symbolize a clash between scientific inquiry and military discipline.

Oppenheimer is tall and thin, Groves a lumpy presence whose uniform, as described in Martin Cruz Smith's *Stallion Gate* (1986), "bulged everywhere with the pressure of soft fat" (38). As depicted in Robert Olen Butler's *Countrymen of Bones* (1983), Oppenheimer is a magnetic force, high-strung, exuding energy and self-confidence, inspiring the confidence of his fellow scientists. "Oppie" is the agent of scientific intellect, Groves the instrument of military authority. In the closed system of Los Alamos, Oppenheimer is in charge of creativity, while Groves is responsible for secrecy, restriction, and paranoia. Oppenheimer advocates openness of intellectual dialogue; the very idea is abhorrent to the security-minded general, who, in Roberta Silman's *Beginning the World Again* (1990), displays an "almost pathological need for secrecy" (60).

In Smith's *Stallion Gate,* Groves is Oppenheimer's equal. Bulging form and military bearing notwithstanding, the general is a man well aware of history. He has a mission to fulfill, and his strength, determination, and worldly wisdom render him a force to be reckoned with. In most other accounts, Groves is regarded lightly by the scientists, who take no pains to conceal their indifference to military discipline. Groves views the scientists as prima donnas who do not understand the imperatives of war; he tolerates them because he must.

The wartime effort helped make legends of other Los Alamos personalities, too — Louis Slotin, victim of a deadly nuclear accident; Klaus Fuchs, a congenial scientist convicted of selling nuclear secrets to the Soviets; Richard Feynman; Edward Teller; and Niels Bohr, discoverer of the atom and a proponent of rational measures to curb the arms race.

While the men worked in secrecy atop the Hill, an unlikely legend emerged at the foot of the mesa, in the person of Edith Warner, who welcomed weary scientists to her tearoom by the Rio Grande. Fictionalized as Helen Chalmers in Frank Waters's *The Woman at Otowi Crossing* (1966) and Pamela Bye in Silman's *Beginning the World Again,* the historical Edith Warner is most accessible in an admiring biography by Peggy Pond Church, *The House at Otowi Bridge* (1960). While Waters engages in extensive improvisation, involving his character in an affair and endowing her with uncanny psychic powers, Silman's Pamela Bye is a milder version of Warner.

LITERATURE, LEGEND, AND TRUTH

Frank Waters's portrayal of Edith Warner was regarded by many friends and acquaintances as a slanderous distortion of Miss Warner's life and character. Observed Claire Morrill of Taos, "It would be hard to imagine two more completely different books written about the same person than Peggy Pond Church's biography, *The House at Otowi Bridge,* and Frank's novel, *The Woman at Otowi Crossing.*" Morrill reports that Waters's portrayal was "a matter of great distress to Edith's friends" and a source of controversy, as readers compared Waters's novel to the portrait fashioned in Church's gentle narrative (Morrill, 153).

This controversy raises a question of more general significance with respect to treatment of known persons in works of fiction. Is the writer responsible for her or his portrayal of a real person in a creative work, particularly when that portrayal exerts an observable and perhaps malignant influence on popular perceptions of the person?

Surely Waters's detractors are entitled to their opinions, but it is doubtful that many who value creative expression would deny him the prerogative to explore the myth that already had grown up about Miss Warner's life, as a brief note preceding the text says he proposes to do. He can hardly develop the ideas he finds worthwhile in the myth without referring the reader, however obliquely, to the person upon whom his character is based. In *Grant of Kingdom* (1950), Harvey Fergusson takes pains to stipulate in a foreword that, despite its obvious origins in history, "This book is a fiction and neither its characters nor its incidents are to be identified with real ones" (vi). Despite that disclaimer and the efforts of both authors to distinguish between a historic person and a fictional character, neither Waters nor Fergusson could prevent readers from incorporating the attributes of fictional characters into their perceptions of actual persons.

More serious consideration is required in the matter of Willa Cather and a purposely brutal portrayal of Padre Antonio José Martínez. No doubt the character served Cather's literary purpose by providing a bold antagonist to test the resolve of the more delicate and pious French priest, Jean Marie Latour, but at what price? Without troubling to rename her character, Cather conjures up an ogre surpassing in decadence and treachery the most unflattering account of Martínez to be found in historical sources. Archbishop Jean Baptiste Lamy, the basis for Cather's Latour, also satisfies Jon Tuska's criterion for legendary status. He can be portrayed as good or bad or both — as humble servant or overbearing conqueror — but Cather's character is the picture of long-suffering, progress, and piety.

Cather's treatment of Martínez long has been a source of resentment in northern New Mexico; in their objections, Martínez's defenders have found some allies. For Patricia Clark Smith, Cather's fairness or lack of it is a legitimate issue: "I think we cannot dismiss the problem of Cather's treatment of Padre Martínez, and of her whole condescending stance toward the nonwhite populations at large in the novel, by saying that the work is, after all, an 'imaginary construct,' not history, or by saying that, as with Milton on the subject of women, Cather, for one reason or another, simply didn't know any better" (Smith, 107).

Smith notes that such constructs of the imagination "have, in themselves, shaped history" and that they have in some instances served to create and perpetuate divisive stereotypes. "Since 1927," she observes, "many people in the United States and abroad have derived their ideas about the Southwest and its native cultures largely from her enduringly popular novel, and few people outside the Southwest know anything at all about Padre Martínez and the 'American' conquest of New Mexico except by way of Cather" (107).

In *But Time and Chance: The Story of Padre Martínez of Taos, 1793–1867,* Fray Angelico Chavez persuasively rejects many of the notions advanced in Cather's portrayal of Padre Martínez, but Chavez's ponderous biography was released by a small regional publisher in a modest edition which apparently satisfied demand for the work without difficulty. By 1978, on the other hand, the hardcover trade edition of Cather's novel was in its forty-eighth printing. In 1997, *Death Comes for the Archbishop* was available in at least two U.S. hardcover editions, a trade paperback, and a pocketbook, not to mention books-on-tape, large print, and foreign editions. The book has been read by literally millions.

The phenomenon of myth making, so vital to artists and writers, seems most bothersome to historians. Frustrated by the persistence of a public perception of Kit Carson as a "monstrous Indian slayer," Marc Simmons no doubt speaks for many of his colleagues when he decries the power of myth in the edited volume, *Kit Carson: Indian Fighter or Indian Killer* (1996): "The answer in part can be found in the old truism: Myths will not yield to facts. Once a myth has taken hold in the popular mind, no amount of empirical evidence is likely to overthrow it. Because Americans have long held that the voice of the people is the voice of truth, once a fantasy or myth becomes accepted in the street, it receives automatic validation" (85).

As already has been observed, bad history is as much to blame for many of the mythic constructs that have "taken hold in the popular mind" as are artists, fiction writers, and propagandists. Be that as it may, one can only sympathize with the reader whose desire is to find the truth — be it the literal truth of history or the ideal truth of art and literature — for, in many cases, the posse has trampled lots of signs while looking for the trail. The pursuer of truth will do well to proceed with caution, as does Rhodes's wily Jeff Bransford, whose advice to a younger companion in *Good Men and True* (1910) bears repeating: "You shouldn't believe all you read and only half what you see" (8).

Bransford's defenses against hasty and unfounded conclusions include a healthy skepticism and a penchant for critical thinking, habits which will prove indispensable to the reader who wants to ride out the rough country where lives and legends meet.

9 THE WILD WEST, THE AGRICULTURAL WEST, AND THE REAL WEST

aving mortally wounded a careless cattle rustler, Louis L'Amour's Conn Conagher gives the man's companion one brief chance to forsake the outlaw trail, then sends him back to his gang, promising to aim for his guts at the next opportunity.

"You're a hard man, Conagher," the boy allows.

"This here's a hard country," replies Conagher, "but it's a good country, Scott, and it'll be even better as soon as we hang or shoot a few more thieving skunks." (1969, p. 85)

A loner who uses courage and violence to bring order to a primitive society, Conagher belongs to the Wild West, one of two contrasting notions of the American frontier, as described by Henry Nash Smith in *Virgin Land: The American West as Symbol and Myth* (1950). The other West, the agricultural West, is represented by the pioneer farmer — a hero to some and a lowly drudge to others.

The Wild West was a vast frontier of natural hazards, exotic peoples, and panoramic vistas beyond the line of settlement. It was a land where hunters, trappers, and scouts, direct descendants of James Fenimore Cooper's Natty Bumppo, moved about freely, conducted themselves according to their own sensibilities, and lived lives of untrammeled freedom. It was, Smith wrote, "an exhilarating region of adventure and comradeship in the open air" (52).

The natural descendent of the trappers and scouts who first peopled the literary Wild West was the American cowboy. The cowboy went about on horseback and moved freely over the unfenced range. Unencumbered by home, hearth, or family, he was free to give his loyalty to the brand and just as free to ride into the sunset when it pleased him to do so. In the later dime novels and pulp Westerns, the cowboy was, more often than not, a loosely drawn character who could handle a horse and a gun but who had no visible means of support and no apparent bovine responsibilities.

By contrast, the agricultural West followed the line of settlement and was populated by farmers, whose lives were characterized by immobility, entangling family obligations, conformity to the rules of organized society, and a preference for personal safety. According to Smith, "The agricultural West was tedious; its inhabitants belonged to a despised social class," meaning that they had to stay in one place, work for a living, and carry on the mundane functions of civilized society (52). They raised families, built schools, joined fraternal organizations, voted, and went to church.

The farmer was more easily admired than envied; he was place-bound, his work was drudgery, and he was acutely vulnerable to hail, drought, and pestilence. Unlike the cowman, who might push his herd from drought-singed range to better grass, the farmer could not move wilted crops to a place where it was raining. The agent of the Wild West is admired for courage and action, the farmer for what he can endure without folding up.

Richard Slotkin, in his 1992 study of the mythology of the American West, notes that some frontier historians, including Frederick Jackson Turner, made the farmer the hero of the westward advance. He was exalted as the industrious agent of civilized society, stimulating settlement and bringing along such institutions as school, church, law, and family.

This was not a new idea. In 1755, Jean Jacques Rousseau, explaining how mankind came to exchange freedom for progress, wrote, "The first man who, having enclosed a piece of ground, bethought himself of saying *This is mine,* and found people simple enough to believe him, was the real founder of civil society" (38:348). It worked like this: "The cultivation of the earth necessarily brought about its distribution; and property, once recognized, gave rise to the first rules of justice; for to secure each man his own, it had to be possible for each to have something" (38:353). One thing led to another, and before you knew it, industrious societies were printing currency, levying taxes, regulating commerce, organizing bridge clubs, and building shopping malls.

Daniel Webster spoke more directly to the situation developing on the American frontier, noting in a speech to the legislature of Massachusetts in 1840: "Man may be civilized, in some degree, without great progress in manufactures and with little commerce with his distant neighbors. But without the cultivation of the earth, he is, in all countries, a savage. Until he gives up the chase, and fixes himself in some place and seeks a living from the earth, he is a roaming barbarian. When tillage begins, other arts follow. The farmers, therefore, are the founders of human civilization."

But as Slotkin notes, if the farmer was a hero, he was a hero *en masse;* it is difficult, if not impossible, to conjure up the names and faces of legendary farmers of the frontier West.

By contrast, the hunter, the trapper, the scout, and their spiritual heir, the cowboy, achieved heroic status for their exploits as individuals. The durability of numerous legendary figures among them proves it. Francis Parkman, Theodore Roosevelt, and others cast the independent man of the frontier as the hero of the westward movement, Roosevelt contrasting the frontiersman's virtues of courage and daring with the farmer's role as a passive developer of gains won by others. "In this," writes Slotkin, "his preferences were shared by the readers of American nineteenth-century popular fiction, for in romances and dime novels the farmer was a secondary figure while the hunter/Indian-fighter was at the center of action" (33).

Written mainly by Anglo-Americans and focusing primarily on the notion of an advancing American frontier, literary accounts of the farmer and the cowboy are, for the most part, accounts of westering Anglo men. In the agricultural West, women share — and sometimes carry — the load. The Wild West describes a man's world in which women, if they appear at all, are either exploited or patronized.

THE WILD WEST

When the cowboy made his appearance as a hero of popular western fiction, he inherited the mythic persona of the dime-novel frontiersman. According to Henry Nash Smith, his invention as a heroic figure was motivated largely by a perceived need to clothe the hero in more contemporary garb. The makeover was purely cosmetic, as the central features accounting for the hero's appeal were retained. The cowboy hero moves about in a magnificent western landscape, behaves according to his own code of honor, and helps bring order to a lawless country. He intervenes on the side of right in conflicts between forces representing good and evil, even if he has to go outside the law to do it. If there is a fair young miss within a hundred miles, he will find her; he may end up marrying the girl, but he is just as likely to choose his independence over the entanglements of married life. The cowboy is courageous, and he is not reluctant to use violence in pursuit of virtuous ends. He rarely works cattle, but he is comfortable on a horse and handy with a rope and a gun. He weathers numerous hazards and acts of treachery, but in the end he always wins.

C. L. Sonnichsen has called this "the West that wasn't." There is some historical basis for the Wild West as a place of ad hoc justice and violent conflict, certainly; but the complaint is that these elements are enlarged and exploited in the production of literature which is meant only to entertain readers.

Sonnichsen and others have taken pains to distinguish between the "low road" of western fiction, which runs from the earliest beginnings of western writing to the present; and the "high road," which generally is traced to the 1902 publication of Owen Wister's *The Virginian: Horseman of the Plains.* The difference, however, is a difference of degree more than of kind; the so-called "high road" does not necessarily represent a departure from the mythology upon which the popular western formula is based.

As analyzed by John Milton in *The Novel of the American West* (1980), *The Virginian* includes all the essentials of the western formula. The cowboy appears as a drifter who chooses to live apart from society. His character is that of a gallant hero. He confronts violence caused by evildoers, and he responds with violence to defeat the perpetrator and restore justice. The story embraces a moral system based on clear delineation of good and evil, and good always wins. A love interest is provided for the hero. Cattle ranching, while superficially part of the western setting, has little or no relationship to the plot. The story unfolds against the backdrop of the frontier West, a land of immense scale, natural purity, and promise. It is a land up for grabs. As the frontier heroine observes in Zane Grey's *Sunset Pass* (1931), "Our West is in the making" (349).

The hero, violence, love, and the western landscape survive as essential ingredients of the western formula, and of these, says Milton, "it is violence that has been refined, not into an art but into a pattern of action and a condition of effect which the standard western cannot do without" (1980, p. 21). Initially justified in terms of vengeance, survival, and the pursuit of justice, violence came to be appreciated for its own sake, and its incidence as part of the western motif increased.

Violence is, in fact, one of the hallmarks of the popular Western. This can be demonstrated easily enough by looking through a rack of paperback Westerns. In nearly 100 percent of cases, the cover illustration includes a gun, usually in the hands of a male figure. The gun is there for a reason; it tells the reader who wants to hear the familiar refrain of the Wild West that this book is for him. In some cases, the high incidence of violence has become a selling point. Publishers of the popular "Edge" series state on each cover that theirs are "the most violent Westerns in print." This is not an apology, but a boast.

The author who ignores the preference for violent action does so at his peril. Frank O'Rourke, who lived in Taos for five years and used the area as a setting for many of his books, wrote more than two dozen popular Westerns. He aspired to create more serious works as well, but Random House disparaged the manuscripts he proffered as "off-trail" efforts. On more than one occasion, the publisher retitled O'Rourke's Westerns to give them the desired market appeal. Explaining the publisher's preferred title of *Gunsmoke Over Big Muddy* for an O'Rourke novel, editor Harry Maule wrote, "The people who read westerns don't want geographic titles like *The Rolling Hills.* They want action and violence."

The first notable writer to take the high road in western fiction when dealing with New Mexico subjects was Eugene Manlove Rhodes. Writing from exile in Upstate New York, Rhodes idealized the vanished West and made it the subject of numerous magazine stories, novelettes, and novels.

Rhodes detested the treatment given his works by the eastern publishing establishment. Those whose business was to sell books thought they needed to fit their products to established genres that consumers could recognize easily. Rhodes's books obviously were Westerns, but to him they were Westerns with a difference. Rhodes resented the unmerited popularity of authors whose books he thought were "false on every page in letter and in spirit" (Hutchinson, 245). By contrast, he felt that his own works faithfully portrayed a West he had seen with his own eyes.

More to the point, Rhodes held and expressed a point of view in his stories of the West. Courage, loyalty, and resourcefulness were qualities he admired, and he built them into the characters who rode through his novels. They were "good men and true," with the accent on loyalty rather than goodness. L'Amour's Conagher would have qualified on the basis of a stage driver's frank appraisal: "I think you're a no-account saloon brawler who'd rather fight than eat, and the only things I can say good about you is that you do your job, you're honest, and you never backed off from trouble" (L'Amour 1969, p. 146). In the Wild West, that's about all the good there is to be said about a man.

Men with overactive scruples were of limited value. "Really good men, they never do much of anything — not when it's risky," explains Rhodes's Pres Lewis in *The Trusty Knaves* (111). Effective action requires men who are undeterred by danger and who are not cowed by the law or its agents, both of which are notoriously susceptible to error and corruption. Rhodes expressed contempt for people of wealth and authority; in his view, they tended to display an unfortunate penchant for corrupt behavior. He admired the ordinary men of the range, and he preferred their brand of justice, which did not always proceed according to the letter of the law.

If the literary properties of Rhodes's novels placed him above most other writers of Westerns, his stories still conformed to the traditional western formula. The hero stands tall in defense of right and triumphs over wrongdoers; if there is a girl to be had, he gets her. Rhodes makes judicious use of violence, but it serves approximately the same purpose in his stories as it does in other western tales.

Winning Rhodes's approval as riders of the high trail were such contemporaries as Frederick Bechdolt, Bertha Muzzy Bower, Jackson Gregory, Emerson Hough, Peter B. Kyne, George Patullo, and William MacLeod Raine, all of whom penned western novels and stories with New Mexico settings. Rhodes regarded their stories as truth-telling Westerns in which fictitious people and horses resembled the real ones of his experience.

Frank O'Rourke and Louis L'Amour also deserve consideration as travelers of the high road. Their best works exhibit an appreciation of history and place, and offer the reader something more than a formulaic treatment of western themes. O'Rourke's adventure Westerns set in Taos, or "Rio Arriba," reflect the author's intimate knowledge of northern New Mexico and a concern for freedom that was evident in his personal life as well as in his works.

L'Amour, noted for his fidelity to the western landscape, evokes New Mexico places in several titles, including *Radigan* (1958), *The Daybreakers* (1960), *Flint* (1960), *Killoe* (1962), *Shalako* (1962), and *Conagher* (1969). Bert Murphy of Roswell has checked up on L'Amour, tracing the steps of L'Amour's characters across New Mexico; he reports in *Trailing Louis L'Amour in New Mexico* (1995) that virtually every feature referred to in

L'Amour's novels may be observed on the ground as described. L'Amour's heroes exhibit individual strength and character, in accord with the expected formula; the author also admires characters who struggle and overcome obstacles — both internal and external — in order to succeed.

Consigned to the low road in Rhodes's judgment — "the three worst," he said — were such celebrated western writers as Zane Grey, Charles Alden Seltzer, and Clarence E. Mulford (Hutchinson, 219). These were joined by dozens, if not hundreds, of writers who turned out countless Westerns for a market that demanded little in the way of originality or literary quality. Books of this ilk typically hew to the tried-and-true formula, plying readers with tales of heroic loners who blow away menacing antagonists. These stories include stereotypical heroes, villains, virgins, Indians, and "Mexicans," and are unlikely to jangle the sensibilities or threaten the values of a reader who is committed to the western myth.

Notable in many of the lesser Westerns is the absence of anything approaching a sense of place. In many cases, stories are vaguely located, employing a generic western setting and revealing little of the geography, historical context, attitudes, and values by which a particular place and its people may be made known to the reader. Some stories are nominally laid in "New Mexico Territory," but it really doesn't matter, because the author provides nothing to illuminate the fictional setting or to set it apart from any other place in the Wild West.

There are exceptions, of course. Zane Grey, highly successful as a writer of commercial western fiction, was criticized roundly for his portrayal of a mythic West bearing little resemblance to the real thing. Still, Grey's *Fighting Caravans* (1929) and *Knights of the Range* (1939) manage to convey much of the lore and appeal of the Santa Fe Trail and the Cimarron country.

At the bottom of the low road in fiction of the Wild West are the adventure series novels. These include the stories of Edge, Slocum, Longarm, Bolt, the Trailsman, and other hard-core western heroes. Some of these presumably are published under house names, with individual titles farmed out to writers who may be just as happy to remain anonymous. Like the later dime novels, these tales stretch the limits of the traditional formula, incorporating more violence, more explicit sex, tougher and more ruthless heroes. The protagonists of these stories are highly mobile, finding action all over the West and as far afield as Florida.

The western formula has proven remarkably durable, pleasing consumers of dime novels, story papers, pulp magazines, "straight western" novels, movies, television, and mass-market adventure Westerns, for more than a century. But one cannot help wondering what the future holds. For at least twenty years, the traditional Western has been in a steady decline. In 1978, C. L. Sonnichsen wrote that "the Western novel has fallen farther and faster than any other type" (4). Sonnichsen held out the possibility of a resurgence, but so far none is evident.

Speaking at a cowboy symposium in 1996, Max Evans reported on his effort to gauge the popularity of the paperback Western by measuring the shelf space devoted to Westerns at the local supermarket; over a three-year period, he found a decrease of two-thirds. Unless there is another Louis L'Amour lurking somewhere in the sagebrush, the Western may be down for the count. Certainly, in their efforts to explore new depths of sensationalism, the stories of Edge, Slocum, and the like reveal the sense of desperation that their writers must feel. With the elements of a threadbare formula stretched to absurd extremes, one wonders whether there is anywhere left for the adventure Western to go, or whether its *macho* hero at long last is riding toward his final sunset.

THE AGRICULTURAL WEST

In Henry Nash Smith's terms, "the Wild West beyond the frontier lent itself readily to interpretation in a literature developing the themes of natural nobility and physical adventure, but the agricultural West . . . proved quite intractable as literary material" (211). One technique for making the western farmer an acceptable literary subject involved portraying him as an ignorant bumpkin whose speech and manner were both picturesque and appalling. Unlettered, gullible, speaking in a dialect indicative of his degraded status, he was a comical character and an object of ridicule. If the farmer could not inspire readers with his daring, he could amuse them. The timid reader back east might not admire the lowly sodbuster, but at least he could feel superior to him.

In the two most notable novels about Anglo farmers in New Mexico to attain the blessing of the eastern publishing establishment, the characters are indeed comic figures. But the humor in these books comes at the expense of the struggling farmer; readers are invited to laugh at the ignorance and misfortune of the nester and his family. They are funny for their untutored manner of speech, their misbegotten ideas, and for their struggles to get ahead in the face of a never-ending series of set-

backs. At the same time, readers are meant to admire the heart and durability of these simple folk, to struggle with them, and to rejoice in their
accomplishments.

In Lorraine Carr's *Mother of the Smiths* (1940), Si and Sabe Smith come
to the Taos Valley from Texas to settle and raise a family. Si is a loafer and
a dreamer who expects to make his fortune finding gold nuggets. It is big
Sabe who turns in and gets it done for her family, trading for a piece of
land and building an adobe house. Sabe does the washing, cooking, hunting, and plowing. She hauls the wood, nurses the babies, and fends off
creditors. Whenever a neighbor is sick, the call goes out for Sabe Smith.

Sabe's own desires are simple. She wants a blue gate and a big bowl of
apples on the kitchen table. Other needs, however, keep getting between
Sabe and her dream. Two of her six boys die, but Sabe lives to see one son,
Sammy, become a doctor and return to work among the plain folk of the
valley. One can only hope that Sabe has her reward in heaven, having
shouldered her earthly burdens with faithfulness and good cheer.

Among fiction writers, John L. Sinclair became the chief chronicler of
the New Mexico dirt farmer, turning out three novels about struggling
farm families. Sinclair studied agriculture as a youth in Scotland, but it
was after he crossed the ocean and landed in southern New Mexico in the
early 1920s that he got to know the people who inspired his stories. As a
cowboy in Lincoln County, he saw hopeful families traversing the plain
below Capitán Mountain and was determined to know their stories. "I
looked down there and saw those people," he recalled, "and I wanted to
get to know them and to hear their stories and listen to their lingo and to
watch 'em fixing-up and cultivating; getting fences up and stock a'going.
And I did!" (Kimball, 1–2).

The first and best of Sinclair's stories is *In Time of Harvest* (1943), a tale
of Estancia Valley bean farmers. Tod and Faybelle McClung move to the
valley from Oklahoma in 1919, hauling all they own in a wagon, hoping to
homestead and grow beans. The McClungs settle in on a section of land
and see bountiful years and lean years as their family grows.

Sinclair's story should resonate with readers whose family heritage includes the experience of the westering farmer. The McClungs form part of
a rural community of the sort that was common from the coming of the
farmers until the Great Depression. Work, children, neighbors, religion,
gossip, and dances at the community schoolhouse make up the substance
of their lives. Like many others of their time and social class, the McClungs

at first view education with suspicion, but a likable teacher persuades them to let their two youngest attend school.

Of their six children, one dies a rounder, one becomes a whore, one lands in the penitentiary, and another hits the road with his guitar; but the last two seem headed toward responsible and productive lives. All of this leaves Tod to look back over the years and conclude, "It ain't till maturity that any of us can figure what we raise is a success crop or a failure. I've had my happy moments and my years of grief since the day I started keeping company with you-all beans. We've had our short and bumper crops together" (212).

In Sinclair's *Death in the Claimshack* (1947), the hardluck Hendricks family—Pappy, Maw Maw, and Nythalda Fay—have hopes of homesteading near the Datil Mountains. But before they can make the trip from Lincoln County, Pappy catches pneumonia while slopping the hogs and dies in the tumbledown claimshack in which they have lived. The epitaph penned for Pappy Hendricks by the book's illustrator will do for all the fictional nesters who have left their homes to pursue elusive dreams of a better life: "He done the best he could."

Mother of the Smiths and *In Time of Harvest,* both published in the early 1940s, are of value in part because they provide rare portrayals of an era. Before the Depression, many families lived the lives of the Smiths and the McClungs—large families taking advantage of free or cheap western land, working small farms, living in small communities organized around country schools and churches. Carr and Sinclair understand the culture of the pioneer farmers, their motives and attitudes, their hopes and disappointments.

It is doubtful that either book could have been written in the 1990s. The pioneer farm family, as conceived of in 1996, instead is embodied in the Conklins of Karen Osborn's *Between Earth and Sky* (1996). Like Mother Smith, Abigail Conklin is saddled with a weak and worthless husband, and she carries the load with competence and dignity. Like Tod and Faybelle McClung, she achieves mixed results as a parent of three children. But unlike either the Smiths or the McClungs, Abigail is an educated and articulate pioneer, retaining the refined manner and sensibilities of her Virginia upbringing even as she stands up to the rigors of life in New Mexico.

Hispanic farmers appearing in novels of village life share the degraded status of the Anglo farmers. Poor and poorly educated, they see their earning power erode as the family lands are further subdivided with each succeeding generation, and as competition from more efficient producers increases. The Trujillo brothers of Raymond Otis's *Little Valley* (1937) fight a losing battle, struggling to eke out a living on small plots of tillable land. As the Depression devastates small farming all across the Great Plains, it deals a death blow to the capacity of the farmers of Vallecito to provide for themselves.

Following the great westward migration, the Homestead Act, the Depression, the creation of an ambitious agricultural extension program, the implementation of federal controls on price and production, the development of improved methods of irrigation, and the rise of corporate farming interests, the small farmer ends about where he began. Having fed the nation and having made major contributions to the settlement of its western lands, the farmer remains unacceptable as a heroic character in western fiction. The best he can do is win the admiration of readers for his determination to better his circumstances and for his perseverance in the face of adversity.

THE REAL WEST

Two novels published in 1956 signaled a move away from traditional portrayals of the American cowboy in works of fiction set in New Mexico. One was *The Brave Cowboy*, by Edward Abbey; and the other was *The Diamond Hitch*, by Frank O'Rourke. Neither book could be considered a "Western" in the traditional sense, but both reveal a great deal more about the West than do most Westerns. The main characters in these books are cowboys in the broad sense — one actually is a sheepherder and the other a horse breaker — but they do not conform to the conventional mythology of the cowboy hero. They do not live in a black-and-white world of moral values as most cowboy heroes do, and they are not indomitable figures who employ violence to overcome evil. They are real people living in a real world.

The Brave Cowboy reveals the traditional cowboy hero as an anachronism in contemporary society. Accustomed to move over the unbroken western landscape on horseback, the mythic cowboy embodies a spirit of freedom and independence. Jack Burns, Abbey's brave cowboy, steers his horse into Duke City — Albuquerque — where heavy traffic and angry motorists frighten the horse and seriously impair the cowboy's mobility and style. Moreover, when Burns goes to war over a moral issue, the issue turns out to involve shades of gray, and his antagonist is not an individual or a gang, but a far-flung, technologically sophisticated, and heavily armed

Doughbelly Price and
Frank O'Rourke.
Photo by Verne Sackett.
Courtesy Edith Carlson
O'Rourke.

conglomeration of law enforcement agencies and military forces, backed
by the authority of several governmental entities. When Burns attempts
first to spring his friend from jail, then to flee alone over the ridge above
Duke City, he finds himself overpowered. His moral sense is keen and his
courage admirable, but this cowboy is in the wrong place at the wrong
time; if the traditional mythology ever worked for the cowboy hero, it no
longer works for Jack Burns.

Once free of Random House and its insistence on fidelity to the western formula, Frank O'Rourke turned out some of the best fictional accounts of cowboy life on record. *The Diamond Hitch* involves none of the
wrenching moral and philosophical implications of Abbey's book, but it
reveals rodeo and ranch life as experienced by a likable young hand.
O'Rourke was not a cowboy or anything of the kind; the book owes its authenticity to the author's research and to the contributions of Doughbelly
Price, on whose early life the book is based.

Set in the mid-1920s, *The Diamond Hitch* involves no shooting and very
little that could be called violence, unless the bone-crunching work of a
bronc rider qualifies. Dewey Jones is hanging out in Raton, nosing around
for work, when he is offered the job of camp cook and horse breaker with
a packsaddle outfit in Arizona. After chasing wild cattle on the Flying A
Ranch all summer, Dewey entrains for Las Vegas, New Mexico, where he

wins top money in the Cowboy's Reunion Rodeo. In the twilight of his reckless youth, Dewey has the good fortune to win the love of a lady and land a job managing a horse ranch in the Moreno Valley.

Another novel of the real West, also attributable to O'Rourke's friendship with Price, is *The Last Ride* (1958). The book tells more than most readers may want to know about cinches and surcingles and hobbles, and about the tedium and loneliness of ranch work, but it is at bottom the story of an aging cowboy finding common ground with an aging stallion who loves freedom as much as the cowboy does. O'Rourke picks up his characters — cowboys on the move and looking for work — in the vicinity of the village of Maxwell. John Hatton's pursuit of the lone stallion takes place in the Vermejo country of northern New Mexico.

Max Evans continued the trend toward more realistic portrayals and found both humor and pathos in the lot of the luckless cowboys who populate his stories. Evans's comic treatment of Dusty Jones and Wrangler Lewis in *The Rounders* (1960) was a resounding success, possibly overshadowing revealed truths about the everyday lives of working cowboys. Introducing a 1983 paperback reprint of Evans's novel, C. L. Sonnichsen wrote, "*The Rounders* is, in truth, a serious, even a sad book. Behind the banter and horseplay is an exceptional feel for place and people, a keen ear for talk, a warm heart for struggling human beings, a wry and wise sense of the human predicament" (v).

Like Henry Blanton in Jane Kramer's nonfiction narrative, *The Last Cowboy* (1977), Dusty and Wrangler are trapped in a condition of perpetual servitude, beholden to an owner whose only real virtues are stability and business sense. In theory, Dusty and Wrangler would like to escape their lives as ranch hands for something better, but they are victims of their own excesses and their own impulsive generosity. The cowboys maintain a measure of freedom to act as they please, but by refusing to moderate their behavior and conform to accepted social norms, they also spoil their chances to better their circumstances.

Evans's book also serves to point up important differences between the cowboy and the rancher who owns and operates a cattle-raising business. Unlike the cowboy, who prides himself on freedom from encumbrances, the rancher shares some circumstances with the farmer. His commitment is long-term, and his enterprise is bound by place; he also has a greater stake in the development of community and society. By virtue of his dependence on hired workers, bankers, and buyers, he also may be more inclined to moderation and compromise.

In Jack Schaefer's *Monte Walsh* (1963), a young cowboy lives through the last days of the open range and becomes a top hand, but he sees the world pass him by as he stays with the life he loves. Monte's friend, Chet Rollins, foresees big changes and forsakes the cowboy life, attaining success as a family man with a thriving business. Monte, however, slides on into his twilight years, an aging saddle bum out of place in the modern world. Monte's reputation as a horse breaker follows him through his declining years, prompting a listener to ask why he never tried the rodeo circuit. "Monte?" replies a knowledgeable bystander. "He ain't that kind. He's real" (469).

Ignacio Ortiz, a Mexican orphan reared on the D Cross A Ranch in Norman Zollinger's *Riders to Cibola* (1977), is another product of the Real West. Taken in by the McAndrews family of Ojos Negros, Ignacio becomes a trusted hand, superseding Douglas MacAndrews's irresponsible son as the stabilizing force of the D Cross A. Ignacio rides for the brand through good years and bad, escaping the outfit's demise by his death in the 1950s.

What John Hatton, Dusty Jones, Wrangler Lewis, Monte Walsh, and Ignacio Ortiz have in common is the unvarnished life of a working cowboy. According to western myth, they live lives of freedom and independence, riding the range and spurning society's expectations. In reality, all are economically dependent on men of inferior courage and intelligence. While the cowboy is impetuous, skillful, stubborn, and proud, the boss attains his superior status through planning, judgment, business sense, and self-discipline. The cowboy remains, mostly by choice, a member of an underclass of hired men who share many of the risks but few of the rewards of the enterprise.

As for the cowboy's supposed preference for freedom from the entanglements of marriage and family, one has to wonder whether it is just that, or whether he is, in reality, a socially dysfunctional character who can't connect or commit. When Dewey Jones quits the cowboy life to wed Mary Ashford in *The Diamond Hitch*, it is hard not to feel that he has been delivered from a life that offers less and less as the years pile up. Either way, there is much to weigh, and very little to envy, in the solitary life of a working cowboy.

THE COWMAN AND THE FARMER

A song in the musical, *Oklahoma*, admonishes that "the cowman and the farmer should be friends." The indication is that they are not, by natural inclination, friends or anything like it. The most notable works of fiction contrasting the cowman and the farmer suggest that their differences go much deeper than a simple conflict over competing uses of land; as groups, they hold different values and exhibit differences in attitude, character, and culture.

In a classic confrontation between cowmen and farmers in Conrad Richter's *The Sea of Grass* (1937), there is bitter conflict over competing uses of the vast range claimed by Col. Jim Brewton. Most of the land is public domain and so is open to homesteading, but Brewton vehemently opposes the notion of farming the high, dry prairie. "I have sympathy for the pioneer settler who came out here and risked his life and family among the Indians," he declares,

> and I hope I have a little charity for the nester who waited until the country was safe and peaceable before he filed on a homestead on someone else's range who fought for it. But . . . when that nester picks country like my big vega, that's more than seven thousand feet above the sea, when he wants to plow it up to support his family where there isn't enough rain for crops to grow, where he only kills the grass that will grow, where he starves for water and feeds his family by killing my beef and becomes a man without respect to himself and a miserable menace to the territory, then I have neither sympathy nor charity! (23–24)

Brewton sees the farmer as Theodore Roosevelt did, as the passive developer of gains won by others. In Richter's novel, the farmer is a weak character who cannot stand up to the attacks of the cattlemen; he has to hide behind the law and the U.S. Cavalry. He arrives with family in tow, already domesticated and encumbered with obligations.

Brewton, on the other hand, came to the frontier as a single man and fought for the land he now occupies. He brought a bride from the East only when the country was safe from the Indians. This, in his view, is the behavior of an honorable man. This is the cowman's way.

Rudolfo Anaya treats the cowboy and the farmer as competing influences in the life of young Antonio Marez in *Bless Me, Ultima* (1972). Antonio's father is descended from *vaqueros,* men who enjoy the freedom of the *llano,* who thrill at the power and swiftness of horses. His mother is of the Lunas, farmers who inhabit the fertile valley of Puerto de Luna, who glory in the harvest. In contrast to the restless *vaqueros,* the farmers value family and security, and their cardinal virtue is not freedom, but commu-

Conrad Richter.
Photo by Elliott Erwitt.
Courtesy Harvena Richter.

nity. Clearly, Antonio is the product of two very different traditions: "The men of the *llano* were men of the sun. The men of the farms along the river were men of the moon" (25).

As Antonio is left to reconcile the divergent strands of his heritage and find his own identity, so might every reader contemplate the archetypal farmer and cowboy — characters whose impulses inhabit us all to one degree or another. Every reader finds some part of himself in these mythic figures of the American West. In the homebody beats the heart of a farmer; in the restless loner, that of a cowboy. In those who join clubs and build communities, we see the farmer at work. When the middle-aged rebel tells the boss to take his job and shove it, truck payment and retirement be damned — well, that's the cowboy way. The mythic images of the cowboy and the farmer may not perfectly mirror reality in this changing world, but they do focus attention on two sides of human nature, as different and inseparable as the people of the sun and those of the moon.

10 LIVING WITH THE BOMB

When the scientists and technicians of the Manhattan Project ascended to Pajarito Plateau with their families beginning in 1943, they comprised a foreign element in the social matrix of New Mexico. Hidden away behind the high fences and entry stations that guarded Los Alamos and its secrets, they formed a community apart, an enclave surrounded by mountains, pueblos, valleys, villages, and towns that had evolved over several centuries. In nearby Santa Fe, there was concern that the new people would ruin the city's unique southwestern ambiance. This threat may have been exaggerated, but there is no doubt that the newcomers taxed supplies of scarce consumer goods, exacerbating shortages for the local people and fueling resentment (Brode, 157–58).

The differences between residents of the Hill and the locals were striking. For a century, New Mexico had been peopled mostly by Native Americans, Hispanics, and Anglo-Americans. Native American religious traditions endured alongside the Catholic faith of the Spanish conquerors and Protestant denominations introduced by Anglo-Americans. The Manhattan Project brought to Los Alamos eminent scientists who had fled western Europe rather than perish or serve the cause of Adolf Hitler; many of those who came were Jewish.

The project attracted a stunning concentration of scientific intellect. Several Nobel Prize winners were in residence, along with some bright young scientists who later would attain distinction, in part on the strength of their contributions to the Manhattan Project. The people of Los Alamos came from both coasts and around the world and had far more formal education than most people in the region. They were, on the whole, youthful, energetic, highly intelligent, relatively affluent, and possessed of a sense of urgency in keeping with the priorities of a nation at war.

If Los Alamos, with all that it symbolizes, at first shocked those accustomed to the relative serenity of the Upper Rio Grande region, the lore of Los Alamos, Trinity Site, and the bomb since have been accepted as essential parts of the story of New Mexico. Nor did the state's involvement with technology research and development end with Los Alamos. When the war was over, Los Alamos continued as a center of atomic research and later became a national laboratory pursuing a variety of scientific activities. Los Alamos National Laboratory, Sandia National Laboratories, White Sands Missile Range, the large-array radio telescope near Magdalena, and the Stealth aircraft based at Alamogordo's Holloman Air Force Base give weight to New Mexico's claim to preeminence in technology research and development.

Scientists, journalists, politicians, historians, military leaders, and pacifists all have had their say concerning the events of 1943–45 and their aftermath. Robert Oppenheimer, Edward Teller, Richard Feynman, and others have chronicled the major events and noted personalities of wartime Los Alamos, but the spouses and children of the scientists and technicians who lived at Los Alamos also have recorded reminiscences of those memorable days. These latter are, in many ways, just as interesting as those of the scientists and technicians who made the bomb.

Fiction writers quickly recognized the literary possibilities inherent in wartime Los Alamos. The story of Los Alamos and the bomb featured fascinating characters, it was shrouded in mystery, and it involved the pursuit and protection of vital national secrets. In working with lethal materials and dealing with experiments of uncertain consequence, the scientists also faced an element of danger. The lore of Los Alamos has inspired numerous mystery novels and spy thrillers — for example, *The Search* (1986), by Robert Mayer; and James Kunetka's *Shadow Man* (1988). A more ambitious mystery treatment is the 1998 novel, *Los Alamos,* by Joseph Kanon. Kanon poses a murder to be solved on the Hill — a place that does not exist for local law enforcement agencies. The case requires special handling, so Kanon has created Michael Connolly, an intelligence officer who pursues the case with cool efficiency and utmost discretion.

There also have been lighter treatments, as in Dorothy Hughes's references to the Hill and the danger of "los rayos gammos" in *The Big Barbe-cue* (1949), a novel set near Santa Fe. Writing as Patrick O'Malley and us-ing his familiar gumshoes, Hoeffler and Harrigan, Frank O'Rourke pro-duced a mystery spoof involving an attempt by foreign spies to purloin the strategic secrets of Los Alamos in *The Affair of the Red Mosaic* (1961).

More to the point, the literature includes some serious novels that doc-ument the tense days preceding the blast at Trinity Site and detail the ex-periences of life at Los Alamos. Writers also have found food for thought and material for serious literature in the moral dilemmas confronted by participants in the Manhattan Project. The fictional accounts of wartime Los Alamos undoubtedly have relied heavily on available memoirs and other authoritative nonfiction writings. The best novels of Los Alamos plumb the souls of those involved and bring to light ethical questions that should trouble all who believe in the moral superiority of human beings and who are concerned with the survival of the species.

LIFE ON THE HILL

If the new residents of Los Alamos were not universally welcomed in New Mexico, neither were many of the newcomers overjoyed to be there. Most did not choose to come to New Mexico; they came out of duty to a country at war. For many of the scientists, the Manhattan Project rep-resented an unwelcome interruption in prestigious careers in academia, but one they could not well refuse. When the war was over, many would leave as suddenly as they had come. Trained to probe the mysteries of the universe and in the process reap professional gratification, prestige, and profit, they found themselves converted into glorified technicians labor-ing at the behest of the military, in a cause of which many became in-creasingly wary. For some, of course, the call to Los Alamos represented a rare opportunity — a chance to work with the great scientific minds of the age in a venture of unquestioned importance.

The call to service involved not only the scientists, support staff, and military personnel, but families as well. Reactions to the decision to ac-commodate families were mixed. Presumably, those needed for the war work were more willing to come and more content to stay because they could go home to those near and dear to them each day. At the same time, the arrangement produced a glaring disparity between the scientists, whose time and attention increasingly were absorbed in their work, and the families, for whom the experience was largely one of boredom, isola-tion, and exile.

Los Alamos offered few comforts to those who came to work — mostly men — or to the spouses and children who came to wait. Uprooted from their homes, swept away to a strange and distant land, they were deposited in an outpost hidden away from the world and guarded by barbed-wire fences and armed soldiers. As described in Thomas Wiseman's *Savage Day* (1981), Los Alamos is a makeshift village thrown together in haste, with no consideration for aesthetics and no thought of permanence.

> The town that had sprung up had a ramshackle, temporary air — as if nobody expected it, or required it, to last very long. One building was put up in one place, and then another was stuck onto it (with a communicating first-story covered bridge) as an afterthought. There was a five-bed hospital; when more beds were needed, the original single straight-line structure became an H structure. Whenever more accommodation was needed (and more accommodation was always needed) the Army added another of its expandable government cara-vans to the vast unsightly sprawl on the western outskirts of the com-pound. (19)

For the scientists and their wives, fresh from comfortable lives in the city, inconveniences were constant and annoying. Wives newly arrived on the Hill were urged to "adjust," and there was plenty to adjust to, as is evi-dent in Dexter Master's 1955 novel, *The Accident:* "The mesa was what it was; the houses were at first nonexistent, then bad, and finally inadequate; the water ran out, was carted in, ran short, and was carted in; the road broke down, was repaired, broke down, and was rebuilt; walks which were paths turned to mud in the rains; and until the spring of 1946, by which time six thousand people had moved to the mesa, there were thirteen bathtubs in all of Los Alamos" (45).

Many of the fictional newcomers are surprised to find themselves liv-ing in an army camp, the whole settlement ringed by a high-security fence and the laboratory area further fortified against intrusion. The fences sym-bolize a division that goes far beyond mere physical separation. If Spanish Colonial New Mexico had its "two majesties," so too does Los Alamos. The scientists and military heads eye each other warily, each resentful of the other.

"You're an undisciplined lot, all of you," fumes the general in Pearl S. Buck's 1959 *Command the Morning* (154). The general is identified only as "old Bubble-guts," but presumably the character is based on Gen. Leslie Groves, military head of the Manhattan Project. The object of the general's outburst is Burton Hall, a character suggesting physicist and project director Robert Oppenheimer.

> "General," says Hall, "I can see my chief role in the Project. I'm to be a buffer between you and the scientists."
> "They're a damned cocky bunch," the general retorts, "They think they're God's little wise men." (155)

The resentment is mutual, as the scientists, possessed of indispensable knowledge and unaccustomed to encroachments on their intellectual prerogatives, chafe under the authority of military command — authority which, to their way of thinking, often is exercised in a mindless and overbearing manner. On the morning following an accident which will claim the life of a young scientist in *The Accident,* David Thiel knocks at the door of Col. Cornelius Hough, telling him: "We beef about the military mind, because the military mind, even yours, subordinates people to routines, and refers decisions elsewhere, and makes an art of buckpassing. It hasn't any interest in what is, or might be, but only in what has been, and only in what's been officially sanctioned out of that" (33).

Clashes of ego also occur among the scientists themselves, many of them renowned public figures who feel no compulsion to subordinate themselves to a military command structure.

Fictional portrayals of the physical appearance of wartime Los Alamos closely resemble those in nonfiction memoirs and historical works, presumably because the writer has consulted these accounts. Such descriptions are interesting and informative, but the writer also is interested in the inner lives of those who experienced the tense days just before the world learned what the men in Los Alamos were up to.

In fictional Los Alamos, the primitive conditions are sufficient to support the work of the bomb makers; but there is a psychic price to be paid, and it is paid mainly by the wives and children of the scientists. Cut off from past associations and neglected by their husbands, the women are left to wait the war out, keep a stiff upper lip, and make the best of it. Some take refuge in contrived amusements, including silly plays in which the women play men's roles as well as their own. Alcohol flows freely, and for some women like Ruthie Friedman in Robert Cohen's *The Organ Builder,* it becomes the anesthetic of choice. When a psychiatrist hangs out his shingle in Los Alamos, she and other wives flock to him.

When the Trinity test is over and Helen Coast again has her husband's attention in Buck's *Command the Morning*, she tells him, "While you and your scientists have been busy at your private life, there's been another sort of life going on. You can't lock a lot of people up on a mesa like this without having things go on" (290).

What Helen presumably has in mind are the secret liaisons that appear to be commonplace in fictional Los Alamos. Bored and tense, some of the wives seek comfort in extramarital affairs. They need love and intimacy, and if they can't get the attention they crave from their distracted husbands, they will get it where they can. Clandestine sexual encounters occur not only in Buck's story, but in Roberta Silman's *Beginning the World Again* (1990) and other novels of life on the Hill. C. L. Sonnichsen thought that Thomas Wiseman risked being sued for libel for his portrayal of Helen Bamberger — a character logically identified with Kitty Oppenheimer — in *Savage Day* (66). Helen is the dutiful Los Alamos wife in public, but her boredom leads to torrid sexual encounters with two of her husband's colleagues.

This is not to say that all Los Alamos wives were neurotic or promiscuous. Nonfiction memoirs of life on the Hill tell of spouses who endured the hardships without complaint, led reasonably happy lives, and were supportive of their husbands' efforts.

On the positive side, many couples seem to have taken Los Alamos as an opportunity to start families. In her memoir of life on the Hill, Bernice Brode reports, "So many babies were born that the hospital had at one time nearly half its capacity used as a nursery" (141). Neighbors crowded the windows of the small hospital to see the new babies and wish their mothers well; but, according to at least one source, the military brass were not so pleased. In *Los Alamos Experience* (1985), former resident Phyllis K. Fisher reports that one of the generals, alarmed at the post's burgeoning population, ordered the commanding officer to "do something about it" (95). What the officer did is not recorded.

In a fictional treatment of wartime Los Alamos, Roberta Silman offers her interpretation of the baby boom. As Lily Fialka sees it in Silman's *Beginning the World Again*, the Los Alamos mother is making a statement, an affirmation of life: "For having a child was the most positive thing a wife here at Los Alamos could do, I suppose. And maybe making a baby had everything to do with making a gadget. For when your husband is working on a weapon capable of unknown and perhaps unprecedented destruction, perhaps the only thing a woman can do to convince herself of a future is to have a child" (233). Fialka also observes, on more than one occasion, that the tensions of life on the Hill made for some very good sex between husbands and wives.

SOUL SEARCHING

When the scientists were summoned to Los Alamos, they could hardly refuse to lend their expertise to the war effort. They suffered disruption of their lives, surely, but who didn't? They were subjected to the inconveniences of life on the Hill and the annoyance of subordination to military authority, but they did not face enemy fire on a daily basis. Nor did their families live in fear of a death message brought to them by a man in uniform. Moreover, their careers as intellectuals depended on the liberties for which the enlisted recruit was sent to fight and possibly die. Compared with the soldiers who suffered on Bataan, stormed the beaches at Normandy, and fought their way through Japanese fire to gain a foothold in the Pacific, they had little to complain about.

Even so, some of the scientists came reluctantly, and some did not come at all, due to concern about the moral and ethical consequences of the task they were asked to assume.

In the novels of Los Alamos and Trinity, wary scientists are quick to see where their work will lead. Stephen Coast sees it when he is prevailed upon by his mentor to join the project in Buck's *Command the Morning.* Coast at first resists the call to duty but later agrees to participate, based on the naïve premise that his involvement will allow him to influence the use of a weapon whose creation is, in any event, inevitable. By conviction, Coast is a resolute pacifist, but the shocking reality of Pearl Harbor brings him to compromise on principle and retreat to the uncertain refuge of wishful thinking.

In the novels of wartime Los Alamos, much of the impetus to build the atomic bomb comes from a fear that Germany is already well along in the development of such a weapon. If the Germans should succeed in creating a superbomb and catch the Allies with no comparable threat, then what? None of the scientists has a good answer for this, so most of them heed the call to national service.

Under duress of patriotic duty, the scientists begin their work, but the moral questions will not leave them alone. A question is raised, then another and another. As the project proceeds, doubts keep appearing, like snakes loosed in the dark spaces of the mind to slither amid the thoughts of the guilt-stricken scientists. Not all the scientists experience anguish; some accept no responsibility at all for the uses others may make of scientific principles which are, after all, extracted from nature. The moral questions are, therefore, divisive. They incite disagreement among the scientists themselves and set the "concerned scientists" at odds with military and political authorities.

A divide also exists between generations, as some of the scientists find that their actions and decisions are scrutinized critically by their own children. "You are all a bunch of stinkers," Burton Hall hears his son say in Buck's *Command the Morning;* "a bunch of old men plotting to kill off my generation!" (142).

Informed by his father that some things are more important than life, Tim Hall replies, "I don't know what they are, and if they're so damned precious, why don't you old fellows do the fighting. You've had your lives and we haven't" (143).

When it becomes clear that the Nazis do not have the capacity to produce a superbomb, some of the scientists see no reason to continue. Harvey Pillsbury, a physicist troubled by gnawing doubts about the project in Martin Cruz Smith's *Stallion Gate,* confides to a colleague his thoughts of quitting. "Nobody remembers," he says, "we started this project only because Hitler had his project, so he couldn't blackmail us with his bomb. Now it looks like he never made one. Now we say we're going to use it on Japan, which doesn't have any project" (90–91). The probability that Japan would have no compunction about using such a weapon if it were available makes no difference. Pillsbury insists there is a moral choice to be made, and faith to be kept with the original intent of the project. "Joe," Pillsbury tells his friend, "I didn't leave Amarillo to become a physicist to atomize a hundred thousand human beings" (91).

The scientists are not unanimous, however, in their responses to moral and ethical issues arising out of the war work. In *The Organ Builder,* a young interviewer questions one of the scientists years after the war, asking him why the project continued once its "ethical base" had evaporated. "The whole point of the project was to beat Hitler to atomic weapons wasn't it?" she asks. "And once he'd been beaten, didn't that call for some kind of reevaluation?" (129). Hostile in the face of the young woman's implied indictment, Dr. Ziobro unleashes a response: "'I didn't allow myself such sentimental notions,' he said. 'I didn't at the time, and I don't now. What is this ethical base you use like a bludgeon? Was it unethical of the apple to hit Newton on the head? Who says science grows from ethics? The thing was technically sweet. It worked. That was the thing that mattered'" (130).

Clearly the project took on a life of its own for many of the scientists. As they became more deeply engrossed in the intellectual and technical challenges, the linkage between task and purpose became hazy. The men pressed on, driven by their desire to see the great experiment to its logical conclusion. Recalling his Los Alamos childhood in Bradford Morrow's *Trinity Fields* (1995), Brice McCarthy characterizes the scientists as men driven "by their own love of a scientific challenge, a warm lust to push the envelope of theoretical and applied physics to the limit, as if to test its own tensile strengths, and all under the cloak of patriotism" (30).

David Bamberger confesses as much to a colleague in Wiseman's *Savage Day.* "If you really want to know," Bamberger admits, "the reason we are doing it is because it's an organic necessity. A scientist wants to know what lies underneath, that's what being a scientist is all about, and it's something you cannot stop because it's getting you into dangerous waters" (202). Bamberger explains that there is a great drive to finish off an experiment that is "technically very sweet." The skeptical colleague responds, "Would you feel obliged to discover bubonic plague if it didn't exist — just because you'd gotten some germ culture that was technically very sweet?" (202).

As the day of Trinity approaches, tensions build; those most concerned with the consequences of their labors turn their attention to the issue of control of the devices they have created. In Silman's *Beginning the World Again,* Erik Traugott, a character based on Niels Bohr, presses the notions of openness and international control with respect to nuclear weaponry, but his ideas are lost on American and British political leaders. Deeply distressed, Traugott leaves Los Alamos and returns to England to await the inevitable.

Once the bomb has been dropped, few of the scientists have occasion to survey the damage in person. One who does is Benno Halverson in Michael Amrine's *Secret* (1950), one of the first books to probe the meaning of the bomb. Having agreed to go to Japan and view the consequences of his work at first hand, Halverson lies in bed beside his sleeping wife and comes to the realization that the bomb has fallen on real people — that, even now, those irradiated beyond recovery are lying in their beds "awaiting the gradual dissolution of their living cells" (77). Halverson walks among the ashes, sees the bones of the dead and looks into the hollow

Dexter Masters.
*Courtesy Consumers
Union Archives.*

faces of the living. He returns to the United States shaken, bereft of his faith in science as an instrument of human progress.

Japan's surrender does not bring an end to the scientists' troubles. Some who might have countenanced the bomb's use at Hiroshima cannot reconcile themselves to the use of a second bomb so quickly. To some, including Silman's Lily Fialka, the bombing of Nagasaki seems a gratuitous and unforgivable travesty.

The scientists' continuing concern over control of nuclear weapons leads some of them into a political crusade of sorts. In Amrine's *Secret*, Benno Halverson travels to Washington to assume an active role in the Federation of American Scientists, also known as "The League of Frightened Men." Halverson promotes the principle of civilian control of atomic energy, speaking to groups and lobbying members of Congress, but he succeeds mainly in raising suspicions about his own loyalty.

Neither does the coming of peace write a finish to the ambitions of the scientists and the military officials who egg them on. Having helped win the war, many of the men return to their homes and jobs, but some stay to investigate other possible uses of atomic energy and to work on an even more powerful weapon. One of those remaining is Louis Saxl in *The Ac-*

cident (1955), a powerful novel by Dexter Masters. Based on a famous incident in which Louis Slotin took a massive and fatal dose of radiation in a laboratory accident, the novel chronicles the agonizing death of Saxl, an engaging young scientist whose life is tragically and painfully cut short. As Saxl lies feverish in the small hospital at Los Alamos, sliding toward delirium and death, his colleagues reflect anew on the dangers they have wrought, and on their loss of direction as men of science. Saxl is not one of the nameless, faceless masses whose fate it is to die across the ocean at the conclusion of a long and terrible war. He is one of their own, and his death due to forces unleashed at Los Alamos underscores the apprehension with which his colleagues and countrymen must attempt to resume their normal lives in a frightening new age.

AFTER THE HOLOCAUST

In *Nuclear Holocausts: Atomic War in Fiction, 1895–1984* (1987), Paul Brians lists several hundred novels and stories contemplating nuclear war and its aftermath. They reflect a penchant among writers and publishers for that which is novel or sensational, but they also express the very real fears of people living in a nuclear age. Many are science-fiction pieces written to entertain the reader who prefers star wars and otherworldly creatures, but many others are thought-provoking projections into an ominous future in which nuclear weapons again are loosed upon the world. In the latter group, the writer undertakes to imagine an eventuality that is widely regarded as unthinkable.

Virtually all of these works hark back to the chain of events involving Los Alamos, Trinity, Hiroshima, and Nagasaki. New Mexico is not as central to these works as it is to those concerning the development of the bomb, but this body of literature does include random glimpses of the region in the aftermath of nuclear war.

One of the most sweeping holocaust novels is Walter M. Miller's *A Canticle for Leibowitz* (1959), a science-fiction classic. In three parts depicting events separated by several hundred years, the book reveals the experience of the monks of the Order of St. Leibowitz. Miller checks in on the brothers every five hundred years or so, over a period of nearly two millenia following the "flame deluge."

The monks live in an abbey in the desert Southwest, where they work to preserve what remains of human knowledge after the deluge. The location of the abbey is indefinite, but the scanty geographical references point to New Mexico as a likely setting. Dom Paulo de Pecos, an abbot serving in the thirty-second century A.D., is addressed care of the Monastery of the Leibowitzian Brethren, Environs of Sanly Bowits Village, Southwest Desert, Empire of Denver. The abbey is also described as lying along a road supposed to have been "a portion of the shortest route from the Great Salt Lake to Old El Paso" (4).

The events recorded in Miller's novel reveal two enduring and apparently immutable impulses of mankind. They are the urge to pursue knowledge and progress, and the propensity for violent conflict, the effect of which is to destroy that which has been created. In the centuries immediately following the flame deluge, darkness descends on the human spirit; barbaric tribes inhabit the land, preying on weaker and gentler inhabitants. At length there is a resurgence of scientific and intellectual activity and, with it, the resumption of wars among nations. The cycle is completed as nuclear war breaks out in the thirty-eighth century. The monks of St. Leibowitz, guardians of knowledge, launch a colony of space travelers, sending along the precious "memorabilia" in the hope that future generations may use the learning of their forebears more wisely.

Nearly forty years after publication of *A Canticle for Leibowitz* came an astonishing sequel, *Saint Leibowitz and the Wild Horse Woman* (1997). The book is substantially the work of the reclusive Miller but was completed by science-fiction writer Terry Bisson after Miller's death. The profound effects of a holocaust long past are still evident in the thirty-third century A.D. Birth defects have created a society apart in the Valley of the Misborn, and warring factions contend for dominance in the region. Still, in the story, Miller expresses considerable hope, depicting two lovers who remain devoted to one another despite events and obligations that keep them apart. A map prepared at Bisson's direction establishes much of the action in New Mexico, with the Abbey of St. Leibowitz located near present-day Abiquiu.

In *Good News* (1980), Edward Abbey blames the outbreak of nuclear war on a breakdown of social values — the result of unbounded industrial development, severe degradation of the environment, and a massing of people under stress in great, inhospitable cities. Jack Burns, a character last encountered as "the brave cowboy" in Abbey's second novel, has made his way from New Mexico to look for his son among the ruins of Phoenix. He finds the city a smoldering, socially dysfunctional ruin, dominated by a self-appointed autocrat known only as "the Chief." The Chief has delusions of grandeur, including the conquest and reunification of a fragmented American nation.

Instead of learning from the catastrophe, the Chief vows to rebuild and complete the subjugation of the earth and its creatures. As the Chief explains, his will be "a thoroughly technological state": "The conquest of Nature, once far advanced, now temporarily interrupted, will be resumed and completed. Not a single square foot of soil, nor a single living creature, will ever again be allowed to escape the service of humankind, society, and the State" (96). The fate of the Chief's quest is unknown. As in *The Brave Cowboy*, Jack Burns defies overwhelming odds to oppose the political authorities, with uncertain results.

The most realistic portrayal of post-holocaust New Mexico occurs in *Warday and the Journey Onward* (1984), by Whitley Strieber and James Kunetka. "Warday" refers to October 28, 1988, when a thirty-six-minute nuclear exchange has destroyed the cities of New York, Washington, and San Antonio, along with selected military targets. Heavy losses also have been inflicted on the Soviet Union. A new national capital has been established at Los Angeles, but the federal government remains ineffectual. A new Hispanic state of Aztlán has been declared in the vicinity of El Paso, Texas. With the U.S. weakened and politically fragmented, Japanese influence is felt as never before.

Appearing in the book as themselves, Strieber and Kunetka tour the country in 1993 to survey the impact of the world's first nuclear war. Starting from Dallas, they traverse the West, then head back across the country to New York before returning home. Even a limited war, they find, has produced severe and lasting consequences. Some 250,000 people are still dying each month from the effects of radiation. Transportation and communication remain crippled, in part because of massive electromagnetic pulse radiation generated by the Soviets on Warday. Millions of electronic devices have been disabled; automobiles equipped with electric starters — those manufactured before 1977 — are still on the road and in great demand.

The authors make a point of visiting Los Alamos, birthplace of the bomb. Without the accustomed infusion of government paychecks, Los Alamos quickly withered following Warday. Much of the sophisticated laboratory equipment and many of the scientists have been taken to a new atomic city in Japan. Locally, scientists are objects of scorn. Those who remain have turned to farming, using their skills to develop better methods of cultivation. The visiting writers observe that "Los Alamos, for all its modern history, is returning to ancient ways" (110).

LIVING WITH THE BOMB

Is life worth living in a world under constant threat of nuclear annihilation? This question is asked and partially answered by Pulitzer Prize–winning author Robert Olen Butler in an early and generally unsung novel, *Countrymen of Bones.* (1983). Unlike the science-fiction futurists, Butler looks to the past, rather than to the future, for answers.

In Butler's novel, as Robert Oppenheimer prepares for an initial test of the fabled "gadget," Darrell Reeves, an archeologist from the University of Santa Fe, probes a most unusual discovery in the New Mexico desert, in the shadow of Trinity Site. Racing against time, Reeves and his assistants uncover the bones of a westering party of native Mound Builders — people who apparently fled before the ominous advance of the Spanish. His world shaken by a negation of its known boundaries, besieged by an awesome new power, the chief of the Mound Builders has chosen death, taking three sacrificial virgins along to the hereafter.

Warned of the impending blast, Reeves digs on while his own world awaits the emergence of another new and menacing force. As the countdown to Trinity proceeds, Reeves and his companion, Anna Brown, face a choice which is analogous, if not precisely comparable, to that of the ancient tribe whose fate is told in the pit of bones. They can surrender to the ominous threat of nuclear holocaust and die, or they can choose life, with all its risks and uncertainties. They choose to live, freewheeling toward the nearby mountains in an army sedan and disappearing over the ridge as the predawn sky explodes with light.

In a nonfiction work, *Living with the Bomb* (1985), Dorothy Rowe examines the psychological stresses inherent in life in a nuclear age. One need only consider the passions that have raged for centuries in remote corners of the world to be assured that conflict and danger abound in all times and places. Yet one needs only to contemplate the destructive power of the weapons created at Los Alamos to conclude that the stakes for peace have been raised to a new and frightening level. If the natives are edgy, who can blame them?

Rowe considers the threat of nuclear war to be an actual and potential cause of clinical depression, and she ponders the courage required to live with the prospect of such terror — courage to confront fears, to struggle with the demons that afflict contemporary society, to connect across geographical and cultural boundaries, to change, and to love.

The fictional characters of wartime Los Alamos — scientists, technicians, spouses, and children — live not only with the omnipresent threat of holocaust, but also with their own conflicted recollections of the bomb's creation. Though young at the time of the Manhattan Project, many who were present on the Hill as children of the bomb makers find that they cannot outlive their memories of the project. Nor has time healed the wounds that some have suffered.

Herschel Freeman, though a successful New York businessman, is still among the walking wounded when, as an adult, he visits New Mexico to sift through the shards of a shattered childhood, in Robert Cohen's *The Organ Builder*. The son of a gifted scientist at the time of the Manhattan Project, Hesh witnessed his family's own private implosion as his father vanished from the Hill and his mother became an alcoholic.

Haunted by the "why" of his lost youth, Hesh gropes for answers. None are to be found in his mother, a burned-out, unresponsive shadow of a woman who lives quietly in a Santa Fe nursing home. But in the discovery of his father's spiritual rebirth as a craftsman who found peace far from the tensions and moral contradictions of Los Alamos — whose scientific knowledge and passion for life were merged in the creation of beautiful pipe organs — Hesh finds partial reconciliation.

Lily Fialka's memories of Los Alamos have slumbered quietly in a distant corner of her mind for nearly forty years when they are awakened by her grown son's antinuclear activism, in Silman's *Beginning the World Again*. Lily's husband is a man at peace with himself — a septuagenarian who has spent his life after World War II teaching and pursuing peaceful uses of atomic technology. Weary of defending the past, Peter Fialka has no appetite for protest. He considers many of his son's ideas naïve, but he does not begrudge his wife and son their sentiments.

It is Lily who needs to bring closure to the part of her life that began on the Hill. With her son, Tony, and with friends from her days as a Los Alamos wife, she walks amid a throng of marchers who have gathered in New York to call for nuclear disarmament. The conflicting emotions of Lily's life are reconciled as she comes to appreciate her husband for the war work they thought would bring peace to the world, and her son for the acts of conscience in which she finds renewed hope. Lily is hopeful, but she is not so naïve as to believe in simple, final solutions to the scourge of human conflict. "For, unlike war," she concludes, "peace has no drama, no end. In peacetime you need more than faith and brains; you need the strength of Atlas, of all the Gods on Mount Olympus, all the gods in every religion, everywhere" (414).

Frank Waters.
Photo by Martin Shaffer.
Courtesy The Harwood
Museum, University of
New Mexico, Neg. 168.81.

There are lingering issues to be resolved, too, by children of Los Alamos in Bradford Morrow's *Trinity Fields* (1995). Brice McCarthy and Kip Calder grow up as friends on the Hill, then take divergent paths, one fighting in Vietnam and the other becoming a war resister. Both are haunted by the legacy of Los Alamos, where their fathers helped to create the atomic bomb.

Following a long estrangement and Kip's return from Vietnam, they rendezvous at El Santuario de Chimayo for a time of reconciliation and healing. Kip relates his view of the war in Vietnam, which he sees as a fitting antidote to the American arrogance born at Los Alamos. Brice, as a middle-aged husband and father, has made peace with his legacy as a child of Pajarito, but he knows that, once out of the bottle, the atomic genie cannot be put back. Resigned to the inevitability of human conflict, he acknowledges a depressing reality: "The arsenal Trinity fathered is vast and there are despots not born yet whose pleasure will be to make it vaster and threaten to give us another glimpse of its fearful magic" (426). There is just so much one can do to exorcise the demons of the past, when they remain so much a part of the present.

Only Frank Waters seems able to find anything edifying in the detonation of a hydrogen bomb — a device many times more powerful than the atomic bombs dropped on Hiroshima and Nagasaki. In *The Woman at Otowi Crossing* (1966), Waters juxtaposes the scientific quest for atomic weapons with the ancient wisdom of the Rio Grande pueblos and comes up with the metaphysical equivalent of Einstein's theory of relativity.

While observing a thermonuclear blast in the Pacific, Edmund Gaylord cannot but think of the dying Helen Chalmers, a remarkable visionary who has befriended the men on the Hill, providing a safe haven from their labors in her tearoom by the Rio Grande. As Gaylord beholds the explosion of light and energy over the island of Elugelab, he experiences an epiphany. The spectacular release of energy from the hydrogen atom is for him as the release of Helen's indomitable spirit from her frail earthly body. In the monstrous ball of fire, Gaylord sees not death only, but light and life. Life and death, he sees, are not contradictory and inimical forces, as is commonly supposed; they are but two faces of a perfect and indivisible whole.

That's a thought to hold, surely, should the forces of Armageddon ever escape the fragile bonds of reason and restraint, to rain fires of holocaust on the people of planet Earth.

11 THE HOLLYWOOD SPIN

Once the motion-picture industry roared to life and cameras started to roll on films inspired by the legendary American West, it did not take discerning writers long to see how the land lay. Eugene Manlove Rhodes saw a half-dozen of his early stories produced as blood-and-thunder one- and two-reelers and pronounced the West, as portrayed on the silver screen, "too much of the old hokum bucket" (Hutchinson, 143).

Rhodes's contemporary, Bertha Muzzy Bower, expressed her dismay with Hollywood through Luck Lindsay, a plucky young producer of western movies in her 1916 novel, *The Phantom Herd*. Luck swims against the tide of his industry, because his one shining principle in movie making is realism. If his film calls for Indians, he wants Indians — not painted, costumed white men. If a scene calls for a stampede, he wants a real stampede, "not a bunch of galloping tame cows urged to the foreground by shouting and rock-throwing" (22). Disgusted with the claptrap he has been grinding out under the watchful eye of studio managers, Luck is in New Mexico to make the kind of realistic western that he wants and believes the public wants:

"The West — the real honest-to-goodness, twelve-months-in-the-year West," Luck ventilates, "has been mighty little used in films. Ever notice that?

"It's all gone to shooting, and stealing the full product of all the gold mines in the world, and killing off more bad men than the Lord ever sent a flood to punish. For film purposes, the West consists of one part beautiful maiden in distress, three parts bandit, and two parts hero. Mix these to taste with plenty of swift action and gunsmoke, and serve with bandits all dead or handcuffed and beautiful maiden and hero in lovers' embrace on top. That's your film West, boys — and how well I know it!" (42–43)

Despite Luck Lindsay's protestations, the formula described by Bower in 1916 continued to serve the commercial interests of Hollywood throughout most of the twentieth century. The early history of the motion picture industry's use of stories with New Mexico settings, in fact, consisted mainly in the production of inconsequential films adapted from inferior literary properties. But as the industry matured, so did the body of literature available for adaptation. As the century wore on, Hollywood proved a discerning judge of literary material. Some very respectable films eventually were made from some of New Mexico's best novels, but all bore the unmistakable imprint of the Hollywood treatment.

A SECOND AND DIFFERENT TELLING

Novels have been a dependable source of good story material for motion pictures for approximately as long as the industry has been in business. In a good novel, suitable for adaptation, much of the creative work already has been done. Interesting characters have been developed, scenes have been suggested, and, presumably, an engaging plot has been devised to hold the attention of the audience. Seemingly, the producer need only bring sufficient talent and material resources to bear in order to translate the story into the medium of film.

The process seems simple enough, and the prospects for success would seem to be weighted heavily in Hollywood's favor, since the movie maker has the advantage of an appealing story which may have achieved sufficient acclaim to generate anticipation of the film version.

Why, then, do so many adaptations of literary works fail to live up to the expectations of readers eager to see a favorite novel brought to life on the screen? Why do so many film industry professionals seem to treat the author's literary purpose with such disregard? And how is it that a vibrant motion picture sometimes can be inspired by a slight and poorly crafted work of fiction?

The answer seems to lie in the major differences inherent in the two media, literature and film. The novel and the film are distinct creatures, calling for different creative talents and requiring different approaches and techniques. They are as different from each other, says George Bluestone, "as ballet is from architecture" (5). Given the innate dissimilarities, he argues, it should come as no surprise that significant changes occur in the transformation from novel to film. Such changes, in his view, are not only probable, but inevitable. "In the fullest sense of the word," Bluestone says, "the filmist becomes not a translator for an established author, but a new author in his own right."

Mature professionals like John Nichols and Max Evans understand this. In a protracted memoir on the trials of getting *The Milagro Beanfield War* made, Nichols (1987b, p. 15) concurs in the conventional wisdom that, to successfully adapt a literary work for the screen, "you buy the book and throw it away." Despite his passion for ideas expressed in his novel, Nichols acknowledged and accepted an inevitable divergence in his interests as author and those of the filmmakers.

Invited to comment on adaptations of three of his novels, including *The Bravados,* Frank O'Rourke acknowledged to an interviewer that screenwriting was "an art in itself," one that he had no desire to pursue. He believed that the purchase of film rights entitled the filmmaker to a good deal of discretion: "I don't have much sympathy for writers who say, 'Oh, they ruined my book.' That's not true, they *have* their book. The movie belongs to the film people, the book is yours and your book is still there after the movie is made" (Ross, 364).

Patricia Skarda (1996) characterizes the film as "a second and different telling," relative to the literary work upon which it is based. Film is multidimensional, incorporating visual images and sound, along with dialogue and limited text. Image and sound may be used to impart information and convey meaning, taking the place of verbal descriptions in the printed text; they also can be used to convey symbolic content.

For Bluestone, the critical distinction between novel and film concerns the thought process of the reader or viewer. While the motion picture audience receives meaning through direct perception of images, language, and sound, the written word of the novel requires something more of the reader. The printed text "must be translated into images of things, feelings and concepts through the process of thought." As noted by Gerald Peary and Roger Shatzkin (1977), opinions vary concerning the levels of intellectual energy required of those attending to the two media. While the reader must conjure up complex images from the text, the cinema viewer sometimes is called upon to decipher equally complex symbols encrypted by the filmmaker.

There are other significant differences which influence the process of adaptation. The novelist can proceed at a leisurely pace, spinning out lengthy descriptions of time and place, introducing and developing numerous characters, and weaving multiple plots and subplots. The screenwriter, on the other hand, must get the story told in something less than 140 pages of text; this entails considerable compression, likely involving the elimination of minor characters and simplification of the plot. This effect is evident, for example, in the film version of *The Milagro Beanfield War*. In a novel covering some 445 large pages of small type, Nichols is free to create a mind-boggling array of characters. In the film, some are omitted, while others presumably fade into the cast of extras who people the village of Milagro.

Screenwriter Ben Brady observes (1994) that the novel is a recounting, while the film is a recreation of events. The novelist usually speaks to the reader in the past tense, but the film happens in the present, unfolding before the eyes of the viewer.

The dramatic film requires plot and action — elements that are, to some degree, optional for the novelist. Writing in 1957, Bluestone observed, "It is a commonplace by now that the novel has tended to retreat more and more from external action to internal thought, from plot to character, from social to psychological realities" (46). The novelist reveals the inner lives of his characters with ease, but, because the film audience knows screen characters only by observable actions and dialogue, the revelation of their secret thoughts is more difficult for the filmmaker. Similarly, when much that is of interest to the novelist goes on in someone's head, there may not be much for the filmmaker to show; the film medium calls for action.

The film also needs a plot as the focus of the viewer's attention — preferably one centering on a conflict to be resolved. The problem belongs to the protagonist, with whom the audience is invited to identify; the protagonist's problem becomes the viewer's problem as well. It is the task of the screenwriter, Brady believes, to "isolate the *struggle* that will involve the protagonist" (6).

Given such considerations, the episodic or plotless novel poses obvious problems. In the absence of a compelling dilemma, the reader must be patient and invest a good deal of her or his own intellectual energy in the story. This is something that motion picture companies rarely are willing to expect of their audiences. This, in part, explains why fine literary novels like Willa Cather's *Death Comes for the Archbishop* (1927), William Eastlake's *Dancers in the Scalp House* (1975), and Abbey's *The Monkey Wrench Gang* (1975) have yet to appear on the screen, despite their many virtues, including some highly animated action sequences and likely visual appeal. Cather develops a rich portrayal of Father Jean Marie Latour and conveys her admiration for the faith and sacrifice of many of the early missionary priests, but she does so through an accretion of small incidents; no compelling dilemma demands resolution.

As "regional" literary works are adapted for film, the screenwriter is likely to focus on a central conflict of assumed universal appeal, discarding much detail that is of merely local or regional interest. Amid the pressure to condense the original work, such material may be considered expendable; in addition, the screenwriter must appeal to a large and diverse audience, not a regional one. This may help to explain why Harvey Fergusson's *Wolf Song* (1927) and *Hot Saturday* (1926) were transported from New Mexico to California when adapted as motion pictures, and why the producers of Zane Grey's *Fighting Caravans* took little interest in details of the Santa Fe Trail and Lucien Maxwell's feudal estate on the Cimarron River.

The filmmaker also is influenced by current fashion in the film industry and may feel compelled to shape a story from a literary source to conform to the expectations of a particular film genre — Western, *film noir,* or family-oriented comedy, for example.

Some filmmakers have made more extensive use than others of the creative license afforded them by their acquisition of rights to adapt a popular novel for the screen. No group of movie makers, though, has taken greater liberties with the literary antecedents of their films than have the early purveyors of the Wild West.

THE FILM WEST

The classic western story, with its cowboy hero, clash of values, and violent resolution, grew up alongside the emerging motion picture industry. According to Will Wright's *Six-Guns and Society: A Structural Study of the Western* (1975), it was in film that the western myth found its fullest expression. It has been through film, Wright observes, that "the myth has become part of the cultural language by which America understands itself" (12). Zane Grey, Louis L'Amour, and other masters of western myth have taken their tales to millions, but movies and television have reached their tens of millions.

It is also true that some essential elements of the western formula are better expressed on film than in print. Of the four essentials named by John Milton — the hero, violence, love, and the western landscape — violence and landscape are eminently suited to expression on film. Violence implies motion and action, attributes favored by the filmmaker; even when one knows what is coming, it is difficult to ignore the animation and percussive effect of a good fistfight or gun battle. The rugged landscape of Utah's Monument Valley has become almost trite as a western setting, but it is a rare Western that has not made some use of mountain, desert, or rangeland in panoramic footage meant to convey the boundless freedom and danger of the frontier West.

A fifth element of the western formula, particularly as it is expressed in film, is the horse. By its presence, says Jane Tompkins in *West of Everything: The Inner Life of Westerns* (1992), the horse "has an extraordinary influence on our experience of Westerns. The sheer energy of the posse, chasing the bandits at breakneck speed, pulling up short, the horses' mouths foaming, bridles clanking, saddles creaking, hooves churning the sand; the fleeing villains stopping at a lookout point, wheeling around, pausing for a moment, then turning and galloping off again in a cloud of dust — these images are the heart and soul of a Western" (90).

Moreover, observes Jenni Calder, the horse is a powerful symbol of freedom, as well as a status symbol for its rider (1975). We see this notion at work in literature as well as in film. In at least three novels — Lawrence's *St. Mawr* (1925), Harvey Fergusson's *Proud Rider* (1935–36), and Conrad Richter's *The Lady* (1957) — the horse functions as an object of power and mystique.

More than fifty novels and stories with New Mexico settings have been adapted as motion pictures. Of these, at least three-fourths are Westerns. These run from early silent films to movies made for television and encompass numerous B-Westerns, as well as films that challenge the traditional myth.

The novels and stories of Eugene Manlove Rhodes have been used as source material for at least fourteen films, including two remakes. All but one of these are from the silent era, including several one-, two-, and four-reel pictures made in 1914 and 1915. It is doubtful that prints of some of the early silent films survive, but synopses of their plots give some indication of the manner in which the author's works were used. Rhodes needed and welcomed the money he received from motion picture rights, but upon seeing what the screenwriters wrought from his stories of southern New Mexico, he must have wondered why their producers bothered to purchase existing literary works.

In Rhodes's first novel, *Good Men and True* (1910), John Wesley Pringle is one of four men from the Rainbow Range who journey to El Paso and Juarez to rescue a friend, Jeff Bransford, who is held captive by agents of a corrupt judge, the dishonorable S. S. Thorpe; Bransford is the focal character of Rhodes's story. In the film version, Pringle is the main man, running for sheriff against Thorpe, and the person in need of rescue is his girl, Georgie Hibbler. The romantic angle, uncommon but not unknown in Rhodes's stories, is, in this instance, a fabrication of the screenwriter.

To judge by the scanty accounts in plot summaries, *Sure Fire* (1921), an adaptation of Rhodes's *Bransford in Arcadia; Or, The Little Eohippus* (1914); and *The Mysterious Witness* (1923), an adaptation of *Stepsons of Light* (1921), bore little resemblance to the stories upon which they were based. A 1917 film version of Rhodes's *The Desire of the Moth* (1916) and *The Wallop*, a 1921 remake starring Harry Carey, apparently came nearer expressing the author's intent.

An early silent film of interest for its New Mexico content is *The Penitentes*, produced in 1915 with film industry pioneer D. W. Griffith as "supervisor." According to a notice in the December 3, 1915, issue of *Variety* magazine, the film was about "a group of religious fanatics who inhabited New Mexico during the early part of the 17th century while that territory was still under the rule of the Mexican government." The reviewer identifies as the film's source a novel by R. Ellis Wales. The writer is badly misinformed concerning New Mexico and the Penitentes, and may or may not be mistaken concerning the attribution. The novel may have existed in the form of an unpublished manuscript, or it may have been published in a small and obscure edition. Wales was real enough, publishing sporadically in periodicals in the early decades of the twentieth century, but the novel is apocryphal.

Other silent-era adaptations of works originally set in New Mexico include *The Enchanted Hill* (1926), from Peter B. Kyne's novel of the same title; and two films adapted from novels by William MacLeod Raine. Hoot Gibson starred in *Burning the Wind* (1929), from the 1914 Raine novel, *A Daughter of the Dons;* and Buck Jones was featured in *A Man Four-Square*

(1926), from Raine's 1919 novel of the same name. Tom Mix starred in a 1919 adaptation of Charles Alden Seltzer's *The Coming of the Law* (1912). Filmed on the cusp of the talking-picture era, Fergusson's *Wolf Song* was produced in an unusual format; the movie was mostly in the familiar silent mode, but one reel introduced audiences to the innovation of sound. An off-screen romance between Gary Cooper and Lupe Velez, starring as Sam Lash and Lola Salazar, reportedly boosted interest in an otherwise unremarkable picture (Swindell, 100).

No writer of Westerns has yet produced more grist for Hollywood's mill than Zane Grey, whose works have provided material for over one hundred films. The first of more than thirty silent features appeared in 1918; a remake of *Riders of the Purple Sage* was produced for television in 1996.

By contracting for limited lease of film rights, Grey was able to maintain control over his stories and sell individual stories more than once. He also insisted on fidelity to the locations of his stories, and at times he used the contract to enforce his will concerning this matter (Kant, 139). Four of Grey's novels with New Mexico settings were adapted for the screen. *The Light of Western Stars* was made four times, *Sunset Pass* three, and *Fighting Caravans* and *Knights of the Range* once each.

Along with the last rendition of *The Light of Western Stars, Knights of the Range* typifies the B-Western of the forties. The 1940 film, with B-Western stars Russell Hayden and Victor Jory, features romance, gun battles, fisticuffs, a galloping orchestral score, and a classic B-Western element, the horseback chase. Having lost her mother and father, Holly Ripple takes charge of the old home ranch, depending on her "knights of the range" to stave off an epidemic of cattle rustling. The hands would do better at this, one suspects, if they did not spend so much of their time harmonizing around the old bunk house. Some Hollywood geography is apparent, as the Ripple ranch is located "on the Cimarron," with Portales and El Paso nearby.

Grey was one of the most successful commercial writers of his time, in part because of his willingness to write for the popular market. According to Jesse Lasky, mogul of Famous Players–Lasky (later Paramount), the studio felt at liberty to invent a new story without even consulting Grey, since it had purchased rights to his entire output and because "the plots were fairly predictable and interchangeable": "We could simply make up a Zane Grey title if we didn't have one and announce it for one of our contract players — probably Richard Dix because he was the outdoor type and good box-office bait. At one point we got so far ahead of Grey that we actually had pictures made and in the can before he started writing the books they were supposed to be taken from!" (198). Bibliographer Kenneth Scott challenges the veracity of Lasky's claim, but the anecdote indicates the extent to which the Hollywood crowd felt at liberty to impose its desires upon the creative processes of writers.

Scholars of literature and film have engaged in extensive analysis of the western formula and its variations. As found in motion pictures, the formula is distilled and simplified. It consists of elements already named, arranged in a morality play which varies little in its philosophical and psychological dimensions through countless evocations of the western myth. A hero, a man who stands apart from society, intervenes to defeat the forces of evil, as embodied in outlaws, rustlers, and other agents of corruption. The hero usually is a reluctant participant — an independent character who would prefer to mind his own business, but who finds himself morally obliged to aid the innocent and bring the guilty to justice. There are multiple variations on this theme, as detailed by Wright. The hero, for example, may be a decent man who has fallen in with outlaws and only needs someone to believe in him. This is the case in Grey's *The Light of Western Stars* and *Knights of the Range,* where a drunkard and a rustler are redeemed by the heroine's love.

A picture recognized as a benchmark in the development of the Western was *Stagecoach* (1939), adapted from the Ernest Haycox story, "Stage to Lordsburg," and directed by John Ford. The film marked Ford's first use of the rugged backdrop of Monument Valley. According to Fenin and Everson, it "rescued John Wayne from the rut of 'B' pictures" (240). The stagecoach, driven by Andy Devine, rumbles through the Arizona desert, headed for Lordsburg, New Mexico. Marauding Apaches threaten the safety of the passengers; and in Lordsburg, a showdown awaits the Ringo Kid, played by Wayne. In a variation on the usual western plot, the Kid, a man on the outs with society, proves himself worthy and is allowed to walk free.

Similar dynamics are at work in *Four Faces West* (1948), a notably unsuccessful film version of Rhodes's *Pasó Por Aquí* (1927). Hollywood set the film not in the Tularosa Basin, but around New Mexico's other Malpais, near Gallup and Grants. Aside from that and a few other modifications, the story follows Rhodes's novel. As the hard-luck bank robber, Ross McEwen, Joel McCrea sacrifices his escape to help a family in need. When

the law catches up and the sheriff sees what McEwen has done for an isolated ranch family under siege by diphtheria, he plays dumb and lets the
outlaw go.

After nearly a century of movie making, numerous changes in style,
and the introduction of films reflecting a revision of western myth, the old
formula still packs a wallop. For Jenni Calder, its origins in a relatively
brief period of American frontier history and its persistence over such a
long time indicate that the traditional myth of the West is, for many Americans, an "instinctive necessity." The Western long since passed its zenith,
but the myth continues to cast a long shadow on Hollywood's portrayals
of the frontier West.

In *The Bravados* (1958), a film adapted from Frank O'Rourke's novel,
viewers at first see the stereotypical western hero. As Jim Douglas, a man
out to avenge the murder of his wife, Gregory Peck says little when he
rides into the northern New Mexico town of Rio Arriba. He exhibits what
Tompkins diagnoses as an unhealthy aversion to language; he is *too* self-
contained. In town to witness the hanging of the four men he believes
guilty of killing his wife, Douglas is on hand when they break jail and take
flight. His struggle consists in bringing them to justice, but he overdoes it,
abandoning a posse to gun them down on his own. He also renews an old
acquaintance with Josefa Velarde, an attractive valley aristocrat who, conveniently, is still unmarried.

Unlike so many adaptations which omit meaningful content relative to
the original story, this one actually adds some. As it happens, the fugitives
are not guilty of the murder of Douglas's wife, though presumably they
are guilty of other, equally reprehensible crimes. Jim Douglas walks away
questioning his own moral judgment, a distinctly unheroic thing for a
western hero to do, but, in the view of Fenin and Everson, he gets off too
easy. Having taken the law into his own hands, he is not held accountable
for the questionable killing of the three fugitives. Instead, he is hailed as a
hero and, per formula, unites with the still-beautiful Josefa.

Peck also stars in the 1968 film adaptation of Theodore V. Olsen's *The
Stalking Moon* (1965), a story which takes the hero from the Arizona desert
to his mountain home near Gallup. Peck is Jim Varner, a cavalry scout —
not a member of the rank and file, but a man apart. Upon separation from
the army, Peck agrees to escort a white woman rescued from captivity
among the Apaches, along with her half-Indian son. Peck soon finds himself more involved than he intended with the mother and son, and locked
in a deadly contest with the boy's father, Salvaje. Intent on reclaiming his

son, the Indian stalks Varner's party to New Mexico, leaving a trail littered with victims. Cunning, strength, and evil are incarnate in the character of Salvaje, who poses a sinister threat to the white hero, much as the character Octavio in Edwin Shrake's novel, *Blessed McGill* (1968), and Buffalo Hump, in Larry McMurtry's *Dead Man's Walk* (1995), do.

While the western formula holds, some stylistic trends are evident in *The Stalking Moon*. Like the popular "spaghetti Westerns" of the period, *The Stalking Moon* incorporates long passages in which meaning is conveyed through sight and sound. Winds howl across the Arizona desert, and later Varner and Salvaje engage in a tense and deadly waiting game at Varner's remote mountain home, set amid soaring rocks and shadowy forest. Dark cabin interiors, sparse dialogue, and an eerie modern soundtrack are reminiscent of the early western films of Clint Eastwood and director Sergio Leone.

The formula was still alive in 1991, when Turner Network Television produced a made-for-television adaptation of Louis L'Amour's *Conagher*, starring Sam Elliott and Katharine Ross. L'Amour is an unabashed admirer of the solitary western hero, embodied here in Conn Conagher, a principled saddle bum who begins living up to his potential when inspired by the love and courage of Evie Teale, widowed mother of two. Conagher stands up to a parasitic band of rustlers in the wilds of west-central New Mexico, and the film proceeds per formula, a creditable production which tracks well with L'Amour's story.

Even as the B-Westerns were thundering out of Hollywood in droves, some divergent views were beginning to be expressed in films about the Old West. In 1945, Gary Cooper was both producer and star of *Along Came Jones*, an adaptation of Alan LeMay's New Mexico novel, *Useless Cowboy* (1943). As Melody Jones, Cooper plays a feckless westerner who hits town and — in a simple case of mistaken identity — finds himself feared by the locals as a bad man with a rep. Jones enjoys the unaccustomed respect until he is exposed by the real outlaw; but in the interim, his actions parody the image of the western hero.

Cooper reportedly was chastised by Cecil B. De Mille for making light of a myth cherished by the public. "If you kid a Western, if you kid a hero," De Mille scolded, "you are doing damage to yourself. People who come to see you — they want to see a fellow who can do no wrong and can come through in tough spots" (Kaminsky, 137). De Mille's dismay notwithstanding, the film was a creative highlight of Cooper's career, precisely because he dared to question the premises of the western formula.

Another awkward fit for the old formula was the 1947 film, *The Sea of Grass,* starring Spencer Tracy and Katharine Hepburn. The production closely follows Conrad Richter's novel, which could have a lot to do with its limited appeal as a film. As cattle baron Jim Brewton, Tracy exhibits some heroic qualities; but, sandbagged by competing principles and priorities, he is unable to focus his righteous anger on a single foe. He hates what the sodbusters represent, tearing up his big *vega* to plant crops he knows will not grow, but he cannot get his hands on the real culprits — misguided government policy and the westward movement of the agricultural frontier. Brewton would like to oppose the farmers who come to homestead, but his regard for himself as a law-abiding citizen will not let him fight the U.S. Cavalry to do it. With its intertwined plots, subtleties of motivation, and ethical ambiguities, *The Sea of Grass* was a departure from the usual western fare.

The traditional mold of the Western was shattered in *Lonely Are the Brave* (1962), an adaptation of Edward Abbey's *The Brave Cowboy* (1956). Supplied by a well-meaning admirer with a paperbound copy of the novel, Kirk Douglas picked it up in a moment of boredom, found himself captivated, and concluded that he had to make the film. The project was fraught with difficulties, but the finished product satisfied both the star and the author (Douglas, ix–xvi). The film's plot closely followed Abbey's novel, and it was shot on location in Albuquerque. Abbey (1994) declared himself delighted with Dalton Trumbo's screenplay and found the screen dialogue "much livelier, heartier, wittier, than my own" (174).

As Jack Burns, Douglas is sufficiently brave, strong, and resourceful to be a western hero; he does not have the killer instinct, however, and, once again, there is no adversary he can get his hands on. His nemesis is not a wild savage or a gang of outlaws, but changing times and a diffuse bureaucratic system. Neither are the moral and ethical issues as clear as the western hero likes them to be.

Max Evans's novel, *The Rounders* (1960) was adapted in 1965 as a moderately successful comedy starring Henry Fonda and Glenn Ford. The setting was changed from northeastern New Mexico to Sedona, Arizona, not because Sedona was more glamorous than Clayton, according to Evans (1995), but because a location-hunting expedition in New Mexico was sabotaged by winter weather, leading the producer to fall back on an established outdoor film location. As luckless cowboys enduring hard weather and harder work, then blowing a season's wages on a weekend binge, Dusty and Wrangler are hardly heroic in the usual sense. Rarely has a film

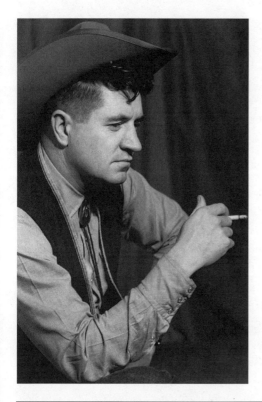

Max Evans.
Photo by Regina Cooke.
Courtesy The Harwood
Museum, University of New
Mexico, Neg. 3.80.

so fulfilled the purpose of an author; Evans calls *The Rounders* "the best *working cowboy film* to date."

Monte Walsh, a 1970 adaptation of Jack Schaefer's 1963 novel, is something of a hybrid Western. Lee Marvin stars as Monte Walsh, an aging cowhand who is increasingly out of place in a changing world. In a West teeming with ranches, cattle, and cowboys, Monte was in his element, but as times change and the old ways vanish, one is left with the sense that Monte has missed a crucial fork in the trail.

This much tracks with Schaefer's novel, but, in the interest of tapping into the appeal of a proven formula, the screenwriters have made some changes. In the book, Chet Rollins leaves his friend, Monte, to the cowboy life and becomes a successful businessman, surviving to mourn the passing of Monte and the era he represents. In the film, Rollins is murdered in his hardware store in the town of Harmony, leaving Monte to track his killer and avenge his wrongful death. In Schaefer's fine novel, the sun clearly is setting on an Old West of endless romance and invincible heroes, but the filmmakers cannot bring themselves to bury a myth that has served Hollywood so well for so long.

In *Dead Man's Walk* (1996), produced as a two-part television movie based on Larry McMurtry's novel, the table is set for Augustus McCrae and Woodrow Call, young Texas Rangers, to assume the role of western hero. They ride out from Austin with the Texan–Santa Fe expedition, intent on conquering new territory and defeating adversaries of inferior intelligence, strength, and courage. The Texans quickly are pitted against a fearsome Comanche Indian, Buffalo Hump, and later they have Gómez, a formidable Apache warrior, to dread. According to the traditional western formula, Call and McCrae are entitled to struggle mightily and then overcome the parched Llano Estacado, the Mexican army, and the Indians. But they don't. Captives of the Mexican soldiers, they leave their companions dead and scattered as they stumble downriver across the unforgiving Jornada del Muerto. Battered and beaten, the remaining stragglers are released at El Paso to find their way home.

Standing on its own, *Dead Man's Walk* would seem the very antithesis of the western formula, its "heroes" humiliated at the hands of foes who had fallen so reliably before the westering white man for decades. But, as faithful followers of Call, McCrae, and the Apostle Paul may know, suffering produces perseverance, and perseverance, character. The ill-fated New Mexico expedition became, for the two young Rangers, an unparalleled opportunity for personal growth — a learning experience that would help mold them into hardened frontier lawmen.

FILM NOIR

A film genre enjoying popularity for a time during the 1940s and 1950s was *film noir*, or "dark cinema." Growing out of the tradition of hard-boiled detective fiction, *film noir* features shadowy crime figures, manipulative temptresses, and undercover cops who move easily in a murky underworld. The atmosphere of these films was predominantly moody and menacing, sometimes nightmarish.

According to Foster Hirsch, *film noir* was at its peak between 1944 and 1950. While *noir* was a cinematic phenomenon associated primarily with the urban East, novels with New Mexico settings provided materials for two respected films in the *noir* tradition.

Hirsch recites a litany of trademark features associated with *film noir*. Cinematically, the films usually incorporate dark, hazy interiors, high contrast between light and shadow, and tight closeup shots — all calculated to heighten the film's sense of moodiness, gloom, and cynicism. A wailing jazz score sometimes is added to reinforce the depressive mood of the *noir* film.

Character types encountered in *film noir* include the sleuth, the criminal, the victim, and the scapegoat. Male characters include weak, easily manipulated men and toughs who talk in terse sentences edged with hostility. A period character commonly found in the genre is the shell-shocked war veteran who returns to society, a disoriented and scary misfit.

Of greater significance to the typical *noir* plot is the sexually potent female — a creature who can attract and manipulate men with ease but whose underlying character is that of a malevolent, scheming bitch-goddess. She can be charming, helpless, or coldly calculating as the situation demands. Cunning and spiteful, she leaves a trail of misery, achieving only a grim satisfaction in her control over others.

Film noir typically expresses a fatalistic vision and adopts a cold, detached view of human tragedy. In Hirsh's view, *noir* expressed the anxieties of the postwar world — a world unsettled by social change, Cold War neuroses, and the threat of nuclear war.

A film rich in the psychological dimensions of *film noir*, but not especially representative of its cinematic properties, was the 1945 production of Ben Ames Williams's *Leave Her to Heaven* (1944). Atypical for *noir* pictures, the production was filmed in color, and the settings are exclusively rural, including scenes in New Mexico, Georgia, and Maine.

The film owes its New Mexico connection to Williams's acquaintance with Oklahoma oilman Waite Phillips, whose New Mexico ranch later became Philmont Scout Ranch. Williams visited Phillips at the ranch in the 1920s and later incorporated much of what he saw there into *Leave Her to Heaven*. The film's "Glen Robie's New Mexico Ranch," called "Rancho Jacinto," was based on the Phillips spread. Readers familiar with the Philmont Ranch will see in the fictional Glen Robie and his son, Lin, much of Waite Phillips and his son Elliott. Phillips's Villa Philmonte home and Rayado River fishing lodge also figure prominently as settings in the novel.

According to Minor Huffman, general manager of Philmont Scout Ranch in the mid-1940s, Fox Studios considered filming the New Mexico portion of Williams's story at the ranch and sent a crew to scout the location. Deterred by the difficulties of wartime transportation and the expense of housing a large crew in a remote location, the studio elected to film the outdoor scenes nearer Hollywood. The studio also requested photographs of Phillips's big ranch home to aid in the construction of authentic sets. Huffman reports that two large volumes of photos were loaned for this purpose; however, there is no noticeable resemblance between the Philmont "big house" and Glen Robie's home in the film (119).

At the New Mexico ranch, writer Richard Harland, played by Cornel Wilde, is enthralled by another of Robie's guests, the beautiful and engaging Ellen Berent, played by Gene Tierney. Richard and Ellen are married almost immediately, but time reveals in Ellen a consuming jealousy of all competitors for Harland's attention, including his work, his invalid brother, and Ellen's own sister, Ruth. Harland's life descends into a hellish nightmare, and he is fortunate to survive tragic personal loss, a frame-up, and prison to make a hopeful new beginning with Ruth, portrayed in the film by Jeanne Crain.

A film more representative of the *noir* tradition is *Ride the Pink Horse* (1947), an adaptation of Dorothy Hughes's 1946 novel. Hughes's mystery novel undergoes considerable modification in the film, with many of the changes bringing the story into conformity with the characteristics of *film noir*.

Hughes's original story brings Sailor, a surly underworld figure, to Santa Fe at Fiesta time to settle a score with the corrupt Sen — Sen. Willis Douglas of Chicago. Uninvited, but also making the scene, is McIntyre, a Chicago homicide detective. Amid the burning of Zozobra and the ensuing revelry, Sailor engages the senator in a deadly game of extortion; McIntyre, meanwhile, does his best to interfere constructively on behalf of the law.

A similar plot is evident in the film, but the characters and situations are altered somewhat. Instead of Sailor, it is Lucky Gagin who gets off the bus in Santa Fe to find and blackmail crime boss Frank Hugo. Hugo dismisses his adversary as a haywire veteran who is resentful because he "fought a war for three years and got nothing out of it but a bunch of dangling ribbons."

Robert Montgomery served as both director and star, doing a bad Jimmy Cagney imitation in the role of Lucky Gagin. But the black-and-white film effectively captures the moody ambiance of *film noir* with its shadowy conversational scenes, unsavory characters, and tight-lipped, tough-guy dialogue. Footage of Santa Fe, Fiesta, and Zozobra, filmed on location at Montgomery's insistence, now qualify as "virtual ethnographic material," in the view of New Mexico film historian Casey St. Charnez (1996). The beloved Tio Vivo carousel, a fixture of Fiesta, was dismantled and reassembled on a Hollywood sound stage for additional filming (51).

The era of the *film noir* was short-lived. Given its preference for the contemporary metropolis, city streets, and smoky cocktail lounges, it is surprising that *noir* found its way to New Mexico at all. Despite its underlying premise of gloom and defeat, however, the *noir* tradition, as embodied in *Leave Her to Heaven* and *Ride the Pink Horse,* marks a refreshing departure from the portrayal of New Mexico as a setting for tired stories of the Old West.

DISCOVERING SOUTHWEST CULTURES

Aside from the Westerns, the film output from fiction with New Mexico settings in the last half of the twentieth century consists mainly of a handful of made-for-television movies and several features exploring the diverse cultures of New Mexico and the Southwest.

The made-for-television features—*The Hanged Man* (1964), a remake of *Ride the Pink Horse; Sweet Hostage* (1975), based on the Nathaniel Benchley novel, *Welcome to Xanadu* (1968); and *Fire on the Mountain* (1981), based on the Edward Abbey novel—are an undistinguished lot.

The spare environs of southern New Mexico and John Vogelin's Box V Ranch are well represented in the location and cinematography of *Fire on the Mountain,* and Buddy Ebsen makes a dandy Vogelin—an implacable old coot with an unswerving sense of justice and a wry sense of humor. But the production suffers from too much Ron Howard and a poorly developed romantic angle conjured up for the television audience.

In Abbey's novel, Lee Mackey is a leavening influence amid Vogelin's confrontation with the government over the taking of the Box V Ranch. A former hand turned businessman, Mackey is Vogelin's equal—both sensible and sympathetic, as he tries to help an old friend through a difficult time. As Mackey in the television version, Howard is a shrill and sleazy dude whose main goal in life has been to get rich quick. Despite his support for the cause, he comes nowhere near matching John Vogelin's stature, and he seems unworthy of the older man's confidence.

One of the first feature-length films to express serious interest in New Mexico's indigenous cultures was not a Hollywood picture, but a production of the U.S. Information Service—*And Now Miguel,* made in the early 1950s under the direction of Joseph Krumgold. The work was filmed on location, at a ranch near the rural village of Los Cordovas in the Taos Valley. The production was intended to show the daily lives of the sheep-raising Chavez family, and its characters were not actors, but family members known in the film by their own names. Krumgold did, however, give the film a dramatic context — an appealing story of a boy's wish to go with the men and help drive the flock to summer pasture in the mountains.

In this case, it was the film that inspired the book — a Newberry Award–winning novel for juveniles, written by Krumgold and published in 1953. A Hollywood adaptation of the story, costarring Guy Stockwell, Michael Ansara, Clu Gulager, and Pat Cardi, achieved moderate success; but the original black-and-white film remains an ethnographic treasure.

Viewers meet the Hispanic Southwest through the eyes of Josh Arnold in *Red Sky at Morning* (1971), the film adaptation of Richard Bradford's 1968 novel. As an Alabama teenager, involuntarily displaced when his father is called to war, Josh comes of age in the New Mexico village of Sagrado, making new friends and learning the ways and values of his Hispanic neighbors. In the view of St. Charnez, *Red Sky at Morning* is a better film of its type than the more highly acclaimed *Summer of '42* (1971). Much of the film was shot in Santa Fe, including scenes in and around the central plaza (1993, p. 25).

And Now Miguel became a source of pride for the Chavez family and their Taos Valley neighbors; but, as Robert Redford has discovered, the outsider's interest is not always appreciated by native peoples. Redford, director and coproducer, with Moctezuma Esparza, of the film adaptation of John Nichols's *The Milagro Beanfield War,* originally wanted to film in the village of Chimayo, just north of Santa Fe. When residents objected and would not be moved by Redford's good intentions or proffered location fees, he took the production up the road to the mountain village of Truchas. A lawsuit filed by land-grant activist Reies Lopez Tijerina, alleging unauthorized use of his life story, further complicated the production, but the issue was resolved, and the finished picture was released to theaters in 1988.

In Redford's view, the film portrays a culture under siege by land developers and other outsiders. It declines to deal with Nichols's deeper concern with the universal issue of class struggle and exploitation. Redford's rationale rests upon the severe limitations of the film medium, which, in his view, require that the filmmaker focus on a point and make it well. "Going much beyond that complicates the film," he told an interviewer (Steinberg, G9). It also may have occurred to Redford that a full-strength treatment of Nichols's socialist inclinations would do the film no good at the box office.

Nichols was pleased with the exposure the film gave his work, and he expressed his hope that viewers would be moved to read *Milagro* and *The*

John Nichols.
Photo by Juanita Franciscus.
Courtesy Juanita Franciscus.

Magic Journey (1978) — two of the most pointed expressions of his political ideas.

Redford found the going no easier when he undertook to produce an adaptation of Tony Hillerman's *The Dark Wind* (1982), a story which takes place mostly on the Navajo and Hopi lands of northeastern Arizona, but which includes a sojourn to Albuquerque and the University of New Mexico. The film, following Hillerman's novel, features a dramatic concluding pursuit which takes place amid a sacred ceremony of the Hopi. Some of the Hopi elders objected to any depiction of Hopi ceremonialism, precipitating some dissension among the Hopi people. Redford finally got the picture made, but it was not released for theater exhibition; it was, however, distributed as a home video release in 1991. Lou Diamond Phillips and Gary Farmer star as the two policemen — Jim Chee, the Navajo; and Cowboy Dashee, the Hopi.

A better film dealing with the realities of contemporary Native American life, and a better vehicle for the talents of Gary Farmer, is *The Powwow Highway* (1989), based on the novel by David Seals. Produced by Hand-Made Films, a British company co-owned by former Beatle George Harrison, the film retains all the wry social commentary and good humor of Seals's original.

As Philbert Bono, a naïve, overweight Cheyenne Indian with no apparent sense of urgency or direction, Farmer follows his hunch that there just might be something more to the heritage of his people than beads and feathers, despair and defeat. With nothing better to do, Philbert accompanies his friend, Buddy Redbow, on a mission to free Bonnie Redbow, Buddy's sister, who has been jailed in Santa Fe on trumped-up marijuana charges. The challenge motivates Philbert to seek his medicine — his power — as a Cheyenne warrior, which he does, taking a detour to Sioux country and the sacred Bear Butte. Redbow is characteristically cynical regarding Philbert's faith in the ways of the past, but Philbert is truly empowered, as the two men leave Dakota and head south to do battle with the white man's bureaucracy in Santa Fe.

Director Jonathan Wacks gets everything out of the material, revealing, in Philbert and his friends, a people who have endured great loss yet persevere in the white man's world with wisdom, dignity, and an indispensable sense of humor. That the film attained no greater public visibility is perhaps a discouraging indication of the difficulty involved in producing a film which does not directly cater to the big middle of contemporary American society.

A picture afflicted with this problem and several others is *House Made of Dawn* (1987), a less than satisfactory adaptation of Momaday's Pulitzer Prize–winning novel. The production attracted favorable attention for its casting of Native Americans in appropriate roles. The film has its moments, but it also illustrates the difficulties involved in using a visual medium to convey a journey which is mostly psychological, and focusing on a cultural group not given to incessant chatter. Film, after all, is mostly sight and sound. In this film, Abel's misery as a displaced and troubled Jemez Pueblo Indian is conveyed mainly through the pained facial expressions of suffering "relocation" Indians. Larry Littlebird, as Abel, can look miserable as well as anyone, but this can hardly be expected to carry a film which is seriously deficient in action and visual appeal. Despite the author's involvement in creating the screenplay — or perhaps because of it — the picture simply cannot approach the power of Momaday's novel.

FILMS AND RUMORS OF FILMS

Rumor and speculation are major byproducts of the motion picture industry. In addition to all the motion pictures made from New Mexico novels and stories, a good many more were supposed to have been made, or were almost made, or eventually might be made.

At the time Dexter Masters's *The Accident* was published in 1955, the *Illinois State Register* reported (April 21, 1955) that MGM already had purchased the motion picture rights, that David O. Selznick was going to spend $2 million on the production, and that Marlon Brando and Montgomery Clift were being considered for the lead role. There must have been some factual basis for the report, but it is just as likely that most of it was wishful thinking. In any event, no such picture was made, possibly because of the doubtful popular appeal of its grim subject matter. If the work ever should be adapted, someone will have to come up with a plot, because what worked for Masters in the book — a montage of flashbacks, philosophical debates, and hospital scenes — is unlikely to work well in a film.

At one time or another, other film adaptations have been reported as imminent. When *The Milagro Beanfield War* premiered in 1988, it was reported that coproducer Moctezuma Esparza would begin shooting a film version of Rudolfo Anaya's *Bless Me, Ultima* "within a year." At the same time, Redford expressed his intention to move ahead with a series of films based on the Tony Hillerman mysteries, starting with *Dance Hall of the Dead.* To date, neither film has seen the light of day.

By 1996, an effort to film Max Evans's *The Hi Lo Country* (1961) had resurfaced, and by the end of 1998 the movie had been made and released, with eastern New Mexico locations providing an authentic backdrop. Persistent rumors again were circulating to the effect that Abbey's *The Monkey Wrench Gang* at last would reach the screen. In the big-money world of Hollywood productions, nothing is for sure, as many long-suffering writers can attest. But it does seem probable that efforts to promote New Mexico as a shooting location will focus increased attention on the state's resident literary properties, and that some of those stories eventually will attain new life in a second and different telling, Hollywood style.

12 WRITING NEW MEXICO

By now it should be apparent that fiction writers have had a good deal to say about New Mexico and its inhabitants in the years since Timothy Flint sent his wandering hero, Francis Berrian, down the Rio Grande in a novel published in 1826. In the beginning, much of the writing was done by people who had little or no attachment to the Southwest and little appreciation for the land or its people. Some had visited the area only briefly, and some had no personal knowledge of the country at all.

But the natural beauty and cultural riches of the Southwest began to attract visual artists toward the end of the nineteenth century, and writers soon followed. Some stayed. By 1916, it was possible to discern the beginnings of a growing community of writers who found in New Mexico an agreeable and stimulating climate in which to live and work. In that year, Alice Corbin Henderson took up residence in Santa Fe; and Mabel Dodge Sterne — later Luhan — discovered a compelling spirit in New Mexico, returning to make her residence in Taos the following year. Both women were writers, but their greater contributions consisted in efforts to inspire and cultivate literary activity in their respective communities. For Marta Weigle and Kyle Fiore, their arrival marked the beginning of an active "writer's era" in Santa Fe and Taos. From this date forward, both communities consistently drew visiting writers and immigrants who stayed to live and write. D. H. Lawrence discovered New Mexico, as did Mary Austin, Myron Brinig, Willa Cather, Oliver La Farge, Raymond Otis, Conrad Richter, Carl Van Vechten, Frank Waters, and many others.

For Weigle and Fiore, the writer's era ends in the early 1940s, with the outbreak of World War II and a shift in the locus of creative energy from the art colonies to the new atomic city of Los Alamos. In fact, New Mexico has continued to attract resident and visiting writers, and at the threshold of the twenty-first century, there are still plenty of writers around. Santa Fe and Taos remain centers of literary activity, but Albuquerque also can point to a dozen or more widely published fiction writers living in the city, including several mystery writers and some noted science-fiction specialists. More surprising is the emergence of Las Cruces as a crucible of literary creativity, with talented writers resident in the English Department of New Mexico State University and in the community.

As for likely objects of attention for present and future observers of life in New Mexico and the West, some suggestions offered to historians may apply equally to fiction writers. According to Donald Worster, the contemporary agenda ought to include at least three objectives. "First," says Worster, "the invaded and subject peoples of the West must be given a voice in the region's history" (16). Indeed, minority perspectives are essential to an understanding of the region. The ones already available are invaluable. Others should be welcomed, not only with respect to history, but concerning every other aspect of life as it is lived in these parts. The second vital theme suggested by Worster concerns economic development and its impact on the environment and the people of the West. Third, Worster suggests that historians examine power structures, identify privileged elites, and consider issues of power and social class. To this list, some surely would add that writers and historians should be paying more attention to the roles and experience of women in the West.

These are all fine suggestions, and Worster may well have named the topics that will dominate discussions of regional identity for the immediate future. Larry McMurtry points out (1990) that these issues have not entirely escaped the attention of earlier historians, however. He names Henry Nash Smith, Ross Calvin, Angie Debo, and Walter Prescott Webb among those who had a clue before the new western history was discovered.

Neither have creative writers failed to recognize and address these issues. It is the nature of art to run ahead of orthodoxy, to question conventional assumptions and challenge authority; fiction writers have been doing this out west for quite some time. The interest of commercial publishers in minority perspectives may be a recent phenomenon, but perceptive Anglo writers have been dealing forthrightly with issues of invasion and conquest in New Mexico since the 1920s, at least. Edwin Corle, William Eastlake, Harvey Fergusson, Oliver La Farge, and Frank Waters all saw and wrote about the tragic consequences of Anglo-American domination for many among the region's native peoples. The federal government's role in the West — a matter of recent, intense interest for the New Western historians — was much on the mind of Edward Abbey in the 1950s and 1960s; Raymond Otis had seen the profound effects of a growing federal presence in the West in the 1930s. Abbey, William Eastlake, and John Nichols were dealing forcefully with the issues of economic development and environmental degradation in the 1970s, and Nichols became intensely interested in examples of class struggle in the region at about the same time. Much earlier works by writers like Emerson Hough, Florence Finch Kelly, and Eugene Manlove Rhodes anticipated some of these issues.

The recurrence of themes and ideas in the substantial body of fiction set in New Mexico is illustrative of the difficulty that writers may face in trying to come up with truly original notions. This is not to say, in the manner of Turner and the Census Bureau, that the frontier is closed and that there are no more new ideas to be explored in the region's literature. Readers undoubtedly will learn much from new literary voices expressing the viewpoints of previously underrepresented female and minority populations. In addition, as the creation and testing of the atom bomb introduced a new, complex, and provocative subject, there are likely to be further developments worthy of literary treatment. Writers undoubtedly will continue to investigate and, in some cases, reinterpret familiar genres and themes in the New Mexico experience.

DIVERSE TRADITIONS, MULTIPLE REALITIES

Not so long ago, the preponderance of English-language fiction about New Mexico subjects was produced by Anglo males from elsewhere. New Mexico continues to attract gifted writers from the outside, but more native New Mexicans and more Native American and Hispanic writers are to be found among those writing about New Mexico and the Southwest. In recent years, the fictional output has been divided about equally between men and women.

Ana Castillo, Denise Chávez, and Demetria Martínez have added their voices — strong feminist voices — to those of established writers like Fray Angélico Chávez, Sabine Ulibarrí, Rudolfo Anaya, Orlando Romero, and Nash Candelaria, who hitherto have provided some of the few available

Denise Chávez.
Photo by Marion Ettlinger,
© *1993. Courtesy Marion*
Ettlinger.

literary expressions of Hispanic experience. A Chicago native, Castillo evokes the cultural heritage of Hispanic New Mexico while recounting the excesses of Anglo society and the travails of four women of Tomé in her novel, *So Far from God.* A more hopeful spirit is evident in Chávez's *Face of an Angel* (1994), as Soveida Dosamantes evolves a philosophy of service that endows her work with meaning and allows her to live a life of humility, wisdom, strength, and dignity. A young Albuquerque woman seeks fulfillment and social justice in Martínez's *Mother Tongue,* winner of the 1994 Western States Book Award for fiction.

Fewer Native Americans have published notable works in traditional English-language literary forms. Kiowa writer N. Scott Momaday won the Pulitzer Prize for *House Made of Dawn* (1968), and Laguna native Leslie Marmon Silko was acclaimed for the poignant novel, *Ceremony* (1977), but those achievements came some time ago. Beyond those two, it is difficult to think of another Native American who has achieved such recognition as a fiction writer working with New Mexico subjects and settings.

Among newer writers with some Native American ancestry are A. A. Carr (Navajo–Laguna Pueblo), Robert F. Gish (Cherokee), Louis Owens

Louis Owens.
Courtesy Louis Owens.

(Choctaw-Cherokee), and Ron Querry (Choctaw), all of whom have produced works with New Mexico settings. Most evocative of native cultures
are Querry's haunting novel of a Jicarilla Apache woman, *The Death of
Bernadette Lefthand* (1993), and Carr's *Eye Killers* (1995), rich in the ceremonial beliefs and legends of the author's Navajo and Pueblo Indian
forebears. In *First Horses: Stories of the New West* (1993), Gish evokes the
cultural mosaic of Albuquerque's South Valley, an area encompassing
significant Anglo and Hispanic populations, as well as the Pueblo Indian
community of Isleta.

The literary record still suffers from a scarcity of works by writers
rooted in minority cultures, but it is no longer the case that "the major
publishers in this country now are closed to Chicanos," as Anaya observed
in 1987 (Rubén Martínez, 20). Neither are they closed to Native Americans. Indeed, works by talented minority writers appear to be in demand
among mainstream publishers. A growing commitment to cultural plu-
ralism and a changing literary marketplace may be partly responsible for
the increasing willingness of publishers to showcase talented minority
writers.

Ron Querry.
Photo by Elaine Querry.
Courtesy Red Crane Books.

Credit is due a handful of small presses — Arte Público Press, Bilingual Press/Editorial Bilingüe, and Tonatiuh–Quinto Sol, to name three — for an abiding commitment to publication of meritorious works by minority writers over a long period when ethnic wasn't cool. These publishers have given life to some fine works ignored by major publishing houses, while providing encouragement to writers whose sensitivity to cultural experience worked against them with the publishing establishment. Rudolfo Anaya is also to be commended for his efforts as an editor, advocate, and mentor for aspiring minority writers during his tenure as director of the Creative Writing Program at the University of New Mexico.

It should be noted that greater exposure does not necessarily lead to greater understanding. Elizabeth Cook-Lynn, a Dakota writer and scholar, worries that it may be nearly impossible to express tribal perspectives through writings blessed by the Anglo-dominated literary establishment, in part because of a bias in favor of European languages and literary forms, to the exclusion of forms preferred by many native writers. Cook-Lynn factors in an editorial aversion to advocacy of Indian interests and a tendency for non-Indians to serve as arbiters of works by native writers, and concludes that the potential for distortion of native perspectives is great (78–96). Cook-Lynn does not advocate abandoning efforts to publish in

Robert Gish.
Photo by Steve McCrank,
© 1998. Courtesy Clear Light
Publishers.

the mainstream press, but she does encourage a stronger and more focused expression of Indian political interests on the part of Native American writers, pointing to Silko's *Almanac of the Dead* (1991) as a step in the
right direction.

THE NEW OLD WEST

In an era characterized by Richard W. Etulain as "postregional," writers examining the West have rejected old myths in favor of a new emphasis on ethnic and environmental themes, new interpretations of cultural conflict, and a heightened curiosity concerning the experiences of
women (xiv).

Serious writers are still interested in the frontier experience in New
Mexico and other parts of the West, but they no longer buy or sell notions
based on Manifest Destiny or the assumed superiority of Western European culture. They are not, for the most part, writing about the Wild West,
and they certainly are not writing about the moral and intellectual superiority of the Anglo male as a conquering hero who brings civilization to a
savage land. To be sure, there are a few diehards writing commercial Westerns, but their numbers are shrinking and their audience is shrinking even

Kate Horsley.
Photo by Michael Reed.
Courtesy La Alameda Press.

faster. Once a mainstay of drugstore book racks, paperback exchanges, and video rental stores, the Western section today often reposes in obscurity, a modest niche located only with some effort.

Where the Old West appears in contemporary literary fiction with a New Mexico setting, the intent usually is to temper, modify, or refute the myth. This is so in McMurtry's *Dead Man's Walk* (1995), Mike Blakely's *Spanish Blood* (1996), and two fine novels written from feminist perspectives, Kate Horsley's *Crazy Woman* (1992) and Karen Osborn's *Between Earth and Sky* (1996). In McMurtry's book, a much-depleted company of Texas Rangers limps home, battered in body and in spirit, having assumed incorrectly that New Mexico and its ignorant savages were theirs for the taking. Another Texan makes the mistake of taking native New Mexicans lightly in Blakely's *Spanish Blood;* armed with a forged law license and plenty of gall, Blakely's protagonist pursues an old land grant in the Sacramento Mountains and pays for his audacity with his life.

In the books by Osborn and Horsley, men lead the way westward but buckle under the rigors of frontier life, leaving stronger women to fend for themselves. Osborn's Abigail Conklin and Horsley's Sara Willoughby behave admirably, displaying remarkable courage and resourcefulness, standing up to the hardships of the frontier with none of the swagger and smugness of the stereotypical male hero. Theirs is an Old West in which men can be not just good or bad, but also weak, confused, and downright incompetent. These works are not necessarily anti-male, but they do work in the direction of revising popular perceptions of women and their roles in the nineteenth-century West.

Although not of the Old West, Cormac McCarthy's *The Crossing* (1994), the middle installment of the author's powerful *Border Trilogy*, portrays life on a slightly different frontier. The frontier, in this case, is the desolate ranch country of far southern New Mexico and the border region of northern Mexico — a vast, primitive country of idiosyncratic characters, mystery, and danger. Here, as elsewhere in the new Old West, the hero has lost his touch. Billy Parham, a resourceful young man in his late teens, makes three forays into Mexico over a period of several years in pursuit of righteous causes but comes home talking to himself — in the words of one reviewer (Mort), "a rootless, restless young man with an uncertain future."

McCarthy's vision of the New West, as expressed in *The Crossing*, is bleak, to be sure, but it gets worse. In the third volume of his trilogy, *Cities of the Plain* (1998), the antiheroic characters of *All the Pretty Horses* (1992) and *The Crossing* are united as friends and fellow ranch hands in the early fifties. The land they work — in the Tularosa Basin next to a missile range — soon will be preempted by the military. The recent world war is seen as a watershed event, and one of the young men is wise enough to observe that the country and a way of life have been changed forever.

John Grady Cole is a nineteen-year-old with a positive genius for working horses, but fate will not allow the realization of his dream of married life with a teenage Mexican prostitute. The boy dares greatly, but he meets an early death in a Juarez back street, cut to ribbons by a dangerous pimp who circles and slashes and taunts him as a "farm boy." John Grady dies an agonizing death in a dirty side street, a stranger in a strange land, attended only by his friend, Billy Parham.

Billy returns to the ranch to settle up, then rides out of the country, a confused and aimless wanderer. He gets along on odd jobs and charity but never gets a handle on life. Looking back over his seventy-eight years, acutely aware of his own mortality, Billy can feel that he has learned little: "In everything that he'd ever thought about the world and about his life in it he'd been wrong" (266).

Having had his way for most of two centuries in tales of western adventure, the once-mighty Anglo hero takes a horrendous beating in the literary Western of the 1990s. At the same time, Hispanic and Native American characters, and women of all kinds, increasingly are portrayed as real people of competence and dignity, who may have done more than serve as extras or antagonists in morality plays celebrating the courage and resourcefulness of the Anglo male.

BORDERS

Borders of various kinds long have been a source of interest to writers dealing with the Southwest. They were of interest to Mayne Reid and his contemporaries, and they are of interest to the men and women who are writing today. In *Beyond Bounds: Cross-Cultural Essays on Anglo, American Indian, and Chicano Literature* (1996), Robert Gish explores the whole notion of "lines, boundaries, and demarcations" as he experienced them as a youth growing up in Albuquerque. Boundaries may be characterized by political, socioeconomic, ethnic, geographical, and political distinctions; as Gish observes, they have a tendency to shift over time. The boundaries themselves imply contrast and conflict; as such, they are likely to attract the scrutiny of writers on the prowl for stories.

Cormac McCarthy's *Border Trilogy* is a recent and emphatic example of the fascination with boundaries. McCarthy's characters live at the fringes of a changing nation and are subject to national forces centered elsewhere, even as they are influenced by the proximity of Mexico — a world apart, characterized by primitive conditions and a fatalistic world view.

Laurence Gonzales evokes the same general forces of time and place in *El Vago* (1983). In the San Andres Mountains of southern New Mexico, overlooking the government missile range, an old man recalls the idealism and chaos of the Mexican Revolution and of his youthful times as a friend and follower of Pancho Villa. The *anciano,* Augustín Mentira, reminisces the night away with his young hunting companion, then witnesses a monstrous explosion, testimony to an ancient and apparently immutable human penchant for conflict and destruction.

Robert Boswell offers a less romantic portrayal of life in the borderlands in *American Owned Love* (1997), drawing attention to the *colonias* — unincorporated rural communities lacking basic amenities like electricity and running water. They are squalid places inhabited mainly by illegal aliens, conveniently forgotten by local government authorities.

Robert Boswell.
Photo by Michael Kiernan.
Courtesy News and
Publications, New Mexico
State University.

Second among significant contemporary geopolitical boundaries is the line separating New Mexico from Texas. McCarthy endows Mexico with a primitive and mystical aura. In comparison, New Mexico's relationship with Texas has the same tension but none of the charm. McMurtry's *Dead Man's Walk* deals with one of the defining events of a tense relationship between Texans and New Mexicans. The Texan–Santa Fe Expedition, the historical point of reference for McMurtry's novel, was an overt act of aggression and an expression of the Texans' assumed superiority to the people of New Mexico. The relationship has never recovered, in part because, to some degree, the same conviction of Texas' superiority and the native New Mexican resentment of it remain in place. New Mexico officially welcomes the tourist dollars that Texans bring, but it hasn't been that long since red and yellow "Tejano No!" bumper strips were common on the roads of northern New Mexico. Texas and New Mexico clash regularly over water issues. The famous lament of Gov. Manuel Armijo, "Poor New Mexico! So far from Heaven; so close to Texas!" still strikes a resonant chord in many New Mexicans.

New Mexico's common borders with Arizona, Colorado, and Oklahoma excite no such passions, but there is literary capital in boundaries involving the state's military installations. In several dozen novels, Los Alamos and the White Sands Missile Range are secret and forbidden places, secure behind well-defined and well-guarded borders; the incongruity of interests between those within and those without the military enclave usually is significant. Borders also have factual and symbolic significance in novels involving land grants and public lands, and in stories involving Indian reservations, where issues of tribal sovereignty and jurisdiction are at stake.

MYSTERIOUS LAND

In a genre sharing some origins with the adventure western novel, New Mexico has inspired notable practitioners since the early 1940s. Gaining popularity in the latter stages of the dime-novel era, mysteries (also called "detective stories") were circulated widely in pulp magazines and "slicks" in the early decades of the twentieth century. In the 1920s and 1930s, they enjoyed great popularity.

The mystery genre, incorporating detective fiction and related tales of suspense, was well established by the time Frances Crane and Dorothy Hughes began to make extensive use of New Mexico settings in mystery novels of the 1940s and 1950s. Crane built a popular series around the likable Pat Abbott and his wife, Jean, proprietor of the Turquoise Shop in Santa Maria, a northern New Mexico town resembling Taos. Hughes produced a number of stand-alone mysteries, including three set in the vicinity of Santa Fe.

Santa Fe writer Richard Martin Stern later created a successful series character in the detective Johnny Ortiz, and Ursula Curtiss produced several New Mexico–based mystery novels featuring women as victims, perpetrators, and heroines. The year 1970 marked the beginning of Tony Hillerman's immensely popular series featuring Navajo detectives Joe Leaphorn and Jim Chee.

Perhaps inspired by Hillerman's success, other New Mexico writers have capitalized on the popularity of the southwestern style to fashion popular mystery series. Judith Van Gieson's Neil Hamel works out of Albuquerque, while Walter Satterthwait's Joshua Croft hangs his hat in Santa Fe; both characters range widely across the western landscape, traveling to such far-flung destinations as the Navajo reservation, El Paso–Juarez, Montana, Beverly Hills, and the remote villages and Anasazi ruins of New Mexico to solve crimes. Rudolfo Anaya's Sonny Baca is a creature of the city, introducing readers to the geographical and cultural diversity of

Albuquerque, as he moves in and out of diverse social circles in pursuit of dangerous killers.

Sculptor and part-time sleuth Mo Bowdre is the creation of Corrales writer Jake Page; the Santa Fe–based Bowdre is blind but has an amazing knack for discovering orderly connections between seemingly unrelated clues, sometimes with the help of his Anglo-Hopi girlfriend. Page makes extensive use of southwestern landscapes and culture, sometimes addressing such sensitive issues as the commercial theft of Native American ceremonial objects (*The Stolen Gods,* 1993) and the commercial and artistic exploitation of native cultures (*The Knotted Strings,* 1995).

Unassuming Bubba Mabry, who resides at the Desert Breeze Motor Inn on Albuquerque's East Central Avenue, stumbles through at least four mysteries by journalist Steve Brewer. And California native Sarah Lovett, a resident of Santa Fe, appears to have a successful series under way with three titles featuring Dr. Sylvia Strange, a forensic psychiatrist in Santa Fe.

Steven Havill might well have achieved the notoriety of the Santa Fe and Albuquerque mystery writers but for the dual sins of living in out-of-the-way Lincoln, New Mexico, and writing about a region more remote still. Havill's unlikely hero through at least six mystery novels is Undersheriff Bill Gerstner of Posadas County, in the sparsely peopled borderland of southwestern New Mexico. An overweight widower nearing retirement, Gerstner leaves much to be desired as a sex symbol, but nevertheless he appeals to readers by virtue of his affability, wisdom, common sense, and good humor. Relying on street savvy acquired during twenty years in the military and twenty more with the sheriff's department, Gerstner labors under the authority of a sheriff who is short on practical experience but who has the patience and ethical flexibility to deal with the political realities of Posadas County.

New Mexico residents Harlan Campbell (*Monkey on a Chain,* 1993), Michael McGarrity (*Tularosa,* 1996; *Mexican Hat,* 1997; *Serpent Gate,* 1998), Louis Owens (*Nightland,* 1996), and Norman Zollinger (*Lautrec,* 1990) also have helped to make the state a hotbed of mystery writing, as have part-time Santa Fe resident Martha Grimes (*Rainbow's End,* 1995) and nonresident Stuart Woods (*Santa Fe Rules,* 1992).

PLANET NEW MEXICO

Aside from a stilted manner of expression and an overtly racist bearing, Thomas Denison's *My Invisible Partner* (1898) is notable as an early novel involving New Mexico settings and subjects. The story involves a murder, characters with varied motives, some subtle clues, and a rather formal ending summary in which the case is solved and all suspects are accounted for. The book also enters the metaphysical realm, as the narrator, George Warren, experiences supernatural visions and transcends his physical body to wander about, thus becoming his own "invisible partner." The story was unusual for its time; but in a later era, Denison might have found a place among a surprising number of writers creating works of science fiction in or about New Mexico.

Science fiction normally does not draw upon familiar settings for its "sense of place"; frequently, the writer is making up an entirely new place amid worlds hitherto unimagined. Even so, New Mexico provides a primary setting for a handful of notable works of science fiction — Fredric Brown's *Rogue in Space* (1957), for example; and *Manseed* (1982), by sci-fi pioneer Jack Williamson of Portales. *Dorothea Dreams* (1986), by Suzy McKee Charnas, unfolds in Taos, where artist Dorothea Howard receives psychic messages from a jurist living at the time of the French Revolution. Roger Zelazny's *Eye of Cat* (1982), if not, strictly speaking, a New Mexico item, is rooted in the homeland and culture of the Navajo people. And Whitley Strieber's *Majestic* (1989), intended as a serious challenge to a suspected cover-up in the 1947 "Roswell Incident," involves human interaction with extraterrestrial beings.

In the anthology she edited, *A Very Large Array: New Mexico Science Fiction and Fantasy* (1987), Melinda Snodgrass demonstrates that New Mexico is a significant producer of science fiction and fantasy literature, claiming such noted practitioners as Charnas, Williamson, Zelazny, Stephen R. Donaldson, George R. R. Martin, and Fred Saberhagen as residents for portions of their professional lives. While New Mexico rarely enters into their stories directly, most of the writers anthologized in the collection are quick to acknowledge their surroundings as stimuli to creativity.

As science fiction frequently involves encounters with alien creatures and cultures, so New Mexico involves encounters among people of different appearances, languages, and cultures. In Snodgrass's view, the opportunity to observe such encounters is one of the attractions for the science fiction writer. "When I think alien," she writes, "I think exciting. New energies, new outlooks, a freshness and vitality that can't be found in more traditional, rigid, and perhaps 'purer' societies." With this in mind, the cultural amalgam of New Mexico provides a rich creative environment. "And as a writer, I find it a heady mix," says Snodgrass. "It conduces to dreaming, and thinking, and asking 'what if?' All of which seem to define a science fiction writer" (248).

EAST MEETS WEST

One consequence of the imposing presence of nonnative writers in the fiction literature of New Mexico is an abundance of works which offer contrasting impressions of East and West.

Such observations come naturally enough to writers who have spent portions of their lives in the varied environs of the eastern U.S. and the great spaces of the West. Says Paul Horgan of the geographical influences that shaped him: "I am a native of New York state and my childhood from twelve years on was spent in New Mexico and the last three years of my adolescence were passed in Rochester, New York. In the three periods of greatest impressionability I was thus exposed to life in both East and West, and my life ever since has reflected this variety" (Milton 1964, p. 27).

Horgan's work also reflects this breadth of experience. For Horgan, the dominant literary theme of the West is that of "man, alone, against the grand immensity of nature — the nature of the land, reflected in his own soul." The East, on the other hand, is characterized by social complexity.

Horgan was one of several writers to take notice of the migration of respiratory sufferers to New Mexico in the early decades of the twentieth century. Differences in values and perspectives among these individuals are illustrated in numerous stories involving easterners suddenly and involuntarily relocated in the West. In the stricken composer, Edmund Abbey, of the 1935 novel, *No Quarter Given,* Horgan draws a character whose life has been molded by influences identified with the East, but who in his final hours finds his spirit renewed in the liberating milieu of Santa Fe. Mary Austin's *Starry Adventure* (1931) and Fergusson's *Hot Saturday* are among other novels in which hopeful lung sufferers discover unsuspected delights and annoyances in the West.

The railroad was a powerful symbol of the connection between East and West for Horgan and Fergusson, as it transported characters between different worlds and brought foreign influences to penetrate and transform the West. For a contemporary writer, Kate Horsley, a Virginia native living in Albuquerque, too, the railroad is such a symbol. In *A Killing in New Town* (1996), the train brings wide-eyed easterners to a country that inspires both awe and fear, changing Las Vegas from an adobe village to a bustling town driven by irresistible forces. So rapidly is the place changing that a woman might one day look out from an adobe house and find herself "surrounded by a landscape from Peoria" (47).

Literary commentary on the contrasting influences of East and West was orchestrated first through the impressions of westering Anglo pioneers and later through the experiences of the health seekers and their families. But in recent years, such observations have come mostly via social dropouts, counterculture followers, and other reasonably affluent Anglo characters who have come to New Mexico seeking personal fulfillment.

The fictional easterner sees the West and its people with new eyes, observing and commenting on matters that to the locals may seem commonplace. Those experiencing New Mexico for the first time frequently find themselves inspired and liberated through their exposure to diverse cultures, divergent attitudes, and the beauty and vastness of the western landscape. New Mexico proved an epiphany for the English novelist, D. H. Lawrence, and he made it that for Lou Witt, a bored and restless young woman who is his central character in the novel, *St. Mawr*. Having tried London, Paris, and the Isle of Capri, Lou finds contentment on a dilapidated ranch in the high country of the New Mexico Rockies. "Now I am where I want to be," she declares, "with the spirit that wants me" (221).

Not all new arrivals are so thrilled, however. Some writers and fictional visitors are put off by what they perceive to be a general disregard for law on the part of locals, others by the gaudy pretensions to southwestern culture that they observe in the homes of patronizing Anglos. For some visitors, Santa Fe and Taos are notable not for an authentic southwestern ambiance, but for their crass commercialism, affectations of mysticism, and abundance of divergent souls pursuing various alternative lifestyles. Edward Abbey's Henry Holyoke Lightcap, an easterner by birth but a westerner by adoption, zips through Taos on a cross-country pilgrimage in *The Fool's Progress* and despairs at finding the town overrun by "hippies, flower children, rock musicians, movie stars, Orientalist mystagogues, minimalist poets, rich idle Eurotrash," ski promoters, and hard-driving entrepreneurs from Texas (235–36). In Santa Fe, New Age healers, spiritualists, and wealthy aficionados of the southwestern style also draw the fire of writers. Santa Fe is chided variously as the "land of the free, home of the occult" and an "adobe theme park."

LOOKING FOR LOVE

Some of the best and brightest young Anglo writers of the 1990s have been concerned with questions of purpose, relationship, and self-worth. Their major characters are an introspective lot — searching, self-doubting, often angst-ridden and insecure. Like their creators, many of these characters are newcomers to New Mexico, and many of them are trying to "find" themselves. They live comfortable middle-class lives; their needs for food, shelter, and other essentials have been met. Neither do they feel physically threatened; and, unlike many who are rooted in minority cultures, they do not feel victimized by social injustice. Their anxieties involve afflictions of the spirit — the need to belong, to relate, to know and realize themselves.

For these lost souls, something is missing, and in many cases that something is love: affection, mutual understanding, and the ability to sustain significant and satisfying relationships — not only with a romantic partner, but with friends, family members, and people in the world at large. The perplexity surrounding these matters sometimes is expressed in the titles of the works — Lee K. Abbott's *Love Is the Crooked Thing* (1986), Mary Cable's *Tell Me the Truth About Love* (1991), and Eddie Lewis's *Ray Had an Idea About Love* (1995), for example.

For the protagonists in these tales, love is not a many-splendored thing. It is, rather, a deceptive, tortured, and thoroughly bewildering thing. In Abbott's stories, sensitive men of the eighties and nineties inhabit middle-class lives in Deming, Las Cruces, and Albuquerque, dealing with hurt, loss, and anger, attempting to make sense of it all. Cable's Alexandra Smithson, mired in a loveless marriage to a Santa Fe banker, finds love in an affair with her husband's brother, suffering predictable emotional conflicts before breaking off the marriage to seek her own happiness. In Lewis's first novel, also set in Santa Fe, yuppie electrical contractor Ray Griffey takes a break from a troubled marriage for an affair with one of his employees. Ray's actions are those of the stereotypical "middle-aged crazy" male, but he concludes that peace is to be found in keeping his marriage together and learning how to make it work.

Most such stories concern characters in their late twenties, thirties, or forties, but C. W. Smith's *Understanding Women* qualifies as a "coming of age" novel. The title is curiously ambiguous, leaving the reader to choose among several possible interpretations. Sixteen-year-old Jimbo Proctor, reared in Dallas, thinks it would be fun to spend the summer with his freewheeling Uncle Waylan and Waylan's new wife, Vicky, in the southeast

New Mexico oil patch town of Hedorville. Jimbo takes the westbound bus in anticipation of a big adventure but stumbles into the eye of a major domestic disturbance and is forced to rely on his own meager reservoir of worldly wisdom. Jimbo leaves Dallas wondering whether he ought to take along his baseball glove and BB gun, but he comes home knowing more about the joy and pain of love than most people may want to learn in a lifetime. He also finds the oil patch culture of the 1950s interesting for the short run but too confining to permit the full flowering of an intellect awakened by two memorable women of his Hedorville summer.

Concern with relationships, reconciliation, and the search for meaning also are evident in novels by Cathryn Alpert (*Rocket City,* 1995), Robert Boswell (*American Owned Love,* 1997), Natalie Goldberg (*Banana Rose,* 1995), Jo-Ann Mapson (*Blue Rodeo,* 1994), Dan McCall (*Messenger Bird,* 1993), John Nichols (*An Elegy for September,* 1992), and Robert Olmstead (*America by Land,* 1993), and in the short fiction of Antonya Nelson and Elizabeth Tallent.

A RIVER RUNS THROUGH IT

It is New Mexico's fortune and fate to be endowed with exceptional resources of a nonmaterial nature. A beautiful landscape, an illustrious history, and a rich mosaic of cultures are among these assets. A sparsely populated state of fewer than two million inhabitants, geographically isolated and economically stressed, New Mexico has provided an apparently inexhaustible fount of ideas and inspiration for writers. The river of words flowing from it is wide, shallow in places and deeper in others. It has been running steady for well over a century and shows no sign of drying up.

Few states of any size can claim works of fiction by the likes of Pearl S. Buck, Robert Olen Butler, Willa Cather, Paul Horgan, Oliver La Farge, Larry McMurtry, N. Scott Momaday, and Conrad Richter — Pulitzer Prize winners all, though not, in most cases, for works closely identified with New Mexico. Among contemporary writers dealing with New Mexico settings and subjects, the achievements of Rudolfo Anaya, Tony Hillerman, Cormac McCarthy, John Nichols, and Leslie Marmon Silko are considerable. Much may be expected of a talented group of younger writers currently at work in the region.

Even in Texas, where they are supposed to have the biggest and best of everything, and where the literati are a good deal more self-conscious about their state's standing in the world of letters, New Mexico's abundant literary wealth is recognized and envied. A. C. Greene, author of *The 50*

Best Books on Texas (1982), writes, "Unfortunately, Texas has not furnished indigenous materials for great novels like La Farge's *Laughing Boy,* Frank Waters's *The Man Who Killed the Deer,* or Bandelier's *Delight Makers,* as did New Mexico. It has drawn out no *Death Comes for the Archbishop,* and few products comparable to Richard Bradford's *Red Sky at Morning*" (5).

Such literary output from a southwestern state of few people and modest means gives rise to a couple of questions: "Why write?" and "Why here?"

Taking the second question first, there simply are not many places that offer the varieties of landscape and climate, the rich history, distinct cultures, and bright mosaic of contrasts found in New Mexico. Nor, as has been demonstrated, are there many places endowed with such an abundance and diversity of types of conflict — the raw material of fiction. All of these factors presumably nourish the creative impulses of artists and writers.

Frank Waters was attracted to the Taos Valley in part by what he characterized as a "biblical aspect" of the immense landscape and the people who moved about in the shadow of the mountains — some mounted, some blanketed in the manner of the Pueblo Indians. Years later, John Nichols found the same area conducive to observations concerning social and economic phenomena — a microcosm in which all the essential forces were present and visible. "It never feels like just Taos to me," he has said. "It feels like some little laboratory where the whole universe is on display" (Nathan, B3). Nichols was impressed with a landscape of incredible beauty, but in the shadow of the mountains he also discovered a history of conquest and exploitation that had to be investigated, understood, and voiced.

Conrad Richter migrated to New Mexico from Pennsylvania for his wife's health, but he quickly developed an admiration for the pioneers who had overcome adversity to build homes and communities in a harsh and primitive land. Richter was already an accomplished writer when he arrived in the Southwest, but in the tales of the old-timers and along the byways of rural New Mexico, he found a new and stimulating literary landscape, and he responded to it with renewed creative energy.

In the 1950s, William Eastlake sought New Mexico, he said, because the West offered the world something new, "an undiscovered country of the imagination" that as yet had not been adequately revealed by truth-telling writers and artists.

Rudolfo Anaya found his voice as a writer when he turned to the materials of his native culture — to the history, world view, indigenous symbols, and collective experience of the cultural milieu whence he emerged.

It is no longer as risky as it once was for writers to be interested in subjects and settings likely to be categorized as "regional." Eugene Manlove Rhodes, Oliver La Farge, and virtually all serious writers whose stories were laid in the West in the first half of the twentieth century felt themselves hopelessly stigmatized in the eyes of eastern publishers and critics. Harvey Fergusson complained that New York reviewers and critics — the taste makers of his day — "care nothing about the West and know nothing about it except that any novel dealing with 'the great spaces' must be treated with a certain condescension" (Milton 1964, p. 24).

Some writers still run from the "regional" label, while others care little. Provincialism is not a problem for Rudolfo Anaya, who is more than capable of addressing themes of universal significance *and* speaking to a particular audience within the region. In Anaya's view, "Every writer attentive to the earth pulse and the human pulse of his place has accessible to him all the symbology, imagery, and archetypes necessary to touch the chords of his people and region on one level, and of humanity on a deeper level" (1975–76, p. 66). Of himself and other Chicano writers, Anaya says, "Why shouldn't we be almost intensely proud of being writers who somehow can speak to a region beyond the limitations of mere local color?" (1988).

Larry McMurtry notes that "fiction proceeds from the particular to the general. You don't create universal fictions just by attempting to write grandiose books about grandiose themes without locating them somewhere" (1978, p. 25). Attentiveness and fidelity to the speech and manner and values of a particular place, he says, "can somehow lead the writer into universality if he attends faithfully enough, and is intelligent enough, and if his emotional resources are sufficient" (25).

Whatever the motive or inspiration, those who have devoted portions of themselves to literate commentary on the human condition and the world around them generally are agreed that such pursuits matter in the scheme of things. To some, writing matters for social or political reasons. Others write to express an artistic impulse, still others to inform or entertain. A select few may even do it for money; but for most, the motivation seems to come from a more personal impulse to create, to tell a story, to probe the mysteries of life, to interpret the world at hand, and perhaps to advance a cause or express a deeply held conviction.

"Speaking for myself," declared Edward Abbey, "I write to entertain my friends and exasperate our enemies. I write to record the truth of our time, as best as I can see it. To investigate the comedy and tragedy of human relationships. To resist and sabotage the contemporary drift toward a technocratic, militaristic totalitarianism, whatever its ideological coloration. To oppose injustice, defy the powerful, and speak for the voiceless" (1984, p. xiv).

Like Abbey, New Mexico's best novelists and storytellers write to make a difference — to tell their stories, full of ideas and images, truths and illusions, that thoughtful readers may sift like so many shards and so much backfill, in search of themselves.

WORKS CITED

PRINTED MATERIALS

Abbey, Edward. *The Brave Cowboy: An Old Tale in a New Time.* New York: Dodd, Mead, 1956.

———. *Confessions of a Barbarian: Selections from the Journals of Edward Abbey, 1951–1989.* Edited and with an introduction by David Peterson. Boston: Little, Brown, 1994.

———. *Fire on the Mountain.* New York: Dial Press, 1962.

———. *The Fool's Progress.* New York: Henry Holt, 1988.

———. *Good News.* New York: E. P. Dutton, 1980.

———. *The Monkey Wrench Gang.* Philadelphia: J. B. Lippincott, 1975.

———. *Slumgullion Stew.* New York: E. P. Dutton, 1984.

Abbott, Lee K. *Love Is the Crooked Thing.* Chapel Hill, N.C.: Algonquin Books of Chapel Hill, 1986.

Aiken, Albert W. *Kit Carson, King of Guides; Or, Mountain Paths and Prairie Trails.* Beadle's Boy's Library of Sport, Story and Adventure, No. 15. New York: Beadle and Adams, March 22, 1882.

Aimard, Gustave [Olivier Gloux]. *The Pirates of the Prairies: Adventures in the American Desert.* London: Ward and Lock, 1862.

———. *The Trail Hunter: A Tale of the Far West.* London: Ward and Lock, 1861.

Alpert, Cathryn. *Rocket City.* Aspen, Colo.: MacMurray and Beck, 1995.

Amrine, Michael. *Secret.* Boston: Houghton Mifflin, 1950.

Anaya, Rudolfo A. *Billy the Kid.* In *The Anaya Reader,* 495–554. New York: Warner Books, 1995.

———. *Bless Me, Ultima.* Berkeley, Calif.: Quinto Sol Publications, 1972.

———. *Heart of Aztlán.* Berkeley, Calif.: Editorial Justa, 1976.

———. Interview by David L. Caffey, February 9, 1988. Notes in the files of David L. Caffey.

———. "Rudolfo A. Anaya." In "The Writer's Sense of Place: A Symposium and Commentaries." *South Dakota Review* 13 (1975–76): 66–67.

———. "Short Autobiography of Rudolfo Anaya." *El Grito: A Journal of Contemporary Mexican American Thought* 5, no. 3 (Spring, 1972): 4–5.

Arnold, Elliott. *The Time of the Gringo.* New York: Knopf, 1953.

Austin, Mary. *Starry Adventure.* Boston: Houghton Mifflin, 1931.

Averill, Charles E. *Kit Carson, the Prince of the Gold Hunters; Or, The Adventures of the Sacramento.* Boston, 1849.

Badash, Lawrence, Joseph O. Hirschfelder, and Herbert P. Broida, eds. *Reminiscences of Los Alamos, 1943–1945.* Dordrecht, Netherlands: D. Reidel, 1980.

Bandelier, Adolf F. *The Delight Makers.* New York: Dodd, Mead, 1890.

Baxter, John O. "The Villista Murder Trials: Deming, New Mexico, 1916–1921." *La Gaceta* 8, no. 1 (1983): 1–22.

Bean, Amelia. *A Time for Outrage.* Garden City, N.Y.: Doubleday and Company, 1967.

Benchley, Nathaniel. *Welcome to Xanadu.* New York: Atheneum, 1968.

Bennet, Robert Ames. *A Volunteer with Pike: The True Narrative of One Dr. John Robinson and of His Love for the Fair Señorita Vallois.* Chicago: A. C. McClurg and Company, 1909.

Bennett, Emerson. *The Prairie Flower; Or, Adventures in the Far West.* Cincinnati, 1849.

Billington, Ray Allen. *Land of Savagery, Land of Promise: The European Image of the American Frontier.* New York: Norton, 1981.

Blacker, Irwin. *Taos.* Cleveland, Ohio: World Publishing Company, 1959.

Blake, Forrester. *The Franciscan.* Garden City, N.Y.: Doubleday and Company, 1963.

Blakely, Mike. *Spanish Blood.* New York: Forge, 1996.

Bluestone, George. *Novels into Film.* Berkeley: University of California Press, 1957.

Boswell, Robert. *American Owned Love.* New York: Knopf, 1997.

Bower, Bertha Muzzy. *The Phantom Herd.* Boston: Little, Brown, 1916.

Bradford, Richard. *Red Sky at Morning.* Philadelphia: J. B. Lippincott Company, 1968.

———. *So Far from Heaven.* Philadelphia: J. B. Lippincott Company, 1973.

Brady, Ben. *Principles of Adaptation for Film and Television.* Austin: University of Texas Press, 1994.

Brewer, Steve. *Witchy Woman.* New York: St. Martin's Press, 1996.

Brians, Paul. *Nuclear Holocausts: Atomic War in Fiction, 1895–1984.* Kent, Ohio: Kent State University Press, 1987.

Bright, Robert. *The Life and Death of Little Jo.* Garden City, N.Y.: Doubleday, Doran and Company, 1944.

Brinig, Myron. *All of Their Lives.* New York: Farrar and Rinehart, 1941.

Brode, Bernice. "Tales of Los Alamos." In *Reminiscences of Los Alamos, 1943–1945,* edited by Lawrence Badash, Joseph O. Hirschfelder, and Herbert P. Broida, 133–59. Dordrecht, Netherlands: D. Reidel Publishing Company, 1980.

Brown, Fredric. *The Far Cry.* New York: E. P. Dutton and Company, 1951.

————. *Rogue in Space.* New York: E. P. Dutton and Company, 1957.

Buck, Pearl S. *Command the Morning.* New York: John Day Company, 1959.

Burns, Walter Noble. *The Saga of Billy the Kid.* Garden City, N.Y.: Doubleday, Page and Company, 1926.

Butler, Robert Olen. *Countrymen of Bones.* New York: Horizon Press, 1983.

Cable, Mary. *Tell Me the Truth About Love.* New York: Atheneum, 1991.

Calder, Jenni. *There Must Be a Lone Ranger: The American West in Film and in Reality.* New York: Taplinger, 1975.

Calvin, Ross. *Sky Determines: An Interpretation of the Southwest.* New York: Macmillan, 1934.

Campbell, Harlan. *Monkey on a Chain.* Garden City, N.Y.: Doubleday and Company, 1993.

Candelaria, Nash. *Not by the Sword.* Ypsilanti, Mich.: Bilingual Press/Editorial Bilingüe, 1982.

Carr, A. A. *Eye Killers.* Norman: University of Oklahoma Press, 1995.

Carr, Lorraine. *Mother of the Smiths.* New York: Macmillan, 1940.

Castillo, Ana. *So Far from God.* New York: Norton, 1993.

Cather, Willa. *Death Comes for the Archbishop.* New York: Knopf, 1927.

————. *The Professor's House.* New York: Knopf, 1925.

Cave, Dorothy. *Go Find the Mountain.* Salt Lake City: Northwest Publishing, 1996.

Champney, Elizabeth W. *Great-Grandmother's Girls in New Mexico, 1670–1680.* Boston: Estes and Lauriat, 1888.

Charnas, Suzy McKee. *Dorothea Dreams.* New York: Arbor House, 1986.

Chávez, Denise. *Face of an Angel.* New York: Farrar, Straus and Giroux, 1994.

Chavez, Fray Angelico. *But Time and Chance: The Story of Padre Martínez of Taos, 1793–1867.* Santa Fe: Sunstone Press, 1981.

————. *My Penitente Land: Reflections on Spanish New Mexico.* Albuquerque: University of New Mexico Press, 1974.

————. *New Mexico Triptych.* Paterson, N.J.: St. Anthony Guild Press, 1940.

Cheuse, Alan. *The Light Possessed.* Salt Lake City: Peregrine Smith Books, 1990.

Christiansen, Paige W. "Of Indians, Spaniards, and Americans." In *Mosaic of New Mexico's Scenery, Rocks, and History,* edited by Paige W. Christiansen and Frank E. Kottlowski, 3–15. Socorro: New Mexico Bureau of Mines and Mineral Resources, 1972.

Church, Peggy Pond. *The House at Otowi Bridge.* Albuquerque: University of New Mexico Press, 1960.

Cohen, Robert. *The Organ Builder.* New York: Harper and Row, 1988.

Cohen, Saul. "New Mexico Novels: A Preliminary Checklist." *Book Talk* 13, no. 2 (March, 1984): 1–12.

Collignon, Rick. *The Journal of Antonio Montoya.* Aspen, Colo.: MacMurray and Beck, 1996.

Cook-Lynn, Elizabeth. *Why I Can't Read Wallace Stegner and Other Essays.* Madison: University of Wisconsin Press, 1996.

Coolidge, Dane. *Comanche Chaser.* New York: E. P. Dutton and Company, 1938.

————. *Under the Sun.* New York: E. P. Dutton and Company, 1926.

Corle, Edwin. *People on the Earth.* New York: Random House, 1937.

Crane, Frances. *The Turquoise Shop.* Philadelphia: J. B. Lippincott Company, 1941.

Curtiss, Ursula. *The Poisoned Orchard.* New York: Dodd, Mead, 1980.

de Aragón, Ray John. *Padre Martínez and Bishop Lamy.* Las Vegas, N.Mex.: Pan-American Publishing Company, 1978.

Denison, Thomas S. *My Invisible Partner.* Chicago: Rand, McNally and Company, 1898.

DeWitt, David A. *Texas Monthly Guide to New Mexico.* Austin: Texas Monthly Press, 1989, rev. ed. 1994.

"Dexter Masters' Novel to be MGM Movie." *Illinois State Register,* April 21, 1955.

Díaz, Elvia. "Statue of Spaniard Loses Foot." *Albuquerque Journal,* January 8, 1998, pp. A1, A4.

Dobie, J. Frank. *Guide to Life and Literature of the Southwest.* Austin: University of Texas Press, 1943.

Douglas, Kirk. "Introduction." In *The Brave Cowboy: An Old Tale in a New Time,* by Edward Abbey. Rev. ed. Salt Lake City: Dream Garden Press; and Santa Barbara, Calif.: Santa Teresa Press, 1993.

Duffus, R. L. *Jornada.* New York: Covici-Friede, 1935.

Eastlake, William. *The Bronc People.* New York: Harcourt, Brace, 1958.

————. *Dancers in the Scalp House.* New York: Viking, 1975.

————. *Go in Beauty.* New York: Harper and Brothers, 1956.

————. *Portrait of an Artist with 26 Horses.* New York: Simon and Schuster, 1963.

Encinias, Miguel. *Two Lives for Oñate.* Albuquerque: University of New Mexico Press, 1997.

Etulain, Richard W. *Re-Imagining the Modern American West: A Century of Fiction, History and Art.* Tucson: University of Arizona Press, 1996.

Evans, Max. *The Hi Lo Country.* New York: Macmillan, 1961.

————. Letter to David L. Caffey, July 21, 1995. In files of David L. Caffey.

————. *The One-Eyed Sky.* Boston: Houghton Mifflin, 1963.

————. *The Rounders.* New York: Macmillan, 1960. Reprinted, Albuquerque: University of New Mexico Press, 1983.

————. *Spinning Sun, Grinning Moon.* Santa Fe: Red Crane Books, 1995.

Everpoint [Joseph M. Field]. *Taos: A Romance of the Massacre.* St. Louis: Reveille Job Office, 1847.

Fable, Edmund, Jr. *Billy the Kid, the New Mexican Outlaw; Or, The Bold Bandit of the West!* Denver: Denver Publishing Company, 1881.

Fackler, Elizabeth. *Billy the Kid: The Legend of El Chivato.* New York: Forge, 1995.

Fellin, Octavia. Letter to David L. Caffey, April 9, 1992. In files of David L. Caffey.

Fenin, George N., and William K. Everson. *The Western from Silents to Cinerama.* New York: Orion Press, 1962.

Fergusson, Harvey. *The Blood of the Conquerors.* New York: Knopf, 1921.

————. *The Conquest of Don Pedro.* New York: William Morrow, 1954.

————. *Footloose McGarnigal.* New York: Knopf, 1930.

————. *Grant of Kingdom.* New York: William Morrow, 1950.

———. *Home in the West: An Inquiry into My Origins.* New York: Duell, Sloan and Pearce, 1944.

———. *Hot Saturday.* New York: Knopf, 1926.

———. "Proud Rider." *Blue Book* magazine, December, 1935, pp. 18–41, and January, 1936, pp. 28–56.

———. *Rio Grande.* New York: Knopf, 1933.

———. "Taos Remembered." *American West* 8, no. 5 (September, 1971): 38–41.

———. *In Those Days: An Impression of Change.* New York: Knopf, 1929.

———. *Wolf Song.* New York: Knopf, 1927.

Fisher, Phyllis K. *Los Alamos Experience.* Tokyo: Japan Publications, 1985.

Flint, Timothy. *Biographical Memoir of Daniel Boone, the First Settler of Kentucky. Interspersed with Incidents in the Early Annals of the Country.* Cincinnati: N. and G. Guilford, 1833.

———. *Francis Berrian; Or, The Mexican Patriot.* 2 vols. Boston: Cummings, Hilliard and Company, 1826.

Folsom, James K. *Timothy Flint.* New York: Twayne Publishers, 1965.

Foster, Joseph. *Stephana.* New York: Duell, Sloan and Pearce, 1959.

Foster, O'Kane. *In the Night Did I Sing.* New York: Charles Scribner's Sons, 1942.

Gallegos, Sallie. *Stone Horses.* Albuquerque: University of New Mexico Press, 1996.

Garrett, Pat F. *The Authentic Life of Billy the Kid, Noted Desperado of the Southwest.* Santa Fe: New Mexican Printing and Publishing Company, 1882.

Gaston, Edwin W., Jr. *The Early Novel of the Southwest.* Albuquerque: University of New Mexico Press, 1961.

Gish, Robert Franklin. *Beyond Bounds: Cross-Cultural Essays on Anglo, American Indian, and Chicano Literature.* Albuquerque: University of New Mexico Press, 1996.

———. *First Horses: Stories of the New West.* Reno: University of Nevada Press, 1993.

Goldberg, Natalie. *Banana Rose.* New York: Bantam Books, 1995.

Gonzales, Laurence. *El Vago.* New York: Atheneum, 1983.

Gonzalez, Nancie L. *The Spanish-Americans of New Mexico: A Heritage of Pride.* 2d ed. rev. Albuquerque: University of New Mexico Press, 1969.

Gordon-McCutchan, R. C., ed. *Kit Carson: Indian Fighter or Indian Killer.* Niwot, Colo.: University Press of Colorado, 1996.

Grant, Blanche C. *Doña Lona: A Story of Old Taos and Santa Fe.* New York: Wilfred Funk, 1941.

Greene, A. C. *The 50 Best Books on Texas.* Dallas: Pressworks Publishing, 1982.

Grey, Zane. *Fighting Caravans.* New York: Harper and Brothers, 1929.

———. *Knights of the Range.* New York: Harper and Brothers, 1939.

———. *The Light of Western Stars: A Romance.* New York: Harper and Brothers, 1914.

———. *Sunset Pass.* New York: Harper and Brothers, 1931.

Grimes, Martha. *Rainbow's End.* New York: Knopf, 1995.

Hall, D. J. *Perilous Sanctuary.* New York: Macmillan, 1937.

Hamilton, W. J. [C. Dunning Clark]. *Mountain Ned; Or, The Flying Scout.* Beadle's Dime Novels, No. 309. New York: Beadle and Adams, June 2, 1874.

Hardy, Thomas. *The Dynasts: An Epic-Drama of the War with Napoleon, in Three Parts, Nineteen Acts, and One Hundred and Thirty Scenes.* Part First. New York: Macmillan, 1904. Reprint, anniversary edition, *The Writings of Thomas Hardy in Prose and Verse.* New York: Harper and Brothers, 1920.

Harrigan, Lana M. *Acoma: A Novel of Conquest.* New York: Forge, 1997.

Haycox, Ernest. "Stage to Lordsburg." *Collier's* 99 (April 10, 1937): 18–19, 68–69.

Hillerman, Tony. *Dance Hall of the Dead.* New York: Harper and Row, 1973.

———. *The Dark Wind.* New York: Harper and Row, 1982.

———. *The Ghostway.* New York: Harper and Row, 1984.

———. "Mystery, Country Boys, and the Big Reservation." In *Colloquium on Crime,* edited by Robin W. Winks, 127–47. New York: Charles Scribner's Sons, 1986b.

———. *Sacred Clowns.* New York: HarperCollins, 1993.

———. *Skinwalkers.* New York: Harper and Row, 1986a.

———. *The Spell of New Mexico.* Albuquerque: University of New Mexico Press, 1976.

———. *Talking God.* New York: Harper and Row, 1989.

———. *A Thief of Time.* New York: Harper and Row, 1988.

Hirsch, Foster. *The Dark Side of the Screen: Film Noir.* San Diego, Calif.: A. S. Barnes, 1981.

Hogan, Ray. *Soldier in Buckskin.* Thorndike, Maine: Five Star Western, 1996.

Horgan, Paul. *Figures in a Landscape.* New York: Harper and Brothers, 1940.

———. *Great River: The Rio Grande in North American History.* New York: Holt, Rinehart and Winston, 1954.

———. *A Lamp on the Plains.* Harper and Brothers, 1937.

———. *Lamy of Santa Fe: His Life and Times.* New York: Farrar, Straus and Giroux, 1975.

———. *No Quarter Given.* New York: Harper and Brothers, 1935.

———. *The Return of the Weed.* New York: Harper and Brothers, 1936.

———. "So Little Freedom." *Saturday Review of Literature* 25, no. 20 (May 16, 1942): 24–28.

Horsley, Kate [Kate Parker]. *Crazy Woman.* Albuquerque: La Alameda Press, 1992.

———. *A Killing in New Town.* Albuquerque: La Alameda Press, 1996.

Hough, Emerson. *Heart's Desire: The Story of a Contented Town, Certain Peculiar Citizens and Two Fortunate Lovers.* New York: Macmillan, 1905.

How, Louis. *The Penitentes of San Rafael: A Tale of the San Luis Valley.* Indianapolis: Bowen-Merrill Company, 1900.

Huffman, Minor S. *High Adventure Among the Magic Mountains: Philmont, the First Fifty Years.* Allendale, N.J.: TIBS, 1988.

Hughes, Dorothy B. *The Big Barbecue.* New York: Random House, 1949.

———. *Ride the Pink Horse.* New York: Duell, Sloan and Pearce, 1946.

Hutchinson, W. H. *A Bar Cross Man: The Life and Personal Writings of Eugene Manlove Rhodes.* Norman: University of Oklahoma Press, 1956.

Ingraham, Prentiss. *Buck Taylor's Boys; Or, The Red Riders of the Rio Grande. A Romance of Life among the Rangers and the Raiders of the Southwest Border.* Beadle's Half-Dime Library, No. 743. New York: Beadle and Adams, October 20, 1891.

———. *Buffalo Bill's Death Charm; Or, The Man with a Scar.* Beadle's Dime Library, No. 863. New York: Beadle and Adams, May 8, 1895.

———. *Buffalo Bill's Road-Agent Round-Up; Or, The Mysterious Masked Man in Black.* Beadle's Dime Library, No. 869. New York: Beadle and Adams, June 19, 1895.

Inman, Henry. *The Old Santa Fe Trail: The Story of a Great Highway.* New York: Macmillan, 1897.

———. *A Pioneer from Kentucky: An Idyll of the Raton Range.* Topeka, Kans.: Crane and Company, Publishers, 1898.

Janvier, Thomas. *Santa Fe's Partner; Being Some Memorials of Events in a New Mexican Track-end Town.* New York: Harper and Brothers, 1907.

Johannsen, Albert. *The House of Beadle and Adams.* 2 vols. Norman: University of Oklahoma Press, 1950.

Jones, Daryl. *The Dime-Novel Western.* Bowling Green, Ohio: Popular Press, 1978.

Kaminsky, Stuart M. *Coop: The Life and Legend of Gary Cooper.* New York: St. Martin's Press, 1980.

Kanon, Joseph. *Los Alamos.* New York: Broadway Books, 1997.

Kant, Candace C. *Zane Grey's Arizona.* Flagstaff, Ariz.: Northland Press, 1984.

Kelly, Florence Finch. *The Delafield Affair.* Chicago: A. C. McClurg and Company, 1909.

———. *With Hoops of Steel.* Indianapolis: Bowen-Merrill Company, 1900.

Kelton, Elmer. *The Time It Never Rained.* Garden City, N.Y.: Doubleday and Company, 1973.

Kimball, Clark. "John L. Sinclair: Epiphany on the Mountain." *Book Talk* 18, no. 2 (April, 1989): 1–4.

Kramer, Jane. *The Last Cowboy.* New York: Harper and Row, 1977.

Krumgold, Joseph. . . . *And Now Miguel.* New York: Thomas Y. Crowell Company, 1953.

Kunetka, James W. *Shadow Man.* New York: Warner Books, 1988.

Kyne, Peter B. *The Enchanted Hill.* New York: Cosmopolitan Book Corporation, 1924.

La Farge, Oliver. "The Ancient Strength." New Yorker 39, no. 28 (August 31, 1963): 26–34.

———. *Behind the Mountains.* Boston: Houghton Mifflin, 1956.

———. *The Enemy Gods.* Boston: Houghton Mifflin, 1937.

———. "Hard Winter." *Saturday Evening Post* 206, no. 27 (December 30, 1933): 5–7, 45–47.

———. "Higher Education." *Saturday Evening Post* 207, no. 13 (March 31, 1934): 8–9, 66–71.

———. *Laughing Boy.* Boston: Houghton Mifflin, 1929.

———. "The Little Stone Man." *New Yorker* 36, no. 19 (June 25, 1960): 32–38.

———. "New Mexico." *Holiday* 11, no. 2 (February, 1952): 34–47.

Lamar, Howard Roberts. "Keeping the Faith: The Forgotten Generations of Literary Turnerians." In *Frontier and Region: Essays in Honor of Martin Ridge,* edited by Robert C. Ritchie and Paul Andrew Hutton, 231–50. San Marino, Calif.: Huntington Library Press; and Albuquerque: University of New Mexico Press, 1997.

L'Amour, Louis. *Conagher.* New York: Bantam Books, 1969.

———. *The Daybreakers.* New York: Bantam Books, 1960a.

———. *Flint.* New York: Bantam Books, 1960b.

———. *Killoe.* New York: Bantam Books, 1962a.

———. *Radigan.* New York: Bantam Books, 1958.

———. *Shalako.* New York: Bantam Books, 1962b.

Lasky, Jesse L., with Don Weldon. *I Blow My Own Horn.* Garden City, N.Y.: Doubleday and Company, 1957.

Laughlin, Ruth. *The Wind Leaves No Shadow.* New York: Whittlesey House, 1948. Expanded version, Caldwell, Idaho: Caxton Printers, Ltd., 1951.

Lawrence, D. H. "New Mexico." *The Survey* 66 (May, 1931): 153–55.

———. *St. Mawr.* New York: Knopf, 1925.

———. "The Woman Who Rode Away." In *The Woman Who Rode Away, and Other Stories,* by D. H. Lawrence. London: M. Secker, 1928.

Lawrence, Lars [Phillip Stevenson]. *Morning Noon and Night.* New York: G. P. Putnam's Sons, 1954.

LeMay, Alan. *Useless Cowboy.* New York: Farrar and Rinehart, 1943.

Lewis, Eddie. *Ray Had an Idea About Love.* New York: Simon and Schuster, 1995.

Lewis, Tom. *Storied New Mexico: An Annotated Bibliography of Novels with New Mexico Settings.* Albuquerque: University of New Mexico Press, 1991.

Limerick, Patricia Nelson. "The Trail to Santa Fe: The Unleashing of the Western Public Intellectual." In *Trails: Toward a New Western History,* edited by Patricia Nelson Limerick, Clyde A. Milner II, and Charles E. Rankin, 59–77. Lawrence: University Press of Kansas, 1991b.

———. "What on Earth Is the New Western History?" In *Trails: Toward a New Western History,* edited by Patricia Nelson Limerick, Clyde A. Milner, II, and Charles E. Rankin, 81–88. Lawrence: University Press of Kansas, 1991a.

Lovett, Sarah. *Acquired Motives.* New York: Villard, 1996.

———. *Dangerous Attachments.* New York: Villard, 1995.

———. *A Desperate Silence.* New York: Villard, 1998.

McCall, Dan. *Messenger Bird.* New York: Harcourt Brace Jovanovich, 1993.

McCarthy, Cormac. *All the Pretty Horses.* New York: Knopf, 1992.

———. *Cities of the Plain.* New York: Knopf, 1998.

———. *The Crossing.* New York: Knopf, 1994.

McGarrity, Michael. *Mexican Hat.* New York: Norton, 1997.

———. *Tularosa.* New York: Norton, 1996.

———. *Serpent Gate.* New York: Scribner's, 1998.

McIlvoy, Kevin. *The Fifth Station.* Chapel Hill, N.C.: Algonquin Books of Chapel Hill, 1988.

————. *Little Peg.* New York: Atheneum, 1990.

McMurtry, Larry. *Anything for Billy.* New York: Simon and Schuster, 1988.

————. *Dead Man's Walk.* New York: Simon and Schuster, 1995.

————. "How the West Was Won or Lost: The Revisionists' Failure of Imagination." *New Republic* 203, no. 17 (October 22, 1990): 32–38.

————. *Lonesome Dove.* New York: Simon and Schuster, 1985.

————. "The Southwest as the Cradle of the Novelist." Therese Kayser Lindsey Lectures, Southwest Texas State University, San Marcos, October 19, 1978. In *The American Southwest: Cradle of Literary Art: Therese Kayser Lindsey Lectures,* edited by Robert W. Walts, 23–42. San Marcos: Southwest Texas State University, n.d.

Maguire, James. "Beginnings of Genres in the West: Introduction." In *A Literary History of the American West,* edited by J. Golden Taylor, 135–40. Fort Worth: Texas Christian University Press, 1987.

Mapson, Jo-Ann. *Blue Rodeo.* New York: HarperCollins, 1994.

Martin, Cort. *Bolt No. 4: The Guns of Taos.* New York: Kensington Publishing, 1981.

Martínez, Demetria. *Mother Tongue.* Tempe, Ariz.: Bilingual Press/Editorial Bilingüe, 1994.

Martínez, Ruben. "Interview with Rudolfo Anaya." *Writers' Forum* 13 (Fall, 1987): 14–29.

Masters, Dexter. *The Accident.* New York: Knopf, 1955.

Maule, Harry E. Letter to Frank O'Rourke, March 12, 1952. Random House Collection, Butler Library, Columbia University, New York City.

Mayer, Robert. *The Search.* Garden City, N.Y.: Doubleday and Company, 1986.

Meyer, Roy W. "The Western Fiction of Mayne Reid." *Western American Literature* 3, no. 2 (Summer, 1968): 115–32.

Miller, Walter M., Jr. *A Canticle for Leibowitz.* Philadelphia: J. B. Lippincott Company, 1959.

————. *Saint Leibowitz and the Wild Horse Woman.* New York: Bantam Books, 1997.

Milton, John R. *The Novel of the American West.* Lincoln: University of Nebraska Press, 1980.

————. "The Western Novel—A Symposium." *South Dakota Review* 2, no. 1 (Autumn, 1964): 3–36.

Momaday, N. Scott. *The Ancient Child.* New York: Doubleday, 1989.

————. *House Made of Dawn.* New York: Harper and Row, 1968.

Morrill, Claire. *A Taos Mosaic: Portrait of a New Mexico Village.* Albuquerque: University of New Mexico Press, 1973.

Morrow, Bradford. *Trinity Fields.* New York: Viking, 1995.

Mort, John. Review of *The Crossing,* by Cormac McCarthy. *Booklist* 90, no. 18 (May 15, 1994): 1645.

Mulford, Clarence E. *Bring Me His Ears.* Chicago: A. C. McClurg and Company, 1922.

Murphy, Bert. *Trailing Louis L'Amour in New Mexico.* Roswell, N. Mex.: MBAR Publishing, 1995.

Murphy, Lawrence R. *Lucien Bonaparte Maxwell: Napoleon of the Southwest.* Norman: University of Oklahoma Press, 1983.

Nathan, Jean. "John Nichols: Writer, Philosopher, Idealist and Shed-Builder." *Taos News,* April 23, 1987, p. B3.

Nelson, Antonya. *In the Land of Men.* New York: William Morrow, 1992.

———. *Nobody's Girl.* New York: Scribner's, 1998.

Nichols, John. *American Blood.* New York: Henry Holt and Company, 1987a.

———. *An Elegy for September.* New York: Henry Holt and Company, 1992.

———. *A Fragile Beauty: John Nichols' Milagro Country.* Salt Lake City: Peregrine Smith Books, 1987b.

———. *The Magic Journey.* New York: Holt, Rinehart and Winston, 1978.

———. *The Milagro Beanfield War.* New York: Holt, Rinehart and Winston, 1974.

———. *The Nirvana Blues.* New York: Holt, Rinehart and Winston, 1981.

Nye, Nelson. *Pistols for Hire.* New York: Macmillan, 1941.

Olmstead, Robert. *America by Land.* New York: Random House, 1993.

Olsen, Theodore V. *The Stalking Moon.* Garden City, N.Y.: Doubleday and Company, 1965.

O'Malley, Patrick [Frank O'Rourke]. *The Affair of the Red Mosaic.* New York: M. S. Mill Company, 1961.

Ondaatje, Michael. *The Collected Works of Billy the Kid.* Toronto: Anansi, 1970.

O'Rourke, Frank. *The Bravados.* New York: Dell, 1957a.

———. *The Diamond Hitch.* New York: William Morrow, 1956.

———. *The Far Mountains.* New York: William Morrow, 1959.

———. *The Last Ride.* New York: William Morrow, 1958.

———. *Legend in the Dust.* New York: Ballantine Books, 1957b.

———. *The Man Who Found His Way.* New York: William Morrow, 1957c.

———. *The Springtime Fancy.* New York: William Morrow, 1961.

Osborn, Karen. *Between Earth and Sky.* New York: William Morrow, 1996.

Otis, Raymond. *Fire in the Night.* New York: Farrar and Rinehart, 1934.

———. *Little Valley.* London: Cresset Press, 1937.

———. "Medievalism in America." *New Mexico Quarterly* 6, no. 2 (May, 1936): 83–90.

———. *Miguel of the Bright Mountain.* London: Victor Gollancz, 1936.

Owens, Louis. *Nightland.* New York: Dutton, 1996.

Padilla, Genaro M., ed. *Short Stories of Fray Angelico Chavez.* Albuquerque: University of New Mexico Press, 1987.

Page, Jake. *The Knotted Strings.* New York: Ballantine Books, 1995.

———. *The Stolen Gods.* New York: Ballantine Books, 1993.

Peary, Gerald, and Shatzkin, Roger. *The Classic American Novel and the Movies.* New York: Frederick Ungar, 1977.

Pike, Albert. *Prose Poems and Sketches Written in the Western Country.* Boston: Light and Horton, 1834. Annotated edition, edited by David J. Weber. Albuquerque: Calvin Horn Publisher, 1967.

Pilkington, William. *Harvey Fergusson.* Boston: Twayne Publishers, 1975.

Poling-Kempes, Lesley. *Canyon of Remembering.* Lubbock: Texas Tech University
Press, 1996.

Querry, Ron. *The Death of Bernadette Lefthand.* Santa Fe: Red Crane Books, 1993.

Raine, William MacLeod. *A Daughter of the Dons: A Story of New Mexico Today.*
New York: G. W. Dillingham Company, 1914.

———. *A Man Four-Square.* Boston: Houghton Mifflin Company, 1919.

Reagan, Albert B. *Don Diego; Or, The Pueblo Indian Uprising of 1680.* New York:
Alice Harriman Company, 1914.

Reid, Mayne. *The Lone Ranch, a Tale of the "Staked Plain."* London: Chapman and
Hall, 1871. New York: Hurst and Company, n.d.

———. *The Rifle Rangers.* London: W. Shoberl, 1850.

———. *The Scalp Hunters; Or, Romantic Adventures in Northern Mexico.* London:
C. J. Skeet, 1851. New York: Carleton, 1880.

———. *The White Chief, a Legend of Northern Mexico.* London: David Bogue, 1855.
New York: Carleton, 1874.

Rhodes, Eugene Manlove. "Aforesaid Bates." *Hearst's International-Cosmopolitan*
85, no. 2 (August, 1928): 34–37, 151–57.

———. *Bransford in Arcadia; Or, The Little Eohippus.* New York: Henry Holt and
Company, 1914.

———. *The Desire of the Moth.* New York: Henry Holt and Company, 1916.

———. *Good Men and True.* New York: Henry Holt and Company, 1910.

———. *Once in the Saddle and Pasó Por Aquí.* Boston: Houghton Mifflin
Company, 1927.

———. *The Proud Sheriff.* Boston: Houghton Mifflin Company, 1935.

———. *Stepsons of Light.* Boston: Houghton Mifflin Company, 1921.

———. *The Trusty Knaves.* Boston: Houghton Mifflin Company, 1933.

———. *West Is West.* New York: H. K. Fly Company, 1917.

Richter, Conrad. *Early Americana and Other Stories.* New York: Knopf, 1936.

———. *The Lady.* New York: Knopf, 1957.

———. *The Sea of Grass.* New York: Knopf, 1937.

———. "That Early American Quality." *Atlantic* 186, no. 3 (September, 1950):
26–30.

Romero, Orlando. *Nambe Year One.* Berkeley, Calif.: Tonatiuh–Quinto Sol, 1976.

Ross, Jean W. Interview with Frank O'Rourke. "CA Interview." *Contemporary
Authors* 118 (1986): 362–64.

Rousseau, Jean Jacques. *Discourse on the Origin and Foundation of Inequality Among
Men.* 1755. Reprinted in *Great Books of the Western World,* vol. 38: *Montesquieu
and Rousseau.* Chicago: Encyclopedia Britannica, 1952.

———. *The Social Contract.* Volume 2. 1762. Reprinted in *The Social Contract and
Discourses,* translated with an introduction by E. D. H. Cole. New York: E. P.
Dutton and Company, 1950.

Rowe, Dorothy. *Living with the Bomb.* London: Routledge and Kegan Paul, 1985.

Rudnick, Lois Palken. *Mabel Dodge Luhan: New Woman, New Worlds.*
Albuquerque: University of New Mexico Press, 1984.

Ruxton, George Frederick. *Life in the Far West*. Edinburgh, Scotland: William Blackwood and Sons, 1849.

Ryan, Marah Ellis. *The Flute of the Gods*. New York: Frederick A. Stokes Company, 1909.

―――. *The House of the Dawn*. Chicago: A. C. McClurg and Company, 1914.

Sagel, Jim. *El Santo Queso / The Holy Cheese*. Hanover, N.H.: Ediciones del Norte, 1990.

Sánchez, Pedro. *Memorias Sobre la Vida del Presbitero Don Antonio José Martínez*. Santa Fe, 1903. Original Spanish text with English translation by Ray John de Aragón. Santa Fe: Lightning Tree, 1978.

Satterthwait, Walter. *The Hanged Man*. New York: St. Martin's Press, 1993.

―――. *Wall of Glass*. New York: St. Martin's Press, 1987.

Savage, Les, Jr. *The Royal City*. Garden City, N.Y.: Hanover House, 1956.

Scarborough, Dorothy. *The Wind*. New York: Harper and Brothers, 1925.

Schaefer, Jack. *Monte Walsh*. Boston: Houghton Mifflin, 1963.

Scott, Kenneth W. *Zane Grey: Born to the West: A Reference Guide*. Boston: G. K. Hall and Company, 1979.

Seals, David. *The Powwow Highway*. Rapid City, S.D.: Sky and Sage, 1979. Reprinted, New York: New American Library, 1990.

―――. *Sweet Medicine*. New York: Orion Books, 1992.

Seltzer, Charles Alden. *The Coming of the Law*. New York: Outing Publishing Company, 1912.

Shrake, Edwin. *Blessed McGill*. Garden City, N.Y.: Doubleday and Company, 1968.

Silko, Leslie Marmon. *Almanac of the Dead*. New York: Simon and Schuster, 1991.

―――. *Ceremony*. New York: Viking Press, 1977.

Silman, Roberta. *Beginning the World Again*. New York: Viking, 1990.

Simmons, Marc. "Kit and the Indians." In *Kit Carson: Indian Fighter or Indian Killer*, edited by R. C. Gordon-McCutchan, 73–90. Niwot, Colo.: University Press of Colorado, 1996.

Sims, A. K. [J. H. Whitson]. *Prince Primrose, the Flower of the Flock; Or, The Grand Coup at Paradise Gulch. A Romance of Silverland*. Beadle's Dime Library, No. 552. New York: Beadle and Adams, May 22, 1889.

Sinclair, John L. *Death in the Claimshack*. Denver: Sage Books, 1947.

―――. *In Time of Harvest*. New York: Macmillan, 1943.

Skarda, Patricia. "A Current Trend: Telling and Retelling of Stories." Presentation at Clovis Community College, Clovis, N.Mex., April 4, 1996.

―――. Interview by David L. Caffey, April 4, 1996. Notes in the files of David L. Caffey.

Slotkin, Richard. *Gunfighter Nation: The Myth of the Frontier in the Twentieth Century*. New York: Atheneum, 1992.

Smith, C. W. *Understanding Women*. Fort Worth, Tex.: TCU Press, 1998.

Smith, Henry Nash. *Virgin Land: The American West as Symbol and Myth*. Cambridge, Mass.: Harvard University Press, 1950.

Smith, Mark. "5 Prefer Deer Hunting to Football Playoffs." *Albuquerque Journal*, November 5, 1997, pp. A1, A10.

Smith, Martin Cruz. *Stallion Gate.* New York: Random House, 1986.

Smith, Patricia Clark. "Achaeans, Americanos, Prelates and Monsters: Willa Cather's *Death Comes for the Archbishop.*" In *Padre Martínez: New Perspectives from Taos,* 101–24. Taos, N.Mex.: Millicent Rogers Museum, 1988.

Smith, Rebecca W. "The Southwest in Fiction." *Saturday Review of Literature* 25, no. 20 (May 16, 1942): 12–13, 37.

Snodgrass, Melinda M., ed. *A Very Large Array: New Mexico Science Fiction and Fantasy.* Albuquerque: University of New Mexico Press, 1987.

Sonnichsen, C. L. "Fat Man and the Story Tellers." *New Mexico Historical Review* 65, no. 1 (January, 1990): 49–71.

———. *From Hopalong to Hud: Thoughts on Western Fiction.* College Station: Texas A&M University Press, 1978.

St. Charnez, Casey. "Noir Classic Captures Burning Spirit of Fiesta." *New Mexico* 74, no. 9 (September, 1996): 48–51.

———. *Shot in New Mexico! Hollywood at Work in the Land of Enchantment, 1898–1993.* Santa Fe: New Mexico Film Commission, 1993.

Steele, Joan. *Captain Mayne Reid.* Boston: Twayne Publishers, 1978.

Steinberg, David. "Redford Felt Uniqueness of Norteños." *Albuquerque Journal,* March 13, 1988, p. G9.

Stephens, Ann S. *Malaeska: The Indian Wife of the White Hunter.* Beadle's Dime Novels, No. 1. New York: Irwin P. Beadle and Company, June 9, 1860.

Stern, Richard Martin. *The Big Bridge.* Garden City, N.Y.: Doubleday and Company, 1982.

Strieber, Whitley. *Majestic.* New York: G. P. Putnam's Sons, 1989.

Strieber, Whitley, and James Kunetka. *War Day and the Journey Onward.* New York: Holt, Rinehart and Winston, 1984.

Swarthout, Glendon. *Skeletons.* Garden City, N.Y.: Doubleday and Company, 1979.

Swindell, Larry. *The Last Hero: A Biography of Gary Cooper.* Garden City, N.Y.: Doubleday and Company, 1980.

Tallent, Elizabeth. *In Constant Flight.* New York: Knopf, 1983.

———. *Honey.* New York: Knopf, 1994.

———. *Time with Children.* New York: Knopf, 1987.

Taylor, J. Golden, ed. *A Literary History of the American West.* Fort Worth: Texas Christian University Press, 1987.

Thomas, Henry J. *The Prairie Rifles; Or, The Captives of New Mexico. A Romance of the Southwest.* Beadle's Dime Novels, No. 175. New York: Beadle and Company, April 13, 1869.

Thompson, David. *Silver Light.* New York: Knopf, 1990.

Tompkins, Jane. *West of Everything: The Inner Life of Westerns.* New York: Oxford University Press, 1992.

Tuska, Jon. *Billy the Kid: A Bio-Bibliography.* Westport, Conn.: Greenwood Press, 1983.

Ulibarrí, Sabine R. *Mi Abuela Fumaba Puros/My Grandma Smoked Cigars.* Berkeley, Calif.: Quinto Sol Publications, 1977.

———. *Primeros Encuentros/First Encounters.* Ypsilanti, Mich.: Bilingual Press/Editorial Bilingüe, 1982.

Utley, Robert M. *Billy the Kid: A Short and Violent Life.* Lincoln: University of Nebraska Press, 1989.

Van Gieson, Judith. *North of the Border.* New York: Walker and Company, 1988.

Van Vechten, Carl. *Peter Whiffle: His Life and Works.* New York: Knopf, 1922.

———. *Spider Boy.* New York: Knopf, 1928.

Waters, Frank. *The Man Who Killed the Deer.* New York: Farrar and Rinehart, 1942.

———. *People of the Valley.* New York: Farrar and Rinehart, 1941.

———. *The Woman at Otowi Crossing.* Denver: Alan Swallow, 1966.

Webber, Charles Wilkins. *Old Hicks the Guide; Or, Adventures in the Camanche Country in Search of a Gold Mine.* New York: Harper and Brothers, Publishers, 1848.

Weber, David J. *The Mexican Frontier, 1821–1846: The American Southwest under Mexico.* Albuquerque: University of New Mexico Press, 1982.

———. *The Spanish Frontier in North America.* New Haven, Conn.: Yale University Press, 1992.

Webster, Daniel. "The Agriculture of England." Speech to the Legislature of the State of Massachusetts, Boston, January 13, 1840. In *The Writings and Speeches of Daniel Webster,* vol. 2. Boston: Little, Brown, and Company, 1903.

Weigle, Marta, and Kyle Fiore. *Santa Fe and Taos: The Writer's Era, 1916–1941.* Santa Fe: Ancient City Press, 1982.

Whittaker, Frederick. *The Black Wizard: A Tale of the Fatal Circle of Invisible Fire.* Beadle's Dime Novels, No. 235. New York: Beadle and Company, August 1, 1871.

Willett, Edward. *Black Eyes; Or, The Three Captives. A Tale of the Taos Valley.* Beadle's Dime Novels, No. 129. New York: Beadle and Company, July 30, 1867.

Williams, Ben Ames. *Leave Her to Heaven.* Boston: Houghton Mifflin, 1944.

Williamson, Jack. *Manseed.* New York: Ballantine Books, 1982.

Wiseman, Thomas. *Savage Day.* New York: Delacorte Press, 1981.

Wister, Owen. *The Virginian: Horseman of the Plains.* New York: Macmillan, 1902.

Woods, Stuart. *Santa Fe Rules.* New York: HarperCollins, 1992.

Worster, Donald. "Beyond the Agrarian Myth." In *Trails: Toward a New Western History,* edited by Patricia Nelson Limerick, Clyde A. Milner, II, and Charles E. Rankin, 3–25. Lawrence: University Press of Kansas, 1991.

Wright, Will. *Six-Guns and Society: A Structural Study of the Western.* Berkeley: University of California Press, 1975.

Zelazny, Roger. *Eye of Cat.* New York: Timescape Books, 1982.

Zollinger, Norman. "Ambushed: The Late-20th-Century Attack on Kit Carson." *Book Talk* 27, no. 3 (July, 1998): 1–6.

———. *Lautrec.* New York: Dutton, 1990.

———. *Meridian.* New York: Forge, 1997.

———. *Riders to Cibola.* Santa Fe: Museum of New Mexico Press, 1977.

FILMS

Along Came Jones. 1945, RKO Radio Pictures. Director: Stuart Heisler.
And Now Miguel. 1953, U.S. Information Service. Director: Joseph Krumgold.
And Now Miguel. 1966, Universal. Director: James B. Clark.
The Bravados. 1958, 20th-Century Fox. Director: Henry King.
Burning the Wind. 1929, Universal. Directors: Herbert Blache, Henry MacRae.
The Coming of the Law. 1919, Fox. Director: Arthur Rosson.
Conagher. 1991, made for television. Director: Reynaldo Villalobos.
Dead Man's Walk. 1996, made for television. Director: Yves Simoneau.
The Desire of the Moth. 1917, Bluebird. Director: Rupert Julian.
The Enchanted Hill. 1926, Paramount. Director: Irvan Willat.
Fighting Caravans. 1931, Paramount. Directors: Otto Brower, David Burton.
Fire on the Mountain. 1981, made for television. Director: Donald Wrye.
Four Faces West. 1948, Enterprise/United Artists. Director: Alfred E. Green.
Good Men and True. 1922, Robertson-Cole. Director: Val Paul.
The Hanged Man. 1964, made for television. Director: Don Siegel.
The Hi-Lo Country. 1998, Gramercy Pictures. Director: Stephen Frears.
House Made of Dawn. 1987, Firebird Productions. Director: Richardson Morse.
Hot Saturday. 1932, Paramount. Director: William A. Seiter.
Knights of the Range. 1940, Paramount. Director: Lesley Selander.
Leave Her to Heaven. 1945, 20th-Century Fox. Director: John M. Stahl.
The Light of Western Stars. 1940, Paramount. Director: Lesley Selander.
Lonely Are the Brave. 1962, Universal. Director: David Miller.
A Man Four-Square. 1926, Fox. Director: Roy William Neill.
The Milagro Beanfield War. 1988, Universal. Director: Robert Redford.
Monte Walsh. 1970, 20th-Century Fox. Director: William A. Fraker.
The Mysterious Witness. 1923, R-C Pictures. Director: Seymour Zeliff.
The Penitentes. 1915, Fine Arts Film Company. Director: John Conway.
The Powwow Highway. 1989, Hand-Made Films. Director: Jonathan Wacks.
Red Sky at Morning. 1971, Universal. Director: James A. Goldstone.
Ride the Pink Horse. 1947, Universal. Director: Robert Montgomery.
The Rounders. 1965, Metro-Goldwyn-Mayer. Director: Burt Kennedy.
The Sea of Grass. 1947, Metro-Goldwyn-Mayer. Director: Elia Kazan.
Stagecoach. 1939, United Artists. Director: John Ford.
The Stalking Moon. 1969, National General. Director: Robert Mulligan.
Summer of '42. 1971, Warner Brothers. Director: Robert Mulligan.
Sure Fire. 1921, Universal. Director: John Ford.
Sweet Hostage. 1975, made for television. Director: Lee Philips.
The Wallop. 1921, Universal. Director: John Ford.
Wolf Song. 1929, Paramount. Director: Victor Fleming.

INDEX

Pages containing illustrations appear in italics.